The Fear in the Sky

Other books by the author

Non-fiction
Bomb on the Red Markers
Fighter! Fighter! Corkscrew Port!
We Kept 'Em Flying (pending)

Peakland Aircrashes Series:
The South (2005)
The Central Area (2006)
The North (2006)

High Peak Air Crash Sites, Central Region
White Peak Air Crash Sites

Faction
A Magnificent Diversion Series (Acclaimed by the First World War Aviation Historical Society)
The Infinite Reaches (1915–16)
Contact Patrol (1916)
Sold A Pup (1917)
The Great Disservice (1918)

Blind Faith: Joan Waste, Derby's Martyr
Joyce Lewis of Mancetter, Lichfield's Feisty Martyr

Fiction
In Kinder's Mists (a Kinderscout ghost story)
Though the Treason Pleases (Irish Troubles)

The Fear in the Sky

Vivid Memories of Operational Aircrew in World War Two

Pat Cunningham, DFM

Pen & Sword
AVIATION

First published in Great Britain in 2012 by
PEN & SWORD AVIATION
an imprint of
Pen & Sword Books Ltd
47 Church Street
Barnsley
South Yorkshire
S70 2AS

ISBN 978-1-84884-648-7

A CIP catalogue record for this book is available from the British Library.

Typeset in 12/14 Palatino by Concept, Huddersfield, West Yorkshire

Printed and bound in England by
CPI Group (UK) Ltd, Croydon, CRO 4YY

Pen & Sword Books Ltd incorporates the Imprints of Pen & Sword Aviation, Pen & Sword Family History, Pen & Sword Maritime, Pen & Sword Military, Pen & Sword Discovery, Wharncliffe Local History, Wharncliffe True Crime, Wharncliffe Transport, Pen & Sword Select, Pen & Sword Military Classics, Leo Cooper, The Praetorian Press, Remember When, Seaforth Publishing and Frontline Publishing.

For a complete list of Pen & Sword titles please contact
PEN & SWORD BOOKS LIMITED
47 Church Street, Barnsley, South Yorkshire, S70 2AS, England
E-mail: enquiries@pen-and-sword.co.uk
Website: www.pen-and-sword.co.uk

Contents

Acknowledgements

To the traced copyright holders authorizing the use of their photographs: Richard Haigh, manager, intellectual properties, Rolls-Royce; Nicola Hunt, intellectual property rights copyright unit, MOD; archives staff, Imperial War Museum; Judy Nokes, licensing adviser, HMSO (Crown Copyright/MOD); archives staff, Royal Air Force Museum.

Craving the indulgence of those for whom all contact attempts have failed.

To Julian Temple and John Lattimore of Brooklands Museum for their Wellington expertise.

To Clive Teale, aviator and grammarian, for proof-reading and technical advice. Similarly to Ken Johnson and Ken Clare for down-to-earth criticism.

To Derwent Living, winter 2010–2011 (the coldest in 100 years): for no central heating, and memorable proof-reading in fingerless gloves.

To the ever-ebullient – and consistently irreverent – personnel of ASDA/ Macdonald's, Spondon; Seasons Café, Park Farm, Derby; Croots Farm Shop, Duffield; Caudwell's Mill Café, Rowsley; and in particular, Ellery's (Hobb's) Tea Rooms, Monsal Head.

To the National Trust staff at Kedleston Hall for both irreverence and forbearance.

To the immeasurable expedition given by Google.

Despite such inestimable assistance, any errors remaining, and all opinions expressed, are my own.

Pat Cunningham, DFM

Introduction

None of the men whose stories appear in this book feel that their wartime aircrew service made them anything out of the ordinary, even as fliers. However, from the outset, I must take issue with this self-effacing assessment. For though my 20,000 hours and forty years in Service and Civil Aviation included several officially-designated operational campaigns flown with the support of a crew, I find great difficulty in imagining my generation enduring the perils facing the wartime aircrews, still less confronting them time and time again.

From the start, the road they volunteered to follow – no flier can be pressed! – was neither easy nor short. For many aspirants the incentive was that, after Dunkirk and the various German blitzes on Britain, the RAF was the only way of directly hitting back at the enemy. Then again, many had been weaned on the heady appeal of Flight. However, having met the medical standards and proven themselves capable of swiftly assimilating a range of technical skills, and keen as they were to do their bit and fly against the enemy, the preparatory courses could take well over a year.

One of the greatest drawbacks to flying training was the British weather, so some would have travelled to Commonwealth countries and even to the then-neutral United States where climatic conditions afforded the all-important continuity.

The final training stage was when the various aircrew specializations came together at the Operational Training Unit where they learnt to work together as a team and to operate the type of aircraft they were to go to war in.

Most operational crews would be destined for Bomber Command but multi-crewed aircraft were employed in all other Commands as well, so that over 500 aircrew fought directly alongside the pilots who so nobly flew Hurricanes and Spitfires in the Battle of Britain; and that is not counting those who supplemented the overall effort by raiding enemy airfields and installations.

Volunteers though aircrew had to be, once they were committed to operations they were required to do a full tour of sorties against the enemy, for the most part, thirty flights, or 'ops'. After that they would be rested for something like six months before becoming liable for a second tour. And even then this rest period was likely to be spent in instructing others; not in itself an occupation without hazard. This consideration aside, however, many crews elected to forgo their rests and continue with a second tour in the company of their tried and trusted crew, not a few referring to the bond built up on operations as being 'closer than kin'!

Just the same, to take the case of Bomber Command, of its 125,000 aircrew only 7,000 embarked upon a second tour. There were men, though, who volunteered for a third tour. But this was rare, whereas to actually anticipate completing that third tour was to strain credulity. As it was, over 60 per cent of crews failed to return.

The hazards they faced included everything the enemy could throw against them in the way of massed and radar-directed anti-aircraft guns and high-performance day- and night-fighters. But there was also the uncertain weather and the lack of radio aids to get them down safely through fog and low cloud on their return. Notably, other than for such specialized units as – some – meteorological flights, there was not even an altimeter that would actually tell them their height above the ground they were overflying! And this became of vital importance if the wind had changed and they had drifted off course during their homeward flight back to a fog-draped and blacked-out near-sea-level Lincolnshire and Yorkshire base and were flying over Peakland's 2,000 foot hills.

Then again there was their inexperience, many finishing full tours of operations before they had logged 500 flying hours, an inexperience further evidenced by the fact that of the 55,500 aircrew lost on operations from Bomber Command alone, 8,300 were lost to accidents rather than to enemy action.

Understandably then, faced with such an array of menaces, one of the major problems facing operational aircrew was that of dealing with fear. Most crew members found their own strategies for coping, through prayer or living an off-duty life of excess, through superstition even, but always, with crew loyalty figuring largely. And yet it remains a source of wonder that essentially disparate crews, from different social backgrounds, even different national air forces, gelled so well. Especially considering the two-tiered makeup of most crews, some being commissioned officers, and others non-commissioned officers (NCOs) who, essentially, went their separate ways on the ground.

In fact, the distinction even extended to the gallantry decorations bestowed, with crosses for both commissioned officers and warrant officers but lower-precedence medals for NCOs; a distinction persisting until 1993! Even then, bearing in mind the typical five-NCOs-to-two-officers structure of wartime crews, just 6,637 Distinguished Flying Medals were awarded as against 20,354 Distinguished Flying Crosses.

Not that either of these things seems to have been an issue, and certainly not at the time. No least because for the most part, the crews were young, with many celebrating twentieth birthdays only after finishing their operational tours. And in the air, at least, the norm was first-name terms, with most former crew members maintaining that all that really concerned them was that they came through and finished their tours.

Of course, there were also technical difficulties, but that hazard, at least, was cushioned by the absolute trust all held in the numerous and variously-skilled personnel who got them into the air. Indeed, former aircrew invariably pay tribute to this trust. Only the inescapable fact is that no matter that the expressions are heartfelt it has never been possible to give ground staff their due credit, the focus always being upon the fliers. And only too often, even in reporting aerial operations of the twenty-first century, to the pilots.

Where fear was concerned, however, everyone could take comfort from reflecting, 'It won't happen to me.' Except that in a mathematically adept Service the statistics of the empty bedspaces could never be ignored.

The moral aspect of aerial bombing, on the other hand – the area that many people since the Second World War have taken so much to heart – barely weighed. But then, unlike their latter-day critics, the aircrew were part of the trauma of the time and remember how they were lauded by a populace who had actually suffered the German onslaught. Even late in the war, aware though they were from training sorties that their own bombing could not possibly be all that accurate, the soulless abandon with which the utterly inaccurate German V-weapons were launched was there to steel the resolve. There was always too the surety that 'they started it!' Then again, for most, the demands of the job, so useful in staving off fear, also left little time for metaphysical reflection.

The men in this book talk of a different age, of course. An age now so distant that as this is written, in 2012, their comradely fellowship, the Aircrew Association, has already been disbanded. Only for some time yet its members will continue to meet, not dwelling on the past, but rather, savouring still their good fortune in having survived the horrors of their youth. If questioning, on occasion, just what their sacrifices, and the ultimate sacrifice of so many of their fellow aircrew, achieved.

Pat Cunningham, DFM, RAF 1951–1973

1

The fear in the sky

Flight Lieutenant Keith Hall, MBE, pilot

When war broke out I had aspirations to become a member of the Institution of Electrical Engineers. These, though, were thwarted when I was unable to get a suitable day release. Then again, the army were not recruiting eighteen-year-olds. Thoroughly fed up, therefore, I turned to my father and his hairdressing salon in Long Eaton, near Nottingham.

Flight Lieutenant Keith Hall, MBE, 1942

Downstairs he had six gents' chairs. Upstairs, though, he'd installed eight ladies' cubicles built of light oak with tastefully arranged leaded light panels, an innovation well in accord with his oft-quoted aphorism, 'Aim for the top of the tree, it's the bottom that's crowded.' As it transpired, my timing was right, for four of his barbers had just been called up and so, after a month's preparation in a Derby establishment, our salon manager allotted me chair No. 6, matching my minimal skills to any need that arose.

Alongside this I became a Home Guard and in company with two First World War veterans nightly patrolled the Trent from Sawley Bridge to Shardlow, the officer carrying the rifle, the sergeant the five rounds of ammunition, and me, the original Private Pike, the flask of soup. After a while, though, I applied to the Royal Navy who gave me a travel warrant to HMS *Arthur* – Butlin's Holiday Camp, Skegness! – to attest as an able-seaman signaller, except that just then the RAF began recruiting aircrew, which appealed more. I applied, and was sent to Cardington for three days' selection.

Here, however, a private education notwithstanding, my academic record did not impress. But then one of the board asked about sport. Rugby? Full back? Ah, a brightening! But doubt too. After all, I was only nine stone nothing soaking wet. Full back, then, for whom? Ilkeston? Ah, a mining town! Delighted smiles all round. Clearly, anyone prepared to face packs of charging miners must be just the sort of fool they were looking for.

So, on 19 August 1941, a trainee pilot, I reported to Lord's Cricket ground – then No. 1 Aircrew Reception Centre – where we were fed in flights of fifty at London Zoo, aircrew feeding-time drawing greater crowds than the animals' bun-fights ever had. It was a hurried spectator sport, however, seven and half minutes during breakfast and tea, if ten whole minutes for lunch!

My next move was to the Initial Training Wing at Torquay, to learn the Ways of the Service. Not least with respect to religious observances. These took the form of Sunday church parade at which the Church of England members were marched off in a boot-crunching body, followed by the Roman Catholics, so leaving the 'odds and sods'. On that first weekend, being a devout Methodist, I was set to scrubbing out the dining hall. By the next Sunday, therefore, I was staunchly C of E. And so one learnt.

Another thing that eased my passage through General Service Training – square bashing – was that policemen, until then in a reserved occupation, were now permitted to apply for aircrew. My intake contained seven stalwarts from the Met who significantly defused any disciplinarian excesses by leading the rest of us in the gradually swelling and mesmerisingly rhythmic chant:

We won't, we won't,
We won't be buggered about,
We absolutely bloody refuse,
We won't be buggered about.

Nor would they be!

Then, in December 1941, it was off to No. 8 Elementary Flying Training School at Woodley, a grass airfield near Reading – where Douglas Bader had left his legs! Unlike most pupils, who trained on biplane Tiger Moths, we had the Miles Magister, a sleek monoplane equipped not only with flaps but with wheel-brakes! Many of the former policemen were quite anxious during flying training knowing that a failure meant returning to the beat. For my part, with no such fears, I had a quietly confident run through, the only setback coming in March 1942 when, instead of sailing off to complete my training in Canada, I was one of five earmarked to become flying instructors. Not a thing any trainee pilot wants. Especially as nobody told us whether we'd been judged as superior student fliers or simply as unworthy of being trusted with a more expensive aircraft!

Still in the dark, we were sent directly to No. 6 Flight Instructors' School at RAF Perdiswell, Worcester, flying Tiger Moths for the balance of the pilots' course. This involved a lot of circuits and landings, cross-countries, practice forced landings, a modicum of formation flying and aerobatics, but little or no instrument flying, although we did do a few sessions in the Link Trainer. At the same time, however, we were burning the midnight oil studying to become word perfect with the 'patter' of flying instruction, the aim being to ensure that the description of the exercise matched the action taking place.

In June 1942, accordingly, I not only got my wings but qualified as a flying instructor! More significantly, emulating the advertisement that enthused, 'Hooray! Hooray! I've got my wings. Now we can look at Bravingtons rings', my girlfriend, Joan, and I did just that. And on 3 October 1942 we were married!

I was now a sergeant pilot, but after eight weeks of instructing I was recommended for a commission, sent on a week's leave, had a uniform fashioned for me by Henry Williams of Nottingham, my father's tailor, and returned to duty as a shiny pilot officer.

Joan 1942

After Worcester my first posting as a flying instructor had been to No. 28 Elementary Flying School at Wolverhampton where I'd soon settled to the regime, repetitively working through the syllabus. My least favourite exercise was restarting the engine in the air. This necessitated diving very steeply until the ever more rapidly windmilling prop brought the engine back to life. Like spinning, this had to be taught to every pupil, though spinning had to be done three times over. Probably aerobatics and formation-flying sessions were my favourites, though the only really satisfying formation flying I did was in May 1943 when the school's instructors did a low-level overflight for the fund-raising Wings For Victory Week.

Most of our pupils progressed to advanced training in Canada but there were also a few intakes of army officers who were scheduled to become Airborne Division glider pilots. Additionally, however, we were training a fair number of Turks. As, indeed, were the Luftwaffe! For both Britain and Germany were trying to entice Turkey into their camp. Certainly, it was held of great importance that we put up no diplomatic blacks in our dealings with them. In the end, of course, Turkey remained neutral. Even so, it was involvement with one of our Turks that tried my mettle as an officer-diplomatist.

I was orderly officer when my commanding officer summoned me to the station dance to get rid of a known good-time girl who, though banned from the station, had, nevertheless, latched on to one of our Turkish officers in town and come as his guest. I decided to tackle the problem by asking the woman to dance, then suggesting that we go outside, when I could get her removed from the station. The plan seemed to work well. Understandably, though, she needed to visit the cloakroom first. Only she never came back. How was I doing? the CO asked a while later. 'It's in hand,' I prevaricated. In fact, it was 4 a.m. next morning before the guardroom checked her out!

Accidents in flying training were not infrequent but the most notable one for me occurred in mid-1943 when a landing Tiger crashed and began to burn as I was taxying out with a pupil. Flicking off our ignition switches we ran to assist, only to find the instructor trapped. Initially unable to lift the debris, we drew away from the searing heat to take stock. Seeing no option, we forced ourselves back again, just as a wing root burnt through and collapsed, so giving us purchase. This time, my pupil, a stout former policeman, gave a gigantic heave, so allowing me to drag the instructor free.

It was all very gratifying, for I was awarded the MBE (Member of the British Empire) 'for gallantry not in the face of the enemy', while my pupil, being non-commissioned, received the British Empire Medal (BEM) on the same grounds. And so, some months later, on 23 November 1943, a now-blossoming Joan and

George R.I.

George the Sixth by the Grace of God of Great Britain Ireland and the British Dominions beyond the Seas King Defender of the Faith Emperor of India and Sovereign of the Most Excellent Order of the British Empire to Our trusty and well beloved Keith James Hall Esquire Pilot Officer in Our Royal Air Force Volunteer Reserve **Greeting**

Whereas We have thought fit to nominate and appoint you to be an Additional Member of the Military Division of Our said Most Excellent Order of the British Empire We do by these presents grant unto you the Dignity of an Additional Member of Our said Order and hereby authorise you to have hold and enjoy the said Dignity and Rank of an Additional Member of Our aforesaid Order together with all and singular the privileges thereunto belonging or appertaining.

Given at Our Court at Saint James's under Our Sign Manual and the Seal of Our said Order this Fourteenth day of May 1943 in the Seventh year of Our Reign

By the Sovereign's Command

Mary R
Grand Master

ant of the dignity of an Additional Member
the Military Division of the Order of the British Empire
Pilot Officer Keith James Hall, R.A.F.V.R.

Award of the MBE

The investiture at Buckingham Palace. My father was already ill

I found ourselves guests of the King – of Dowager Queen Mary, actually – at Buckingham Palace.

As for the survivor, a Warrant Officer Loach, having recovered, he completed his instructing tour. Only, so I heard, to be killed after returning to ops.

Instructing, then, had its highs. Just the same, being stuck in Training Command had never ceased to grate, so in August 1943 I had availed myself of the opportunity given to fretting flying instructors to experience operational life, reporting for a fortnight's observing attachment to RAF Breighton, near Selby, in Yorkshire, a Halifax station.

The first shock awaited me in the officers' mess anteroom. For on the coat rack were airman-pattern greatcoats, the patches left by the sergeant's stripes clearly visible but with epaulettes bearing officers' braid: a sure token that losses here outpaced uniform fittings! It was the height of the Battle of Berlin and Halifaxes had been suffering heavy casualties. Unsurprisingly, therefore, the atmosphere on the station reflected this. Morale was very low, nobody was inclined to chat, and strangers were definitely unwelcome.

A major aim of the detachment had been to get us visitors on an actual operational flight, and indeed, when we arrived we had been advised that should any captain wish to, he could take us along. Only nobody offered. On leaving, therefore, torn between disappointment and relief, I asked why that had been. 'Well,' the squadron commander said dourly, 'if you know you're going to be shit scared, you don't want an audience.'

The visit had been a taste of what I aspired to, but as battle losses mounted so training took on even higher priority, and just before Christmas 1943 I was posted to No. 15 Flying Grading School at RAF Kingstown, Carlisle. The job here was to assess – or grade – the suitability of *ab initio* pupils for further training. For this purpose each aspirant was allocated ten or twelve hours in which to prove himself. Those who met the requirements continued with pilots' courses, those who failed to but were otherwise suitable being offered the chance to remuster into another aircrew specialisation. A vital job, but even less what I really wanted to be doing.

Then, in March 1944, a telegram from my medical-student brother advised me that our parents were both terminally ill. I was given a compassionate posting to Burnaston, at Derby, but Mother died soon after I arrived, Father joining her six weeks later, in April.

Necessarily, my brother and I had much to do with settling family affairs although the salon was in the capable hands of the receptionist cousin who, as it transpired, was to run things until my demob. Though saddened by my double loss I was heartened a little later to receive an operational posting. But I was actually over the moon on 17 July 1944 when a telegram advised me that our son, Robert, had been born.

My own rebirth started at No. 20 (Pilots) Advanced Flying Unit at Kidlington, near Oxford. However, on 6 June 1944, as I stood on the airfield gazing up at the invasion fleets sailing overhead, I was convinced that, even now, I had missed the boat. At least, though, I found myself on the fast track, because as I had logged 1,200 hours it was assumed that the basics could be skipped! Even so, I flew some sixty hours on the twin-engined Airspeed Oxford, good preparation for passing on to heavier, multi-engined types.

My stay, however, also included a detachment closer to home, not back to Burnaston, but to Castle Donington, the other Derby airfield, to do a Standard Beam Approach course. This involved interpreting dots and dashes to find and maintain a radio beam while flying blind beneath a hood; then, as the instructor swept off the hood and took control, seeing the runway dead ahead. A remarkable experience!

But back at Kidlington I had an even more remarkable one. I was cycling along, intent on spending some time with Anthony Trollope's *Phineas Finn* in the Blenheim Palace gardens – to which, as aircrew, we had the entrée – when one engine of a departing Oxford came bounding my way, jarred from its mounting after a stone had shattered its wooden propeller. As for the Oxford, it settled to earth, losing both wings as it slid between two trees. The instructor was shaken enough. But the pupil had emerged from the hood to find himself pushing free of debris! What petrified me was when, with petrol flooding our boots, he produced some cigarettes and a lighter! Luckily, he then thought better of it.

My next posting was to No. 11 Operational Training Unit (OTU) at Westcott, in Buckinghamshire. A most unusual OTU sojourn in that I never collected a crew of my own and did little more than night and day circuits on the Wellington.

The Wellington was all right, but its geodetic construction meant that when you waggled the stick the whole thing would flex. What I really detested, however, was having to hand over to another crew at night with the engines running. Yet this was often done, for after radial engines had been shut down then oil could leak into the bottommost cylinders and create a hydraulic block. This meant that before restarting an engine it had to be checked for freedom by swinging over the prop, an uncleared block – called hydraulicking – being sufficient to wreck it. Even so, sidling past the incoming crew within a hairsbreadth of two whirling great propellers was nerve-racking in the extreme!

The whole thing would flex

After Westcott came the aircrew pool at RAF Stradishall, near Bury St Edmonds where, in December 1944, I finally got a crew. Only to discover that they were in limbo, having been rejected by two other captains. I gathered that each of these had been a relatively senior officer who, after being in an admin appointment, had wanted to fly with more experienced people. Understandable, perhaps, but it left the chaps I inherited with rock-bottom morale.

I grasped the nettle by standing them a meal in Bury. And what a meal! Roast pheasant topped the list, I recall, fairly unobtainable anywhere but deep in the country. It was a start. After that, of course, I grew to know them well. Indeed, we were to do nineteen ops as a crew, so forging a bond that really did approach that of kinship.

But having said that, I must plead anno domini for being unable to put a surname to Roy, my wireless operator, for to us he was always, The Boy. The rear gunner was Sergeant Alan Young, so tall that he had to hunch up in the turret. Because of this trips would be punctuated by his verbalized disgust as, encumbered with four layers of gloves – cape leather, fingerless woollen mitts, a silk pair, then leather gauntlets – he would drop the barley sugar he was trying to unwrap, then be too bulkily clad to reach down for it.

The mid-upper gunner was Sergeant Jim Stanniforth, of Sheffield. Having disembarked after one op it was clear that a sizable lump of flak had pierced his turret. 'I thought it was a bit draughty,' was all he said.

Our flight engineer was Sergeant Wally Rawlings. Competent from the start, he settled very happily with the Lancaster's systems.

At twenty-eight, Sergeant Dick 'Uncle' Copesteak was the old man of the crew. As a conscientious objector he had driven an ambulance throughout the London Blitz. Only to suffer a sea change and become a bomb aimer.

Then, of course, there was my navigator, Sergeant, later Flying Officer, Michael Tavenor – Mike to all but his future wife. As a trainee pilot he had progressed as far as Avro Ansons in Canada. Then he had lost himself and decided to put down in a large field. Only to float, and float, into the one beyond – a field that was too small to be flown out of. And which, it turned out, was in the United States! And this was to be my navigator – and as it transpired, lifelong friend – a chap who not only got lost, but ended up in the wrong country!

Even so, all seven of us gelled.

First, though, we had to pass through No. 1657 Heavy Conversion Unit, on the Stirling. A towering great beast. Even taxying the thing called for right hand on the throttles, left arm to cuddle the wheel back into the stomach and left hand yet further extended to operate the brake lever, so hunching me up that I could no longer see where I was going. How glad we were to move on to No. 3 Lancaster Finishing School at Feltwell, in Norfolk!

We began the conversion in January 1945, approaching it in high spirits, the next stop, at long last, being ops. Nor were we disappointed, for the Lancaster, especially after the Stirling, was bliss! Our posting duly came through on 9 February 1945, to No. 149 Squadron of No. 3 Group, at Methwold, in Norfolk. We settled in with an acceptance trip and a few cross-countries. And on 16 February 1945, we did our first operation.

This was in support of Operation Veritable – the reduction of the pocket at Wessel, on the Rhine – when we were among 100 Lancasters that left the railway area 'smothered in bomb bursts' as the raid report recorded. As indeed, our aiming-point photograph showed.

Those photographs were a real bind, for getting them meant holding straight for yet another ten seconds after we'd dropped the bombs. An interminable time with shadowy – but only too solid – 'friendly' aircraft looming up and flak never ceasing. Indeed, the weaving lines on some photos showed just how hard it could be to hold that run-in heading!

Wessel aiming-point photo, from 18,000 feet

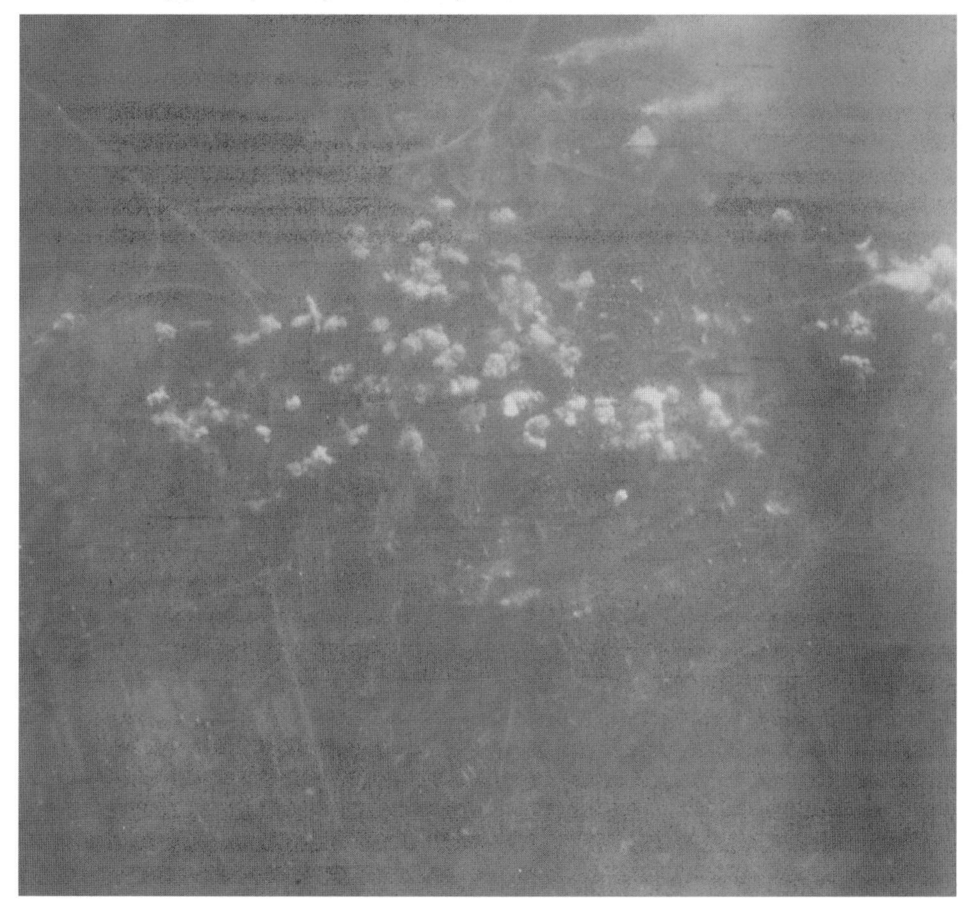

After that first op we were rarely off the battle order. On 21 February 1945 we were one of 514 Lancasters to raid Dortmund, concentrating on the southern half of the city, with fourteen aircraft being lost. And on 23 February it was Gelsenkirchen, attacking the Alma Pluto benzol plant. But the 149 Lancasters employed failed to achieve the purpose, so we went there again on 27 February, this time bombing through cloud using Gee-H.

This was a sophisticated development of the Gee radar-navigational equipment that owed much to the Oboe bombing aid. Using Oboe, an aircraft flew down a beam until a signal advised that it was time to drop its bombs. With the ordinary equipment, however, only one aircraft at a time could use Oboe. Gee-H, on the other hand, could accommodate any number.

It was, of course, all very technical, but the boffins had organized things so that the navigator merely had to line up blips on a scope, then pass headings to keep the pilot on track until the release point was reached. It was much more accurate than visual sighting. But only some aircraft were Gee-H equipped, so these had their tailfins painted with two horizontal yellow stripes. Aircraft without the equipment would fly close to one with a marked tailplane, dropping when it dropped, in the American fashion.

Despite the assistance of Gee-H, the next night we were back at Gelsenkirchen again, this time concentrating on the Nordstern synthetic oil plant, 156 of us. Following that, Group sent 128 of us to attack Wanne Eickel through thick cloud, again, using Gee-H.

Then, on 6 March 1945, it was Cologne, a five-hour effort. The Americans were poised to cross the Rhine and take the city. Our brief, therefore, was to

A Lancaster with (yellow) fin stripes denoting that it is Gee-H equipped

await a signal from the master bomber before dropping. In all, the whole force went around three times without a clearance being obtained. It was chaos, with aircraft everywhere, and flak seemingly filling the sky. Only the clearance never came. In fact, the Americans had indeed taken the city. So, finally, the master bomber called it off, and sent us home. Except that this meant carrying back our bombs. 'How,' wondered a voice from the rear, 'do we land with this lot aboard?'

'Very, very carefully,' I vowed.

On the return from another Cologne visit we had to divert to nearby Tuddenham and land using the FIDO system (Fog, Investigation and Dispersal Operation), which burnt petrol alongside the runway to disperse the fog. It was just my luck that the wind was somewhat across the flare path. Yet as you held off the Lancaster to feel for a three-point landing, any crosswind would drift it sideways. The advice had been, don't try to straighten out or you'll be running over the blazing petrol. Instead, just wait until you're on the grass, then sort things out. Which is what I did. Though drifting over flames like that is not an experience I wanted to repeat!

A Lancaster using FIDO to land in poor visibility

And on 5 March 1945, it was back to Gelsenkirchen once again, on another Gee-H attack by 170 Lancasters. Dessau, though, on 7 March, was an epic in itself! A new target for Bomber Command to confront. But navigator Mike and I had already held our own confrontation. For the last few trips we had been arriving late at the target. And there was no future in that.

The German radars saw to it that the main bomber stream was met with box barrages of anti-aircraft fire. Arriving as part of the stream, then, offered herd protection. Get separated though, and you became the target for predicted flak. The first sign that you had been singled out was a searchlight beam moving towards you, joined just instants later by a second. After that it was only a heartbeat or two before shells began to close in. And shells directed specifically at you! Have that happen and you were just seconds from becoming a statistic!

So I laid down the law. Starting tonight Mike was going to get us there in the middle of the pack, no more lagging, no running in late so that the defences could pay us special attention. If that meant cutting out a safety dog-leg or so, fine. Just so long as we arrived among the leaders.

That night Mike's outbound estimates were hearteningly up to schedule. 'Target should be dead ahead, Skipper,' he finally announced. Except that I could see nothing. But just a little later he insisted, 'Skip, we should be directly overhead now.' Only to be interrupted by rear gunner, Alan, advising, 'Flares are going down, Skipper, but a long way behind us.'

God! We'd overshot! This meant that we had to turn around and go back! First, though, doing a turn wide enough to avoid the incoming bomber stream. Only that would take us outside the protection afforded by the radar-confusing 'Window' and invite the only-too-personal predicted flak – the most rapidly-acting laxative known to man! – to concentrate on us, the isolated blip. And even joining the main stream was hazardous, since our exhaust flames curving in from the side could well be taken for a night-fighter attack. Finally, of course, we'd be running over by-now fully-alerted ground defences. But it had to be done. So, long, long minutes later, by this time virtually alone, we ran in, dropped, held that interminable ten seconds – if forced to weave from counts eight to ten! – and made for home. Only to discover, on arrival, that the entire south-east of the country was out in fog.

But Acklington up in Yorkshire was open! So, with seventy other Lancasters we headed northwards, landing very short of fuel and having been airborne for just ten minutes short of ten hours. Of the 526 Lancasters engaged, eighteen had been lost – 3.4 per cent of the force! True, the target area had suffered widespread damage. But although Jim Stanniforth, phlegmatic though he was when his turret was holed, was always fascinated by the 'chop rate', regularly visiting the office where the squadron's percentage of losses was maintained, none of us could help balancing whatever the damage caused at Dessau against the loss of 126 men!

Only a new ordeal awaited our near-500, deathly-tired aircrew. For Acklington was a training station for 300 WAAFs, and a dance had been

Forced to weave over Dessau at 18,000 feet

hurriedly laid on … Next morning many crews were even more washed out. And, inexplicably, aircraft that on landing had been perfectly serviceable had developed snags overnight! Indeed, some aircraft were only recovered when relief crews arrived to fly them home.

Not long afterwards we were briefed for an operation after a period of persistent fog. The clearance was coming in very slowly, but weather checks had shown that the sky above was gin clear. Certainly, on lining up we were unable to see the end of the runway. The first aircraft though, rolled, lifted off, by arrangement turned fifteen degrees right, then continued climbing. The second lifted off and climbed straight ahead. The third made a left turn. By which time the first of the next trio was on the roll …

And once we broke through, what an experience! Blindingly brilliant sun, that went without saying. But the unbroken snow-white sheet from horizon to horizon below! Except that from every airfield in Norfolk and Suffolk aircraft were shooting through it like so many silvered fishes. Fish that broke free, took stock, then gathered into shoals, Americans into a semblance of formation, British into gaggles; in this instance flocking towards the machines equipped with Gee-H.

Days later, we found ourselves off the battle order for a while, selected from the mob to qualify on Gee-H. And having been checked out, we too had yellow stripes painted on our fins.

Then, on 14 April 1945, the target was Potsdam. Tension ran high, for this would be the first time in a year that Bomber Command had sought to penetrate the Berlin defences. The targets were the barracks and railway facilities, with 500 Lancasters and twelve Mosquitoes taking part. Results were said to be good. But on the run-up we'd had our own little drama.

Mike had brought us there on time, and neatly onto heading, handing over, then, to Dick.

'Steady, steady, Skipper,' Dick intoned. 'Steady …'

Only for Jim, the mid-upper, to break in, 'Skip, there's a Lanc only feet above us.'

'Is his bomb bay open?' I gritted.

'Steady, steady …'

'He's just opened it.'

'Skip,' Dick pleaded, 'just a moment more …'

Only it was no good. And we all knew it. Indeed, the memory was still raw.

Just a matter of days before we'd been running in when those of us up front realized that the lower of two flights ahead of us had inadvertently slipped beneath the higher one. Even as we watched, powerless, the top flight let go their bombs, one dropping squarely on a Lancaster below. There was just an instant's pause, then the bomb exploded, and both dropper and dropped upon

Looking up at someone else's bomb bay!

became so many fragments. It was an experience to turn the strongest stomach. Now I did not hesitate.

'Going round.'

And so we did.

It had been a moment of tight-lipped crew interaction Mike and I would reflect upon many years later, having been disgusted by the portrayal of the supposedly experienced crew in the 1990 film *Memphis Belle*. More recently, the world had been assured that TV celebrity chefs had no option but to launch into obscenity because of the extreme stress they were under.

'What would you have thought,' I asked, 'if I – or the master bomber – had begun effing and blinding?'

Mike didn't hesitate. 'That you'd lost the plot.'

And even now I can hear the master bomber's measured, matter-of-fact tones. And on more than one occasion the ominous cessation before the voice changed as a deputy seamlessly took over …

As it transpired, the Potsdam raid was to be the last major Bomber Command attack on a German city. So we had made a moment of history. Although it took us eight and a half hours to make it.

My passing mention of the Flying Fortress *Memphis Belle* – but thinking now of the 1944 documentary film – brings to mind the somewhat curious relationship we had with our American Allies. Meeting, as we did, in pubs or messes, we enjoyed needling them, belittling their Flying Fortresses for a start. As the Fortress's normal bomb load was 6,000 pounds and a Lancaster's was 14,000, our favourite ditty concluded, 'We're flying Flying Fortresses at forty thousand feet, but we've only got a teeny weeny bomb.' And on air tests we'd pull alongside a Fortress, feather an engine, then, after a while, another, and so on; which they really didn't like. And they thought differently too.

On one occasion we were drinking with a crowd of them in the Golden Lion in Newmarket together with some girls, good-time types, not to put too fine a point on it. Anyway, the Americans suggested we adjourn to a dance at their base. Except that on arriving I immediately realized that it was an officers-only function. Most of my crew were senior NCOs, of course, but on the other hand we knew how democratic Americans were said to be. As I paused at the door, however, I was informed that the base commander wanted a word 'with the senior British officer'.

'Tell me, sir,' he demanded, 'are any of your party enlisted men?'

'No, sir,' I replied. 'They're all volunteers.'

But it didn't wash. And as I led away our social fall-shorts I heard his pained drawl, 'I never thought our ladies would be expected to dance with enlisted men.' The ladies in question, those we'd brought with us, were already dancing, so didn't hear him, but how amused they would have been!

Then there was the occasion when, on a stand-down, crews were checking into a premier London hotel. All went well until a West Indian air gunner reached the desk. When everything stopped. It was impossible to book him in, it transpired, because then the Americans would refuse to stay, and their business was far too valuable to lose. The hotel instantly lost our custom, of course. But, truth to tell, they didn't seem all that much upset.

Crew loyalty of any sort, of course, was deep reaching. So that when Wally arrived back from a run into King's Lynn just as we got airborne with a spare engineer, I was able to avert the wing commander's tantrum, vouching for the miscreant's keenness. Then, when he flew a catch-up op with another crew, the rest of us joined the group of well-wishers at the take-off point. And we were all there again, hours later, when he landed.

The farewell waves ...

What turned out to be our final operation, on 18 April 1945, took us to the naval base on the island of Heligoland. Monty (General Montgomery) we were told, wanted the defences obliterated so that he could get vessels into the German ports. Accordingly, nearly a thousand aircraft took part: 969, in fact. 617 Lancasters, 232 Halifaxes, and 20 Mosquitoes. It was a daylight raid, so although the force bombed on Gee-H, the aircraft we were allocated was not so equipped. Accordingly, tagging on to a yellow tailfin, our aiming-point photo shows that we only just got our bombs on the island. But enough to count, reckoning by the raid results.

Unbelievably, no flak came our way. And we realized that the German garrison, anticipating the onslaught, had taken to boats and were standing off the coast. For my part, I was a little shocked to realize that I was feeling sorry for them. Yet never before had I had ever felt anything like pity for those we bombed. On the other hand, they had always been shooting at us. And even now, with virtually no opposition, three Halifaxes failed to return.

And suddenly, it was all over. In Europe, at least. VE Day! It coincided with the Newmarket Races. So we all trooped along to celebrate. I was leaning on the rails when I became aware that the man beside me had started whistling,

Heligoland aiming-point photo

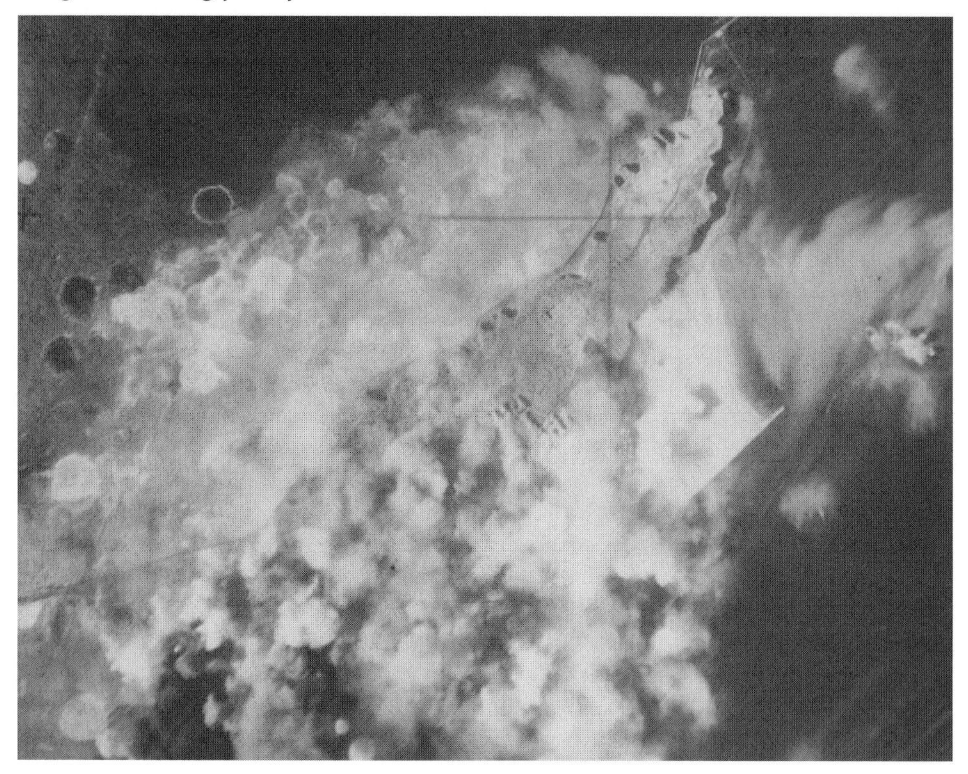

No. 149 Squadron, VE Day; me to the right of the goat

'D'ye ken John Peel'. Looking up, I realized that it was no other than the celebrated tipster, Ras Prince Monolulu, feathered headdress and all. Consulting the race card I saw that 'The Huntsman' was running in the next race. Hurrying, I just had time to put down my ten bob. And 'The Huntsman' romped home!

Prince Monolulu, the celebrated tipster

I worked my way back to Prince Monolulu's side, and again he came up with the goods, 'White for pluck, Black for luck.' Or I'm sure he would have done, had I been able to solve the clue!

It was a respite, but a brief one. Operation Exodus, our first post-war task, however, should have been a joyous occasion, virtually the whole squadron carrying out a series of flights to Reims, France, to help repatriate army, Allied, and RAF prisoners of war who had been gathered there from camps all over Germany. We packed them twenty-four to a Lancaster, each wearing a Mae West lifejacket and sitting on a parachute pack. The trouble was that the airfield had been designed for fighters so that the taxiways were too narrow for heavy bombers. This meant that the stakes pegging down the edges of the perforated-steel-plate decking tended to damage the tyres. Unfortunately, nobody appreciated this until a tyre blew on one of the lead aircraft, the resulting crash killing all thirty-one on board. Following the tragedy, we had our groundcrews check the tyres of each aircraft after it left the taxiway for the runway, the lift being completed without further loss.

But returning to our American allies, it was during Exodus we saw what organizers they were! On the fourth of our lifts, fog set in at Methwold, and once again 70 Lancasters – these carrying some 2,200 bellies – were obliged to divert, this time to one of the American bases. And yet their caterers weren't in the least bit fazed. Before we could blink, as it seemed, food trucks were circulating and everyone was taken care of.

Then again, on the final lift, our common purpose as Allies was forcibly brought home to us. Staying over in Reims we visited a nightclub where the chorus delivered *Lili Marleen* with great vigour. Yanks and Brits in unison

Operation Exodus, April to May 1945, No. 149 Squadron at Reims, ready to load ex-prisoners of war

demanded with equal gusto, 'Encore! Encore!' Only for the enthusiasm to trigger an unthinking '*Ja! Ja!* from the stage', the girls' habituated response of the last three and more years.

Us and both our Allies, American and French. A love-hate relationship. But overall we valued them highly.

One memorable flight still remained, when we flew a Lancaster on a Cook's tour of the Ruhr targets, taking along a couple of the station WAAFs. Flying at low level over the devastation was the experience of a lifetime.

Cook's Tour: left to right: Flight Sergeant Dick Copesteak, bomb aimer; Pilot Officer Mike Tavenor, navigator; unknown flight sergeant, filling-in wireless operator/air gunner; WAAF air traffic control; Flight Lieutenant Keith Hall, MBE, pilot; WAAF air traffic control; Flight Sergeant Alan Young, rear gunner; Flight Sergeant Wally Rawlins, flight engineer

Effectively, the war was over, but the pace of things hardly slackened. We were moved to Benson, near Oxford, and set to aerial map-making across Europe. It was done under pressure, our own powers that be wanting the job completed before the various sovereign governments could collect themselves and object.

Although we were kept busy, still those months at Benson – RAF Shangri La, as we knew it – take on, in retrospect, something of a halcyon aspect. Picnics by the Thames, at Wallingford. And during duty hours, flying a Lancaster utterly without stress.

Map-making photo interpreters

For though I touched upon matter-of-factness earlier, a sure measure of stress on ops had always been the rush for the toilet cubicles on landing. On emerging one airily announced, 'It's that beer in the mess,' and everybody nodded agreement. Only no one was fooled: not the beer in the mess, of course, but the fear in the sky.

Next, we delivered up the money from our escape and evasion kits! And in exchange we received coffee laced with rum, the latter to get us to talk. And it had its effect. For with that inside us and the op behind us even the plainest of WAAF debriefing officers looked like Hedy Lamarr. Only having got us started it was sometimes hard to stop us. Even so, we were very protective of our feelings.

On one occasion I came upon a pilot acquaintance sitting, head in hands. 'I've just done my third turn back,' he told me, 'the Wing Co's bound to see it as LMF.' That is, lack of moral fibre: the acronym stamped on the documents of any aircrew member who refused to carry out an op. Clearly this chap had started turning back short of the target, not because of the weather or a technical problem, but because he could no longer face the strain.

Yet nobody wanted anyone to be so stigmatized. Certainly not the wing commander, not least because any case of LMF reflected badly on his leadership. In this case the chap had just three ops to go, so he was scheduled for what were regarded as easy targets. As it was, he finished his tour, his transient timidity being attributed to what we all knew as 'operational twitch': an eye flicker, or a mannerism.

In fact, we would even play at it. Asked at debriefing what we had done next when things had looked so ropey, we'd clown, 'We p-p-p-p-pressed on regardless.'

Conceivably there may have been more subtle signs. For example, during the critical phases of an operation I always flew manually, ready to get the instant response I might need. On the way home, though, I would often engage George – the automatic pilot. Only the crew would watch for my head to sag to the left, when one of them would call, 'Eng, give the skip a shake, he's dozing off again.' Or maybe I was just tired.

It was at Benson, though, that I first became aware of people arguing the moral aspect of bombing. It started when the atomic bombs were dropped. Yet to our way of thinking anything that ended the war so promptly had to be a good thing. Especially as our aircraft had been painted up to be flown out to the Far-Eastern theatre. Of more concern to us was whether a crew like ours, halfway through its tour, would be sent out, or whether only crews with a full thirty ops to do would go. As it was, the A-bombs rendered the question academic. As for the latter-day do-gooders, well ...

Our most memorable trip from Benson had to be a there-and-back duty carrying passengers to Villacoublay, Paris. Cannily thinking ahead, the crew stocked up with soap and chocolate, arguably better than currency at the time. And on arrival the engineer duly found a snag that obliged us to stay overnight! With easy consciences we repaired to a nightclub where the world-renowned film director and star, Leslie Banks, called us to join his party. Naturally, he was a magnet to the showgirls, one of whom, eyeing the survival whistle on my battleblouse collar, wanted to blow it. I was only too willing, and as she leant close, pursing her lips, I obliged wholeheartedly. Which led to every charmer in the chorus wanting to toot! toot! Until, abruptly, the club was invaded by snowdrops – white-helmeted, baton-swinging American military policemen – responding to the whistle blasts and demanding to know where the riot was.

But halcyon days are, by nature, transitory. And at a moment's notice, with scarcely time for a farewell, another pilot took over the lads, while I was posted to Finningley, near Doncaster, Yorkshire, to the Bomber Command Instructors' School, to learn how to instruct on Wellingtons.

I soldiered on. One did, of course. But with VJ Day a malaise had spread to much more than the clapped-out aircraft. Operational groundcrews had invariably worked around the clock to get their charges serviceable. At Finningley, though, that ethic had gone. So that on one occasion I had to go to four ostensibly on-line aircraft before finding one fit to fly. Only to have its fuel-jettison system dump gallon after gallon onto the tarmac. And then, when the aircraft was once more declared serviceable, nobody had moved it from its pool of petrol! Landing with FIDO was one thing, creating my own inferno on start up was something I wasn't prepared to do.

Lancaster start up

Having qualified at Finningley, I was posted as an instructor to No. 10 Operational Training Unit at Abingdon, back near Benson. But as 1945 drew to a close, demob beckoned. Only there was a choice to be made. I had all the basic requirements to transfer to Imperial Airways. Yet in those days airline crews were rarely at home. And I had spent time enough away from my family. Accordingly, in February 1946, I hung up my flying helmet for good.

What to say of that next six months? Unsettling, would probably suffice. The salon, capably handled by my cousin, was making good money. Yet even the apprentices knew more about the business than I did! After pursuing several false trails, however, I struck gold in Charles Pluckrose, of Wigmore Street, who agreed to accept me on a year's pupillage. And so I learnt my trade.

Over the ensuing years, not least employing precepts laid down by my father, and by the great professional who had tutored me, the Long Eaton salon was joined by seven others. Indeed, only after a 1980 episode called for heart surgery did I decide to call it a day. The company, though, has gathered strength, in 2011, branded KH, comprising twenty-two salons across the Midlands.

It is a long haul from those days over flak-filled skies. Yet the legacy remains with me. Or, being the last of the crew, perhaps I am the legacy. As it was,

The 1948 reunion: left to right (foreground): Keith Hall, pilot; Wally Rawlins, flight engineer; Dick Copesteak, bomb aimer; Michael Tavenor, navigator. Sampling the beer, the fear left far behind them

Navigator Mike carved himself an illustrious career in the world of department stores, notably with Harrods, then with then Bobbys – Debenhams –, contentedly retiring as general manager of the Nottingham branch. Even having made his home in Bath he remained close, leaving us in 2009.

Rear-gunner Alan Young became a policeman in Liverpool. Wireless-operator Roy – The Boy – was commissioned after we finished ops, and stayed on as an education officer. Bomb-aimer Dick Copesteak had been a bus driver with London Transport and returned to become an inspector, but mid-upper Jim Stanniforth, sadly, retained little contact. Of us all, then, Flight-engineer Wally Rawlings alone stayed on as aircrew, only to be lost on 12 February 1954 when his Shackleton disappeared during a maritime sortie from Malta.

They came to me, all those years ago, as it were, under sufferance, but together we experienced – and survived – both the beer in the mess and the fear in the sky. A great crew! Even, I would hazard, the greatest ...

Keith Hall, 2012

2

A matter of getting on with it

Warrant Officer George Ellis Parkinson (Parky), wireless operator/air gunner

Sergeant George Parkinson, 1943

I was born in 1921, left school at fourteen, and became a railwayman. In October 1942 call-up loomed and as I had an aversion to becoming a soldier and as I'd long wanted to be a pilot, I volunteered for the RAF.

I was sent to Padgate for an intelligence test, a medical, and a general examination, but although my maths let me down for being a pilot or navigator I was accepted as a wireless operator/air gunner. After joining up on 11 November 1941 I did my general service training and square-bashing at Blackpool, then began the course at No. 2 Signals School, at Yatesbury, in Wiltshire. This course would make me an aircraftman class one (AC1) with a wireless flash on my sleeve. Unfortunately, as our group completed the basic-radio stage the RAF found itself temporarily flush with trainees but short of aircraft, so, to my consternation, I was one of those detached to the Royal Corps of Signals until the blockage cleared: to the bloody army!

It was a shock for all the RAF recruits affected to go from a peacetime RAF station with well-constructed billets, sheets on the bed, great food, four NAAFI

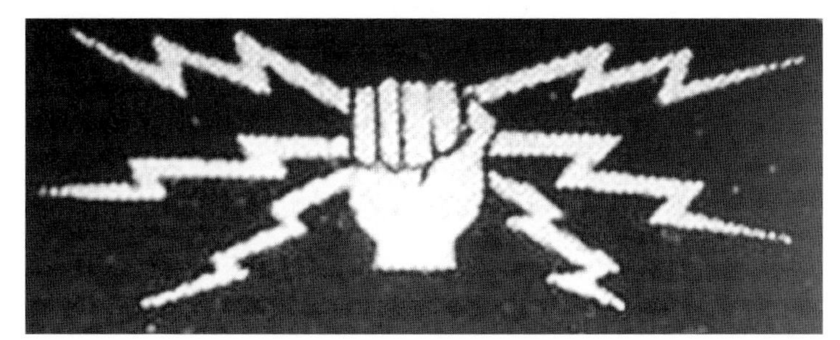

The wireless trade's arm flash

canteens and a station cinema, to shoddy huts, palliasses that had to be stuffed with straw, awful food and few amenities. Not only that, but we had to do army basic training, including an assault course, and route marches! We even wore army battledress. We did, though, have blue forage caps, and as these had the white trainee-aircrew flashes we were often taken for officer cadets and even saluted on occasion!

The highlight of this stint was when we were dropped off in an unknown location in the Truro area and had to map-read our way to a given destination. For security, of course, the signposts had been taken down and all place-names expunged. Our air force bunch, however, discovered that gravestone inscriptions often identified the village, thanks to which we got back in record time, and were praised for our initiative.

I was also pleasantly surprised to find that, although I was a fair shot, I did much better than any of the army recruits on the rifle range. Only slowly did it

The signposts had been taken down

dawn on me that these particular squaddies were determined to avoid being posted for active service. Shooting, therefore, was the last thing they wanted to be seen to shine at.

Alongside such activities our training in wireless-associated subjects went ahead, and although the practical work was more suited to the needs of ground personnel it was interesting just the same.

Beyond that, we were all young and eager, and wherever we went there always seemed to be friendly girls around. Not surprisingly then, we were subjected to a monthly inspection against venereal disease, standing naked by our beds as the medical officer inspected our bits and pieces, moving them aside distastefully with a wooden rule. 'FFIs', these were known as – 'Freedom From Infection' inspections. Or as we rendered it, 'Fit for insertion'.

In December 1942, during a leave period, I went home and got married, though naturally enough, when at camp, I continued to welcome female company. Even, I have to confess, after the following December, when I became a father. No excuses. It was just Youth, I suppose, and what the eye doesn't see . . .

Talking of seeing, though, my home was far from the area where our bomber streams formed up before setting course for raids, but later, when I was on operations, it did concern me that my wife might worry, especially when the baby became due. Indeed, she confessed that whenever an aeroplane flew overhead her heart would come into her mouth. But then from that point of view too, we were all so very young.

Shortly after Christmas 1942 I was recalled to the RAF, reporting to Lord's Cricket Ground where we were accommodated in formerly-private flats and messed in the restaurant of the Regent's Park Zoo.

Mealtimes were great, as with so many airmen to cater for we could go round the food queue twice, leaving a sergeant cook to puzzle at the way the unit's population used to double whenever eggs were on the menu.

After this, it was back to Yatesbury to continue our radio training. Sending messages in morse is long-winded so we had been introduced to a brevity code prefixed by X. Now we had to get used to the military Z Code, and more importantly, to the Q Code, the one we invariably employed. In this, frequently-used messages took the form of three-letter groups prefaced by Q. As an example, if you wanted to know the barometric pressure that would make an altimeter read zero at a given airfield you asked for the QFE.

Once we got onto ops this altimeter information would be broadcast to the returning bomber force at regular intervals. In fact, as the code was international, sending the actual value would have helped the Germans build up the picture of the weather pattern in the UK, so the message would simply be a plus or minus figure on the pressure setting we'd set at take-off.

One extracurricular activity this time around at Yatesbury involved the disinformation that night-fighter pilots were fed on carrots to improve their night vision. This, of course, was aimed at covering up the fact that the RAF possessed radar. Whether the authorities had begun to believe their own propaganda, I couldn't say, but the Yatesbury intakes were used as guinea pigs. Our class was fed carrots until we were sick of them, whereas other classes had none. But although it went on for some weeks I never heard that anything came out of it one way or another.

Radio work was followed by lectures on aircraft recognition and by instruction on the Browning machine gun. Later, at the gunnery school at Porthcawl, in South Wales, we fired at a model aircraft running round a circular track, but I didn't think much of that. We also shot at clay pigeons from a turret, which was better value. Though shooting at clays was most fun using a shotgun, not least because the authorities weren't that hot on accounting for cartridges, which meant that we could make mutually profitable swapping deals with local farmers. The actual air firing we did, though, was much more fun than target shooting of any kind, though the scores were never spectacular

Firing at clay pigeons

Back at Yatesbury, things intensified, and at the course's end I passed out as an aircraftman class one, with a signals' arm badge, having read morse at twenty-four words a minute, taken down Aldis-light signals at eight words a minute, and done semaphore – flag-wagging – to whatever the standard was. I'd also done some basic navigation, and even an introduction to the sextant!

Next stop was No. 3 (Observer) Advanced Flying Unit at Halfpenny Green (formerly Bobbington), near Wolverhampton, where we completed our air-firing while flying in Ansons and Oxfords. Finally, then, we put up our 'AG' (air gunner's) brevets, and our sergeant's stripes, and went on leave.

On reporting back for duty, we were posted to No. 17 Operational Training Unit, at Silverstone, Northamptonshire – the airfield is now the racecourse – where we flew Wellingtons, mostly from Turweston, Silverstone's satellite. We also crewed-up here, the system being to put all the various aircrew into a room and leave them to sort themselves out. I don't think many of us felt that good about the procedure, but I suppose had the pilots been in a position to select people on the basis of course results the last ones chosen would have felt even worse.

Our crew comprised, Sergeant Petite, pilot; Sergeant Jack Peterson, from Winnipeg, navigator; Sergeant Barry Watts from Toronto, bomb aimer; me, of course; and Sergeant Robert Kerr, from Alberta, rear gunner. After some hours of handling, however, the pilot was found unsuitable for heavy bombers. Even

Our crew, left to right: Sergeant Jack Peterson, RCAF, navigator; Sergeant Robert Kerr, RCAF, rear gunner; Sergeant Roy (Puddle) Lake, captain; Sergeant Geordie Baird, flight engineer; Sergeant George Parkinson, wireless operator/air gunner; Sergeant Leslie Major, mid-upper gunner. Sergeant Barry Watts, RCAF, our bomb aimer, took the photo

so they let him solo, unnecessarily putting us all at risk, we felt, before posting him away. His replacement, fortunately for us, was Sergeant Roy (Puddle) Lake, from Croydon.

As a crew, supplemented at the heavies stage by both Flight-Engineer Sergeant Geordie Baird, from Morpeth, in Northumberland, and Mid-Upper Gunner Sergeant Leslie Major, from Camborne, in Cornwall, we were to complete a first, thirty-trip operational tour and then volunteer to commence a second, flying together for a total of forty operations.

Us RAF chaps, of course, couldn't help being aware that the Royal Canadian Air Force bods wore better uniforms and got twice as much pay as us; just the same, we settled well. In fact, from the start we always socialized, hanging together as a pack, doing everything as a bunch, cycling out and about, drinking, and womanizing. Other crews never got close like that but I held it as one of our strengths.

Certainly, we regarded ourselves a good crew, though we were well aware that being good was no guarantee of coming through, for all too many good crews bought it. Not that we ever thought we would buy it, but just the same we put on a confident air rather than speculate on what might be. My own philosophy was that ops, like life itself, was a matter of getting on with it.

We did a lot of local flying and circuits-and-bumps training. The circuits were for the benefit of the pilot, but during all the local flights signallers were expected to get as many wireless contacts as possible. I did particularly well at this and my prowess paid off, for having shown that I was well up to the mark I was able to get compassionate leave when my wife developed high blood pressure.

Once the pilot had got the hang of the circuit it was back to cross-country flights, with an introduction to the radar navigational aid, Gee, and more practice using the loop aerial to get directional bearings, an advantage of the latter being that you didn't have to transmit and so risk giving away your position.

After four months at Silverstone, and a ten-day leave, we were sent to Scampton, Lincolnshire, at that time a holding unit: evidently the RAF was still rather more flush with aircrew

Gee navigational radar

than with aircraft. But at the end of January 1944, with our numbers swelled by Les Major, our mid-upper, and Geordie Baird, our newly-qualified flight engineer, we were posted to No. 1654 Heavy Conversion Unit at RAF Wigsley, on the Nottinghamshire-Lincolnshire border, to fly the four-engined Stirling.

Our pilot, Roy Lake – now commissioned – took easily to the cumbersome bomber, and that was just as well, for as we accelerated down the runway on our first take-off as a crew our new, too-eager, flight engineer called for an over-heating engine to be stopped. Instead, Roy ignored him, getting airborne and continuing to a safe height before throttling it back, after which the temperature returned to within limits.

Just a few trips later we were struck by lightning over The Wash – a notified Danger Area – and, thinking we'd been hit by 'friendly' anti-aircraft fire, Roy put down at the nearest airfield. It turned out to be an American base where

The cumbersome Stirling

we were made much of and fed sumptuously – not least with ice cream, something we hadn't seen for a very long time. The only damage to the aircraft, we found, was that our trailing aerial had been burnt off.

As for the Stirling, I wasn't alone in regarding it as a real crow; certainly, we were all delighted to be posted to No. 5 Lancaster Finishing School at RAF Syerston, near Newark. We were now to fly the beautiful Lancaster, the thoroughbred of the sky, lovely to look at, easy to fly, and very reliable; so that in the 350 hours we were to fly it the only time we had to stop an engine was when we were hit by flak.

The course passed swiftly, and on 25 April 1944, finally operational, we were posted to No. 9 Squadron at RAF Bardney, near Wragby, Lincolnshire.

At that time the squadron worked in association with No. 617 Squadron, the celebrated Dam Busters. Mostly their crews were second-tour men. Although when I came across some of them not that many months later they had sadly shot nerves.

Having joined the squadron we flew some fifteen hours, working up, before being detailed for operations, the first of which came on 1 May 1944 in the shape of a nine-hour round trip to Toulouse.

A heart-warming thing on this first op was that the raid leader circled the target – a French factory – for some time before calling in the bombers, so giving the factory lasses time to evacuate. For my part, I found that I was only a bit scared. Indeed, looking back from this near-seventy years' remove, apart from two thunderstorms and a bit of flak, it was a piece of cake.

Our true baptism of fire, however, was to come on the very next operation: the pre-D-Day raid on the military installation near Mailly-le-Camp, in the Champagne-Ardenne region of North-Central France. This was mounted by a force of 346 Lancasters and 14 Mosquitoes on the night of 3 May 1944. Damage on the target – predominantly a panzer-reserve force poised to cover the coastal area – was substantial. However, we spent twenty minutes loitering nearby before the raid controller, Leonard Cheshire, was satisfied with the accuracy of the markers and called us in.

Largely as a result of this concentration upon getting the markers positioned correctly the only French casualties were those injured when a downed Lancaster fell on their house. But the delay had given nearby night-fighter units time to assemble, and losses on the moonlit return flight were heavy.

I've got a lot of time for Cheshire, but while he was being so meticulous we were left milling about in the dark, which was something we hadn't been prepared for. There was no laid-down direction to turn in, so people were all over the place. In fact, I've always felt that many of that night's losses must have been caused by collisions. Then again, I've never rated the published figure of forty-two Lancs lost (11.6 per cent of the force), personally reckoning losses as more like eighty.

As it was, the pre-raid briefing for this op had unexpectedly faced me with a moral dilemma. We'd been addressed by Squadron Leader 'Willie' Tait, No. 617's boss. He'd started by telling us that the raid had been deliberately timed so that all the enemy soldiers would have returned from the local bars and whorehouses and be back in their quarters. This gave us a laugh. But then he went on, very matter-of-factly, 'Tonight lads, it's not women and children we'll be bombing, tonight we'll be at the real thing.'

I tell you, this took me totally aback! For only then did this aspect of the job come home to me. As it was, after briefing I told the rest of the crew that, regardless of his assurance, I wanted no part of it. And perhaps I would have taken it further: I'm bloody minded enough. But then, between them – crew discussions were part of the way we did things – they persuaded me to carry on, their main argument being that as Germany had started the bombing of civilians then the sooner we beat them at it the sooner the war would be ended. And so, just hours later, I did my best to control my sensibilities – and the butterflies in my stomach – as the first flak rose up about us.

Looking back over the forty operations we were to carry out, some live in my mind more than others. Just the same, of course, there were factors common to all. At night, for instance, seeing the flak flashes ahead, I'd always think, 'How the hell are we going to get through that lot?' But at least, at night, the flash disappeared, and that was that. On daylight raids, however, there was the flash, but then the puff of black smoke. And that hung there, each one feeding on the next as if to fill up the sky before us. In the daytime too, it was easier to see other aircraft going down. And that always chilled the blood. Especially if they burned ...

One eventful trip was that to Rennes, in Brittany, on 8 June 1944. We were told that the target was a pyrotechnics factory, but from the way it went up I rather think other things were being produced there. Having dropped our bombs we were hit by flak, but our real troubles that day were to be weather related.

Bardney was out, we discovered, because of the poor visibility. It was the sort of haze that, on looking vertically downwards through it, made everything appeared gin clear. Looking forwards into it, however, along the slant visibility – the view you faced as you tried to land – you couldn't see a thing. Consequently the whole squadron was diverted way, way up to Scotland, to RAF Turnberry, just south-west of Ayr, the only area that was clear of haze.

Even here though, the ground was blotted out by low cloud. I got a QFE for Turnberry. This was the setting, remember, that would mean that when we landed our altimeters would read zero. As we approached, however, boring along from the south over the various slabs of unseen high ground, we were well aware that the reading on our altimeter would not tell us how far above the ground we were, not until we were actually overhead the field. Not at all a comforting thing to be aware of, but it was the way we did things in those days.

So, with the altimeter set, our navigator, Jack Peterson, played it safe and directed the skipper to let down to the west, towards the sea. Roy dutifully did so, nosing down blind, but on breaking cloud with some very reasonable altitude still showing on the altimeter we were appalled to find ourselves virtually scraping the earth, at which Jack and Roy temporarily fell out. What we'd done, it turned out, was to emerge from cloud directly over Ailsa Crag, an islet off the coast and some one thousand feet high!

That wasn't the end of it, though, for on lowering the undercarriage we got an unsafe indication. Topping up the hydraulic system with the contents of the pee-can did not solve the problem so we were told to land on the grass beside the runway. As it turned out, although we were escorted by two fire engines and an ambulance – not at all a heartening sight – the wheels were fine, safely down and locked: it was just a faulty indicator lamp. As other fliers have told me since, this was a scenario that would be repeated over and over again, and certainly for the next fifty years, the problem invariably being a faulty bulb, or a dirty electrical contact.

That trip to Rennes was an op that should not have taken all that long; in fact, it took us seven hours!

Anyway, Turnberry found itself swamped by some 140 alien aircrew. A dance was laid on, the station's WAAFs being supplemented by hurriedly summoned local girls. Coming off ops we hadn't any money with us, but arrangements were made to make funds available. At a late stage in the proceedings, however, after I'd drunk all I could find to drink, I decided to dance with Turnberry's Station Warrant Officer (SWO), a dignitary who seemed to be not in the least amused.

Nor was he! Therefore, I was awakened next morning – still in flying kit, unwashed, unshaven, and with a massive hangover – by a summons to his office. He wanted me to apologize, but being hungover, and – as I have said – being naturally bloody-minded, I refused.

So I was wheeled before Turnberry's station commander. He listened to the complaint, then, having asked the SWO to leave, gave me a fatherly talking to. He made it clear that he had nothing but respect for the warrant officer, who was, after all, responsible for discipline on his station. On the other hand, he told me, I must understand that the SWO, being a non-flier, 'didn't understand the stupid things operational aircrew got up to'. The commanding officer then promised that if I behaved myself for the remainder of my stay his admonishment would not appear on my records. As it was, we didn't have money enough left to get into any more trouble and so the remaining few days we were forced to spend there were boring in the extreme.

On 26 June 1944 we visited Prouville, some fifteen miles from Abbeville, my logbook recording three hours and thirty-five minutes in the air. The target was an area of caves where V-1 Flying Bombs were being stored. The raid itself went all right but on the return we were coned by searchlights – by twenty-four,

I recorded. This effectively blinded our gunners, but fortunately we had a radar device called 'Monica', which sent pulses backwards and warned us of anything approaching our tail.

And just as well! For shortly afterwards we were attacked by three Junkers Ju88 night-fighters, though how they found us was puzzling, for by the time they attacked we were well clear of the searchlights. Anyway, as each one closed to its firing range of some three hundred yards on Monica's scope, I would call Roy to corkscrew. Our gunners downed one, and claimed to have damaged another. But then our starboard engine began to run rough and had to be stopped and feathered, that is, the blades turned edge-on into the airflow to cut down the enormous resistance a windmilling prop would have caused.

Back at Bardney Roy made a safe landing, after which it was discovered that a propeller blade had been holed, and that the starboard wing had taken several hits. Following that trip he got a DFC – a Distinguished Flying Cross – and one of the gunners was decorated, whereas I, who had kept us clear of so many attacks, was rather miffed not to get as much as a Mention in Despatches.

Even so, I was luckier than I knew, for shortly afterwards it was established that the German fighters were actually homing in on Monica! After that, we left it switched off, and were only too glad when Command scrapped it altogether.

Monica display unit

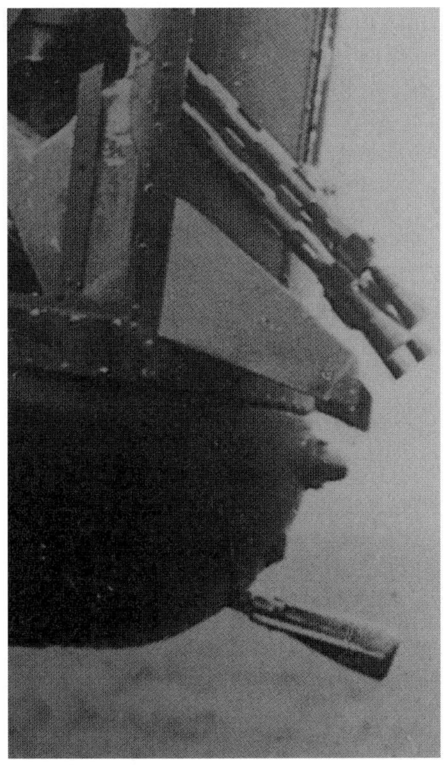

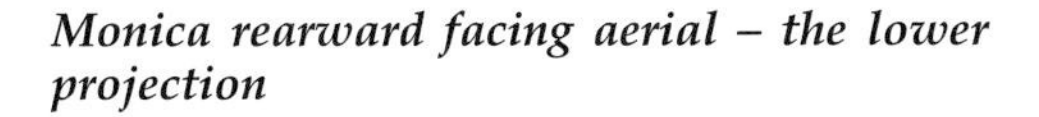

Monica rearward facing aerial – the lower projection

Discounting such aids-to-the-enemy as Monica, there were, of course, no easy ops. And certainly not for us, the tour-and-a-third we did as a crew including half a dozen Ruhr-Valley trips, each of which was double hell. And so we sought refuge in black humour, complaining in mock hurt, 'Someone above or below's always trying to take potshots at us. And merely because we're dropping bombs on them.'

No easy ops then. But many were made even more severe by the weather. Surprisingly, the met men were normally pretty good, for having only a limited number of high-level-recce aircraft to report back on the continental weather, they had little to go on but guesswork. When we were sent on a near-eight-hour round trip to Leipzig, however, they got it really wrong.

We had expected to be flying between cloud layers. Instead, there was just one layer, quite thick, and low down. This meant that from above we were moonlit like moths on a white sheet. If we dropped below the cloud, on the other hand, the flak had us against a clear cloud ceiling. Over and above which the cloud itself was full of ice. We had no option, in the circumstances, but to press on. Losses, though, were significant.

Then, during the return, with the weather problems behind us, Roy wanted to relieve himself. He engaged 'George', the auto-pilot, and leaving his seat, leant to the five-gallon oil container we used as a pee bucket: as was the case with many crews we never used the Elsan chemical toilet situated far back to the rear. Only the moment Roy got going so the auto-pilot disengaged, plunging the aircraft into a steep dive. Both Roy – caught mid-stream – and Geordie, the flight engineer, rushed to pull it out, and finally succeeded, for all that the rest of us thought we were gonners. But what a mess! The pee can's contents had gone all over the nav's station, soaking him and his maps, and Gee was out anyway. But in the end I managed to get a bearing, and we eventually got home.

A series of trips that particularly stands out began on 9 August 1944 when, with the Germans in Brest cut off, we carried out a raid on its U-Boat pens, using 12,000-pound Tallboy bombs. We weren't successful, and so we went back twice more, on 14 and 15 August, again with Tallboys. On 14 August the opposition was slight, and we deduced that the hemmed-in garrison had run out of shells. Next day we came in lower. And they virtually filled the sky with flak! And once again we saw the unsettling sight of other aircraft going down ...

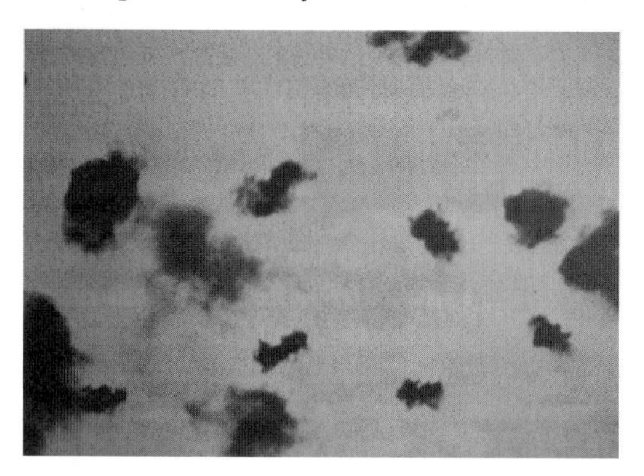

They virtually filled the sky with flak

On the way back things were so tense that, for the first time ever, I decided to ignore procedure and tuned away from the Group broadcast frequency to give the lads some light relief by putting on the BBC Forces Programme. So it was that I didn't receive the warning that the balloon barrage was up over Yeovil, and we virtually scraped it going by: hitting a cable would have been disastrous. As it was, even the near miss put me in a pickle.

The drill with Group broadcasts was that if there was no actual message at the pre-briefed broadcast time then a code number would be transmitted instead, which had to be logged. Fortunately for my hide, on deciding to tune off Group's frequency, I'd left a space in my log. On landing therefore, realizing from our close call that I might have missed something significant, I legged it to another aircraft, grabbed its wireless operator and asked him for the code number. Finding that there had indeed been a balloon barrage warning, I copied that instead and duly entered it before the signals officer could start asking questions. And I got away with it. A fine example of initiative. Or, as I'd rather say, of accepting a situation for what it was, and simply getting on with it.

Ops continued, but in early September we were all taken by crew bus to RAF Woodhall Spa, where, along with No. 617 squadron, we were briefed for an operation against the battleship *Tirpitz*. During the briefing the award of Cheshire's Victoria Cross was announced, and the place fairly rocked with applause, for his squadron worshipped him. And justifiably so: his decoration, remember, was not awarded for a specific op, but for constant valour over a sustained period.

At that time *Tirpitz* was in Norway's Alta Fjord, and the plan was to fly to Archangel, in the Soviet Union, wait until the weather was suitable, then launch the raid from there. We were to drop Tallboys and had specially modified Lancs for the job. These, as well as being pared for weight, had extra fuel tanks encroaching into the bomb bay, for it was to be a long flog. On starting up, therefore, we were brimful with fuel. And even then, before we actually entered the runway, we were given a last minute top-up.

We duly taxied out, but just as we turned onto the runway I felt a judder.

'What the hell was that, Roy?' I asked. Or words to that effect.

Roy checked around the others, but as no one else had noticed anything he decided it must be tailwheel shimmy: not that unusual, and much more likely at this extreme weight. And so we took off.

That went OK, but as we climbed away I felt an unusual draught. Again I told Roy, but he merely called back, 'Stop moaning, Parky.' There was, however, an inspection hatch at my station, and having opened it, I saw that the bomb doors, which should have been locked closed, were quite some way apart.

'Barry,' Roy told the bomb aimer this time, 'have a look and see what the grumpy old sod's on about.'

What the grumpy old sod was on about, Barry discovered, was that the Tallboy had slipped in the sling that held it secure! Now, instead of being held

The Tallboy, instead of being held firmly around its girth ...

firmly around its girth, the great bomb – all 12,000 pounds of it – was pretty well dangling by its tail. Not only that, but the whole great thing was actually swinging about, threatening to pierce the forward end of the extra fuel tank, brimful as it was!

Roy continued climbing, but very gingerly now, until we reached a safe height. By that time we were well over the sea, so he ordered Barry to get rid of the bomb. Only to find that the electrical release mechanism wouldn't work! Roy tried a shallow dive, then brought the nose up, hoping that the pull-out force would throw the Tallboy clear. But nothing doing, it still hung there, swinging even more violently than before.

Now we all had a say, a real crew conference, each one getting his own idea in. Except that the only constructive thing we came up with was to fly back westwards for a while – to make sure we were once more over terra firma – then to turn the aircraft out to sea on the autopilot and abandon by parachute. It was constructive, true. But nobody was all that keen on leaping out. As a consequence Roy dived again, and tried a much more spirited pull-out. At which, thank God! the now-loathsome thing fell away and into the sea, the aircraft, with that much weight gone, soaring upwards.

And so we returned to base, where Roy was interviewed by no less a personage than Sir Ralph Cochrane, the commander of No. 5 Group, to establish why he had turned back. In fact, the subsequent technical investigation showed that we had been doubly fortunate, for it was ascertained that the pin that was meant to hold the bomb in position – the fixing dowel – had either fallen out or had, inadvertently, been missed when the device was loaded. As it was, its noose having slipped, the Tallboy had banged back with such force that it had very seriously distorted the airframe.

The rest of the lads, meanwhile, had eventually found and damaged the *Tirpitz* but did not put it out of action.

Our crew's next job of note came on 15 September 1944 when No. 9 Squadron was tasked to attack the Sorpe Dam, the one No. 617 Squadron had failed to breach during their 'Dams Raid' in May 1943, sixteen months before. We though, would be using Tallboys. By now Roy was a flight lieutenant, and commanding our flight, so as the flight commander's signaller I had an ego boost when I was appointed to send back the raid report. I was issued with a special crystal to ensure that I got the correct frequency, but I didn't use it, priding myself on my ability to tune the set myself. In the event, although our bombs fell close, the attack was not successful, and I was disappointed at having to send 'Failed to breach'.

Tasking model of the Sorpe Dam

By then we'd not only completed the required thirty operations but had decided, after another crew discussion, to carry on rather than take our rest and later risk flying with some unknown bods. Les Major, our mid-upper gunner, however, had decided to opt out, so we'd gained 'Mucker' Morton as a replacement. He'd been burnt at some stage but had still returned to flying. A great character, and a clever cartoonist, he would never fly unless he had drawn a Mr Chad on the aircraft. You remember Mr Chad, of course, the two hands on the wall supporting the long-nosed round head bemoaning, 'Wot! No ——?' whatever the shortage was?

In fact, on one occasion the airspeed indicator failed to indicate as we ran down the runway, so Roy stopped the aircraft and returned to dispersal. There was a spare aircraft all ready to go, and we were rushed around to it, but Mucker absolutely insisted upon drawing his Mr Chad good-luck-charm before he would board.

But then most aircrew had superstitious foibles. Our flight engineer, Geordie, for example, liked to play snooker immediately before an op. And all of us got a bit concerned, and had words with our bomb aimer, when he began getting too close to an obliging lady whose aircrew lovers always seemed to get the chop. Not that I believed in such claptrap myself. Just the same, if I put a sock on

Mr Chad

inside out it stayed that way. Similarly, before every op I made sure my footwear was polished and my cap badge freshly shined ...

On the other hand, at this stage I was seriously beginning to weigh my chances of getting through the war. Up to that time I had never doubted that I would get through – the case, I'd judge, with 90 per cent of us. But now uncertainty was creeping in. After all, when Roy had taken over 'B' Flight he had become the seventh flight commander I'd had while on the squadron. True, ops seemed to be getting less frequent, but each was far more chancy. This war game, I found myself saying, is bloody dangerous. And now I had both a wife and a child to consider.

Having chatted things over, therefore, Barry Watts, our bomb aimer, and Robert Kerr, our rear gunner, both Canadians, joined me in applying to come off ops. The wing commander gave us short shrift, flying into a rage and calling us cowards. He would, he fumed, have us stripped of our stripes and our brevets, and have Lack of Moral Fibre (LMF) stamped all over our records. At which we demanded to see the group captain.

The more senior officer listened to us quietly, and having heard us out, assured us that there was not the slightest question of LMF, telling us that, on the contrary, we should forever hold our heads high, having done even more than the number of operations called for: forty instead of thirty. He then suggested that we take a day or so to reconsider. At the end of that time, however, when he found that we were adamant, he signed the necessary papers.

And so the crew split up. Barry and Robert returned to Canada, while I got a posting to RAF Finningley, near Doncaster, not far from my home. My promotion came through, to warrant officer, and on reporting to Finningley I was put in charge of the reference library. It was in total contrast to ops. But from the start, so boring! Not only that, but as well as messing around with books I found myself being used as a runner! A warrant officer, used as a menial! Certainly, by March 1945 I had had more than enough, and I applied to return to flying duties.

The flying I did at Finningley was not operational, but training flying had its moments, particularly when aloft with one particular instructor who liked to cut three out of the four engines!

On the other hand, there were perks. One of the treats for fliers was energy rations in the shape of the otherwise strictly-rationed chocolate, together with Horlicks and Ovaltine tablets, and canned orange juice. At Finningley we drew our energy rations on every trip, and as we often flew three times a day, soon built up a surplus. And this, of course, could be exchanged in black-market initiatives: after all, I had long exchanged clay-pigeon shotgun cartridges with farmers ...

There was an extra dimension, too, in the flying-associated task of airfield-beacon duty that I took on part-time. Throughout the hours of darkness, whenever aircraft were flying, the pundit beacon flashed an identifying code for the airfield. Looking after the installation was a cushy number, for during daylight hours the attendant was free. Then, when night flying was on, the rations allocated were virtually unlimited. The moment my duty was over, therefore, I would rush off home laden with everything from bacon and butter to pork dripping: to be effusively welcomed by my in-laws.

As for paying bus and train fares to go backwards and forwards, that was never necessary, for the conductors and drivers, women for the most part, would always keep a store of tickets for servicemen, to be produced in the event that an inspector got on.

The remainder of the crew had continued flying, and on 29 October 1944 had finally raided *Tirpitz*, which was, by then, lying damaged in Tromsø Fjord. On that occasion there was no positive result. But they had been part of the squadron force for the return visit on 12 November, and this time the job had been well and truly finished. All had then safely completed their second tours.

As it happened, of the whole crew, I was the only one not decorated. Indeed, shortly after he had returned to Canada, Robert Kerr, who had come off ops with me, was both commissioned and decorated. Only they gave him a DFC – as if he'd been an officer when he earned it. I never did understand that, for to my knowledge he only ever flew on ops as a senior NCO.

Thinking back now, it is just conceivable that his promotion to warrant officer might have been in the pipeline together with his recommendation for the decoration. That, at least, would make sense. But then, who knows, with the RAF?

Tirpitz, ***well and truly finished***

VE Day came, and No. 9 Squadron – for, naturally, I kept my eye on them – actually got as far as India on their way to fight the Japs before VJ Day put an end to the war.

For my part, still at Finningley, I had a rough bout of pleurisy. That passed, however, and even earned me sick leave, so that by December 1945 I was able to take advantage of a Class B release from the Service to return to the railways. After which, just before Christmas, I was sent to Wembley Stadium to hand in my RAF kit and receive my civvies and a leave pass for fourteen days.

My return to civvy street ushered in another life altogether. I soon left the railway, then spent twenty years down the mines. My first marriage failed, as did a second. And before retiring altogether and moving to Youlgreave, in Derbyshire, I ran a pub.

But long before all that, indeed as early as January 1947, it came home to me that I must have had a mental aberration two years before, in 1945, to even consider coming out of the RAF. Had I stayed in I would probably have retained my warrant-officer status, the flying would have been non-threatening, and as for the pay!

Certainly, Roy Lake had left the RAF, but being a pilot, his was a different case; indeed he went on to become a senior captain with BOAC. For my part, I realized that I had cooked my goose. But, as I had discovered during the very worst of our ops, there was nothing to be done. Life was life, and coping was simply a matter of getting on with it.

George Parkinson, 2012

3

I'd have dropped even more bombs

Warrant Officer Charles (Bill) Dowman, flight engineer

When war broke out I was working as a trainee diesel mechanic at Trent Motor Traction. On 30 September 1939, however, the moment I turned eighteen, I followed up an application submitted some time before and reported to RAF Cardington, Bedfordshire, for induction and basic training. That kept me busy, but my main memory of those weeks is of mounting a patrolling night guard on the massive airship sheds. Not that Hitler had much to fear, with one sentry carrying the rifle and the other the bullets.

Aircraftman Bill Dowman, 1939

From Cardington I was sent to South Wales, to St Athan, where I qualified as a fitter, grade two (engines). The course was both well regulated and demanding,

Cardington airship sheds with **R100** *and* **R101***. In 1939 as empty as my rifle*

but in this instance, my mind returns to the girl I met during an off-duty pass to Swansea.

She was my first love, and first love runs deep. In our case it also ran smoothly. Not least when, one idyllic afternoon, the air-raid sirens sounded while we were walking together. Following the people taking shelter we found ourselves crowded into a cinema foyer. The sound of bombs was inexorably drawing nearer. Tension was rising, with panic hovering. And then someone began to sing. The words were incomprehensible to me. But then someone else joined in, and others, a man here, a woman there, and finally the whole crowd, so that within moments the crump of bombs was totally drowned by this impromptu choir singing as only Welsh people can. It was the most moving experience, the memory of which brings a lump to my throat even at this remove.

Unfortunately, there was no cinema foyer and no Welsh crowd to sing away the danger in September 1940, after I had been posted, when the Luftwaffe came again and my fresh young sweetheart was among the fatalities. I suppose I should say that this early tragedy sowed the seed for my desire to retaliate, but I don't honestly think that was ever the case.

When the Luftwaffe came again ...

Once qualified as a fitter, I was posted to No. 92 Squadron, at Biggin Hill, in Kent, where I had the good fortune to be singled out to help look after the machine of the celebrated Bob Stanford Tuck, or, as he became, Wing Commander Robert Roland Stanford Tuck, DSO, DFC and two bars, AFC. My arrival coincided with a series of bombing and strafing attacks on Biggin by the Luftwaffe. On the first of these I was working on a Spitfire out in the open, only just managing to make it to an air raid shelter. In the second, on 30 August 1940, thirty-nine personnel were killed. Next day the nerve centre, the operations block, suffered a direct hit. On that occasion three of our WAAFs kept working to the last, all three receiving the Military Medal for bravery. Much less fortunate

Military Medal holders, Sergeant Elizabeth Martin; Section Officer (formerly Corporal) Elspeth Henderson; Sergeant Helen Turner, RAF Biggin Hill

was a young WAAF officer who, caught in the open, just as I had been on that previous occasion, was shot down.

But eight more raids followed. In one, a corporal I knew, Fred Harris, of No. 32 Squadron, Biggin's Hurricane unit, had arguably better luck. Having been strafed, his head was in such a state that he was put in the station mortuary. Only shortly before his parents arrived to see his body was it realized that he was alive. He then received treatment, and survived, serving on throughout the war, if with only, as he would habitually claim, half a brain. Indeed, many, many years later, applying for a retrospective pension, he was told by a bemused consultant that although his brain was all there, none of it was where it should have been!

After Stamford Tuck left – to gain yet more fame, before being shot down and becoming a POW – I took over a whole succession of sprog pilots. One that comes to mind was a Pilot Officer Welham. I remember him coming down from his first scramble, looking just a little lost as his fellow pilots walked away, hands re-fighting the battles they had just been engaging in. It was clear that he felt somewhat out of it so I hinted to him that if he pulled the fabric protective strips off the muzzles of his guns no outsider would be any the wiser that the opportunity of firing them had eluded him. He was very grateful, I remember, and quickly found his feet.

I remember even more clearly, sometime later, when he had begun to make his mark, that he had a date, but was concerned that, being on standby, he was unable to get away long enough to make his excuses. I elected to help him out and told Chiefy that my pilot's aircraft wouldn't be ready for at least an hour or so. I should have known better, of course, for our flight sergeant had not only got brown knees, as he put it, but lots of sand in his shoes. As it was, he didn't put me on a charge, but the flea in the ear I got about exigencies of the Service, and priorities, made me decide on the spot, never again!

Once the Battle of Britain was over, I applied for overseas service and duly received a posting to South Africa where, under the Joint Air Training Scheme – a South African extension to the Empire Air Training Scheme – RAF and South African Air Force (SAAF) instructors were training both air and groundcrews.

My initial posting was to SAAF Station Wonderboom (pronounced Vunderboom), midway between Johannesburg and Pretoria, just one of thirty-eight SAAF stations devoted to flying training. No. 3 Air School, housed there, was an Elementary Flying Training School equipped with Tiger Moths and Puss Moths, and the odd Anson. I threw myself into the work, and within days, found myself airborne on an air test of a machine I had just serviced.

Although this was a custom, it was not really obligatory, but I loved getting airborne, so that instructors began letting me know whenever a spare ride was going. Not that they were above the odd trick or two. For example, either of the control sticks could be removed by pulling out a split pin. So, on one of my first trips, the instructor suddenly turned his head, waved a control stick in the air, then hurled it over the side. 'You'll have to take control,' he yelled through the Gosport tube. But, having been pre-warned, I too had secreted a spare stick. Now, I held mine aloft. 'Without this?' I yelled back. And threw it too over the side.

After which I found myself totally accepted among the fliers. In fact, from then on I would spend more than half the time during such flights handling the aircraft under the benign tutelage of instructors who looked upon my joy-rides as stress-free relaxation from the normal cycle of their work.

Few of the other groundcrew lads could see the sense in getting airborne like that, especially after witnessing some of the numerous training crashes. But perhaps I had the last laugh, for some time later a group of us were sent down to SAAF Station Bloemspruit, near Bloemfontein, to work at No. 27 Air School and at the neighbouring Central Flying School at Tempe. The other mechanics refused to fly, saying it was too dangerous. And so it turned out that, having left camp a few hours after they had, I was able to look down and see the whole bunch of them, dusty and disconsolate, miles from anywhere, gazing at their lorry, on its side, in a ditch. Grinning, my pilot circled them a time or two, then waggled the wings and carried on to Bloemspruit where, having landed – no wireless, of course! – he organized a rescue party.

In all, I had a great time in South Africa, not least because, as the pupil pilots were happy – being red-hot keen to fly – so everyone else was happy. Certainly this was the case with the African would-be mechanics it fell within my remit to supervise. But what a task! You could spend hours one day showing them how to do a job, only to find that by the next it had totally gone from their heads. Most frustrating! Yet faced with the wide, beatific smiles, one wondered whether their inability to learn wasn't simply an act!

Perhaps the climate had something to do with the lack of will to exert oneself. At any rate it was on a similar head that I came to fall out with one of the sergeants in charge of me.

It wasn't that he was incompetent, just that he had fallen into lazy ways. On this occasion, anyway, I found that he had passed as fit an engine job when he should have had it done over. To my mind it never paid to take chances with aircraft when a minor fault only too often cost someone dearly in limb, or even life. Nor was it the first time I had caught him slipping like this, so now I really let fly at him. Not at all conducive to the good order and discipline required under King's Regulations, of course, but he knew very well that I was in the right. The trouble was as I was letting loose an officer happened along and insisted upon having me charged.

I was duly marched before the CO and asked what it was all about. I avoided tale-telling about the sergeant but argued instead that I hadn't known the reporting officer was commissioned because he had been wearing an airmen's-pattern coat. And so he had been! Being newly-commissioned he hadn't had time to get fully kitted out, and so I got away with the whole thing, and this time someone else got the flea in the ear. Further, left out of the report, the sergeant pulled his socks up.

But, beware of the ladder of life! For a year or so later, when the chance arose for me to apply for aircrew, who was on the board? But, of course: the new officer! And how he quizzed me! But I'll say this for him, that he bore no grudges, for he could have failed me on the spot. On the other hand, on certain flak-filled nights some months later I might have wondered whether he hadn't known full well what he was letting me in for.

As it was, that aircrew board was a real challenge, quite outside my previous experience. At least, until one of the members asked me to talk about some technical thing or other. As it happened I'd just done a course on the subject and had easily come out top, qualifying as a leading aircraftman. And so I began talking, and talking – and talking. Indeed, I think they had to tell me I'd been accepted for flight engineer in order to get me to stop. And just days later, I found myself on the boat.

My tour in South Africa had been kind to me, broadening my outlook and knocking off some youthful rough edges. But it had also made me feel part of things – enormous things. For by 1945 the Joint Air Training Scheme would have produced more than 7,800 pilots and over 33,000 aircrew for the RAF, not forgetting a further 12,000 for the SAAF!

As it was, in late 1943 I reported to St Athan once again, this time for my aircrew course. This was not as technically demanding as the fitter's course, the focus being upon operating engines and systems rather than fixing them. Just the same, when I came to sew on my 'E' brevet and sergeant's stripes, I felt that I had been fairly trained. I hadn't done any flying, but that, everyone seemed to feel, could wait.

Indeed, it had to wait until I had spent a week or so at A. V. Roe's, at Woodford, one of the factories where the Lancaster was being built. This was well worth while, and seeing the pride the men and women of the workforce took in their product amply accounted for the reputation the machine was forging for itself. Here too, I received my copy of the *Flight Engineer's Notes for Lancaster Aircraft*, whose supplementary notes exhorted, 'If you don't know, ASK'. It continued, 'Remember, you are the technical brains of the crew'.

With that in mind, I reported to No. 1661 Heavy Conversion Unit at Winthorpe, Newark, in Nottinghamshire, where my first job was to crew-up by mingling. I was to discover that many crew members found this procedure somewhat daunting, fearing that they might be left on the shelf. In contrast, as an experienced tradesman my attitude was, 'You lot have been flying about on twins, now you need a flight engineer. And I'm it!' As it was, I quickly settled upon my man, and although it was a decision arrived at by nothing but gut-feeling it was one I was never to regret. The crew I became part of, therefore, comprised: Flying Officer Percy (Perce) Fyson, pilot; Flying Officer Frank

Lancaster construction

Geldhart, navigator; Sergeant Bob Larman, Royal Canadian Air Force (RCAF), bomb aimer; Flight Sergeant Peter O'Brien, wireless operator/air gunner; me, Warrant Officer Charles (Bill) Dowman, flight engineer; Flight Sergeant Vic Lever, mid-upper gunner; and Pilot Officer Harold Hebb, RCAF, rear gunner.

On crewing-up most of us were senior NCOs but, for convenience, I've listed the ranks as they were during most of our tour; me as a warrant officer, for example. Then again, Perce was commissioned once we got onto Lancasters.

We were quite a mixture, numbering four Englishmen, one Welshman and, initially, two Canadians. I say initially, because the bomb aimer when I joined, Bob Larman, used to get violently drunk on the ground and tended to doze in the air. He was removed, therefore, before we started flying ops, his place being more than adequately taken by Flying Officer Barry Turnbull, Royal New Zealand Air Force.

I was mildly surprised to find that Winthorpe had Stirlings rather than Lancasters, but as the unit's purpose was to introduce us to four-engined aircraft and Stirlings were plentiful while Lancasters were rated as so much gold dust, it did not make much difference. The bulk of the work fell upon Percy Fyson and me, the rest of the crew getting on with their own tasks while we wrestled with stopping and starting engines, balancing fuel, and keeping on top of the seemingly unlimited stock of snags the screen pilots and engineers had up their voluminous sleeves. So, the Stirling was fine for the task.

Our crew at Winthorpe, beneath a Stirling, left to right: Flight Sergeant Peter O'Brien, wireless operator/air gunner; Flight Sergeant Vic Lever, mid-upper gunner; Pilot Officer Harold Hebb, Royal Canadian Air Force (RCAF), rear gunner; Flying Officer Percy Fyson, pilot; Flying Officer Frank Geldhart, navigator; Sergeant Bob Larman, RCAF, bomb-aimer; Warrant Officer Charles (Bill) Dowman, flight engineer. As explained, Bob Larman was replaced before we began ops, his place being taken by Flying Officer Barry Turnbull, Royal New Zealand Air Force

An interminable number of months later – or so it seemed, although cold logic reckons it at hardly seven months – I was to find myself back on Stirlings, this time to instruct. Just the same, comparing the Stirling and the Lancaster, if I have to, the Stirling was so spacious that you could walk about; the Lancaster was cosy. And a far superior aeroplane in all respects.

At Winthorpe, though, we started the course on 13 March 1944 and finished it a month later, by which time I had logged thirty-six hours in the air – but as aircrew now, as opposed to interested joy-rider! On the down side, because of a training glut, we then spent an unwelcome five weeks or so at the so-called Aircrew Commando School at Scampton. Putting that fiasco behind us, however, we gleefully hurried ourselves off to Syerston, to the Lancaster Finishing School, where we finally began to learn what a thorough lady A. V. Roe's product was.

How it comes back to me! The purr of those sweet-sounding Merlins; running-in to the target, and every gauge on its best behaviour, the airspeed hovering at 165 mph – miles per hour, of course, not your new-fangled knots. Then, hours later, on the approach, reaching to put the flaps down in stages; finally full flap, and the speed gradually falling off, 110, 100, 95, and the slur of the tyres on the tarmac as it brought us safely home once more ... The dear old Lanc!

But back then, in 1944, between beginning the course on 29 April and passing out on 6 May, I had flown a further eighteen hours, so that on reporting to our assigned squadron, No. 106, I had a total of fifty-four hours.

The squadron was stationed at RAF Metheringham, some nine miles south-east of Lincoln. After a spell as a training unit it had been a late joiner in the bomber offensive but had swiftly risen to eminence as an Avro Manchester unit under the command of the celebrated Guy Gibson – Wing Commander Guy Gibson, VC, DSO and Bar, DFC and Bar – who had flown forty-six operations with the squadron before moving on. However, justly celebrated though he was, I managed to rub him up the wrong way on our one and only meeting just a few months later, after a multi-squadron briefing.

Aircrews leaving pre-ops briefing. (In contrast to too many latter-day portrayals, the fliers' smartness is worth noting, some hands-in-pockets notwithstanding)

He had a reputation for despising flight engineers, believing, apparently, that all the front-of-aircraft tasks should be done by the pilot; indeed, common knowledge had it that he even objected to the engineer following up on the throttles! It was also said that you never knew whether he was being sarcastic, toffee-nosed, or just plain arrogant. So, pre-warned, when he addressed me with the pleasantry, 'What do you expect the weather to be like at the target, Flight Sergeant?' I replied shortly, 'Didn't take much notice, sir. I'm not planning a walk.' This raised a great laugh from the aircrews jostling through the doors around us, although I didn't bother looking back to see what he made of it.

On joining we were to find the squadron assimilating a recent change of emphasis in the bombing task. Until that time, we learnt, the main effort had been directed towards German heavy industry, and especially the Ruhr and Berlin. Now, with the Second Front looming, precedence was being given to interdiction attacks on communications networks in France and Belgium, together with the preparatory softening-up of military targets from the Pas de Calais to Brittany.

Our part, as a crew, it transpired, was to carry out a first tour of thirty-four operations before being rested. And thirty-four, rather than the former thirty, for French targets were now held to be less dangerous than German targets. Indeed, as we started operations instructions came that they were to count as only one third of an operation. These instructions, though, were swiftly reversed after the pre-D-Day raids on Mailly-le-Camp and Lille led, respectively, to 11.3 per cent and 13.7 per cent of the force being lost, when we returned to the thirty-four op yardstick.

What we also learnt was that whereas in 1943, the year before, with crews operating maybe two or three nights a week, a tour could take a long time to complete, we, in contrast, would be called upon to fly pretty-near nightly! At first sight this might indicate a quick finish to trauma. In fact, it meant that we could expect relatively little rest. Not that we particularly worried about the prospect at the time, being only too keen to get going. And being volunteers, after all ...

Training, as such, ended on 9 May 1944 when Perce flew an op as second pilot to another crew. But the long-awaited day of our first op as a crew came on the night of the 19 May 1944 when sixteen of the squadron's aircraft formed part of a No. 5 Group force of 114 Lancasters and four target-marking Mosquitoes to raid the railway marshalling yards at Tours. We had been warned that, because the rail centre was surrounded by houses, bombing might be delayed until the markers were judged to be accurate enough.

That, as it turned out, was exactly what happened, for the haze made sighting difficult and the first markers fell to the west of the aiming point. In fact, the planned drop-time had come and gone before the raid leader was satisfied with the marking. Making a tactical decision, however, he then gave the go-ahead. Fortunately no German night-fighters had turned up in the interim.

First impressions? They were of a gigantic and exceedingly colourful firework display! For a start, there were the target-marking flares dropped by Pathfinder Force. These would burn for two minutes, the greens having an intensity of 175,000 candlepower, the reds, 250,000; with others giving the appearance of a vertical chain of slowly descending white balls.

Then there was the flak sparkling in the sky; the bomb bursts and burgeoning fires on the ground; the flailing searchlights; the constantly renewed flares and spots, in red, green, and yellow, with some target indicators and markers burning at low level and others while suspended cloud high: it really was a carnival-like spectacular. A spectacular from which we returned cock-a-hoop, as charmed beings. We had done our first op. We had got away with it! And now we knew the score.

The truth of the matter, of course, was that after that first op we knew so little. Just the same, I had learnt a significant self-truth, for despite being awed I had found myself far too busy to admit to even the possibility of feeling afraid.

And that is a fact. What with my fuel gauges, engines, and all the gubbins both up at the front and to the very rear of the aircraft that might need my attention – to say nothing, on many ops, of having to periodically chuck out the one-pound bundles of radar-clogging, aluminium-foil strips called 'Window' – I had no room for airy-fairy fears. And even after landing I was gratified to find that a swift pint or two in the mess left me fit and ready for the next time. This lack of nervousness might conceivably have waned just a little in the months towards tour's-end, when statistics began to take on a special significance, but by and large, my temperament seemed tailor-made to cope.

Even so, our second op was a rather different story from the first for it took us to mainland Germany for the first time, and to the Ruhr, at that: 'Happy Valley'. The target was Duisburg, a major logistical centre thick with chemical and metal-producing plants. And rather thicker with flak. Once again there was difficulty in marking the aiming point and we had to go around again. This might have been only our second op, but no matter how experienced we became the last thing on earth we ever wanted to do was make a second run over a target. 'Not if I can

Radar-clogging 'Window' being manufactured

Flak thick enough to walk on

bloody help it,' someone would always mutter. Yet on this occasion it was necessary to go around, not once, but *five* times before we were cleared to drop by the raid controller! And yet, we came through unscathed, although the difference between the Ruhr defences and those, which we had thought so formidable, over Tours gave us plenty to think about. Indeed, the flak was so thick that the whimsical notion came to me that it might well prove solid enough for that target-area walk I had told Guy Gibson I didn't intend taking.

Up to this juncture we had carried out high- and medium-level bombing, but within days of the invasion we were called upon to mount our first low-level raid. For this we joined a force of 97 Lancasters dropping from just 6,000 feet on the railway yards at Rennes. Despite a layer of cloud at 3,000 feet the target was well marked by Mosquitoes from No. 627 Squadron and, as it happened, our crew's aiming-point photograph was spot on.

The operation we carried out on 14 June 1944 came rather closer to rattling our equanimity. British armoured elements, we were told, were not only having great difficulty in breaking out of the bocage country beyond the Normandy Beachhead but – having taken heavy losses – of disengaging. It was deemed imperative, therefore, that the German forces concentrated on their flanks be subdued. We were part of the force detailed to attack the enemy armour and personnel gathered at the crossroads of Aunay-sur-Odon.

The opportunity aiming point was a single red spotlight, nevertheless, our bombing photo showed that we had obtained a good result. This, though, was clouded by the fact that, as we had turned away, flak had caught us. But why us? For we had been just one among the 214 Lancasters and four Mosquitoes running-in, and just one of the twenty aircraft of our squadron! And so it was that we suffered an immediate loss of faith in the concept of herd safety.

V-3 long-range, rocket-boosted 150 mm gun

But now came another switch as the force was tasked to deal with the V-1, pilotless, pulse-jet flying bombs, the V-2 supersonic rockets, and the V-3, rocket-boosted, long-range guns, operations generically coded as Crossbows.

Our first intended intervention in this field came in mid-June 1944 when we set out (by daylight!) to raid the V-1 Flying-Bomb site at Watten in the Calais-St Omer area. However, bad weather developing just after we had become airborne led to a hasty recall; and a frustrating non-op. But within the next month we visited Thiverny, just north-east of Paris; the Siracourt cave complex, just west of Arras; and the Beauvoir site in the Île-de-France.

On most of these daylight raids we were amply supported by a large, and comforting, fighter escort that we could

Bois Carré, near Yvrench, the first V-1 launching site in France to be identified

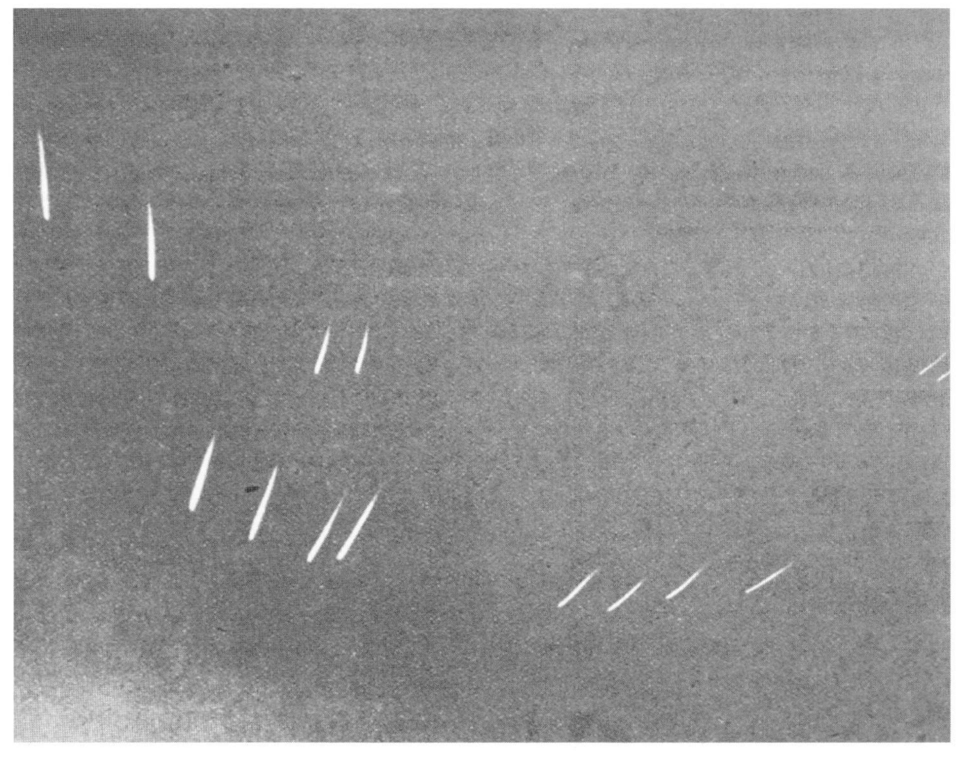

The comforting fighter escort, high above

see wheeling high above as we swept towards the target. What we could also see, unfortunately, were the other aircraft flying so horribly close, with none maintaining height or course for more than a second or two. All in all, what with the heavy and accurate flak, and the constant awareness of collision risk, this was a series of ops nobody particularly enjoyed!

Where locating our targets was concerned, of course, cloud and visibility were always prime factors. With the best will in the world the met men had little enough to go on in a region where weather, and not climate, ruled. We turned to radar navigational aids, therefore, to help us out with unfavourable cloud and smokescreens, the two we made most use of being Gee, and Oboe.

Gee was a radar equipment that took signals from ground stations and allowed a position, accurate to within twenty-five feet, to be plotted on a lattice chart; unfortunately it did not have the range to cover our most distant targets. Oboe, in essence, involved an aircraft flying down a radar beam until a ground-initiated signal showed that it was overhead the aiming point. Both Gee and Oboe were much better than bombing blind, but although clear weather over the target had its obvious drawbacks, a visual sighting of the target was always more satisfying.

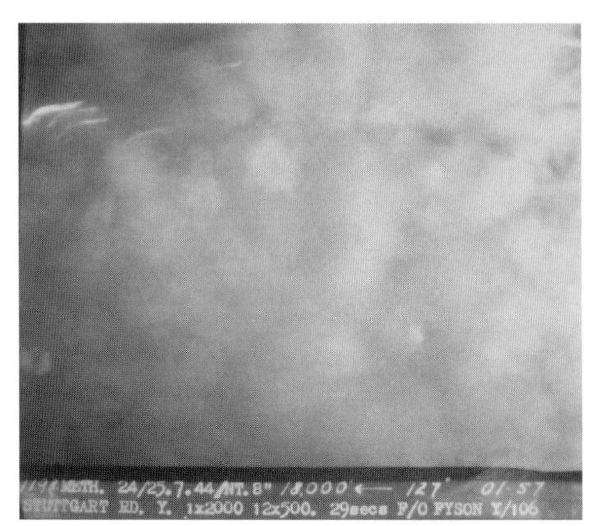

Aiming-point photos: Stuttgart, 24 July 1944, 9/10 cloud cover; Le Havre, 11 September 1944, partial smokescreen; Poitiers, 13 June 1944, a visual sighting of the target was always more satisfying

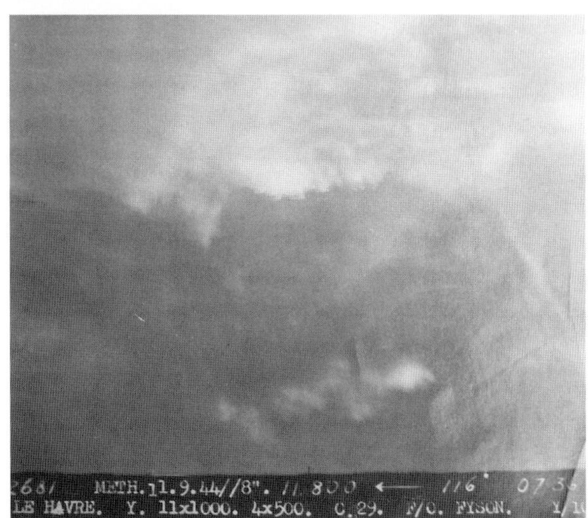

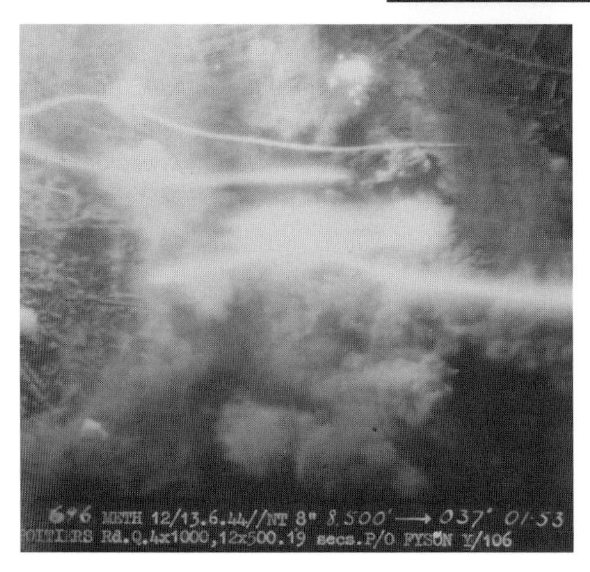

People have asked me – if only in the last few years – what moral stance I took about dropping bombs, particularly when I was well aware of the limited accuracy our best efforts could obtain. To tell the truth it was not something I had thought of overmuch, but as people wanted an answer I had to admit to a long-standing regret that our bomb bays hadn't been bigger, that given my way I'd have dropped even more bombs. There was a bloody war on, for Christ's sake! But I'm told that saying that is not PC – whatever that's supposed to mean.

But then querulousness is not the only quality that comes with age, for there is forbearance too. So let me make a concession. Only this would have to be that, had the questioner felt the grief I did after that Swansea air raid; and had they seen, as I did, the bodies of the WAAFs and airmen at Biggin Hill; and perhaps had they posed the question when crouched alongside me at Perce's shoulder over the Ruhr with all hell going on outside and their legs – like mine – crossed against what might coming upwards through the floor; then perhaps – just perhaps – I might have a different answer to give.

Far more germane, to my mind, was what it was we dropped. Typical bomb loads for each Lancaster on railway targets were four 1,000-pounder bombs and twelve 500-pounders, while on industrial targets it would be one 2,000-pounder and twelve clusters of incendiaries.

Certainly, the latter was the load we carried to Gelsenkirchen's Scholven-Buer oil plant. On that occasion, having routed out over the Wash, all 120 of us, together with our four Oboe-Mosquitoes, dropped below the radar screen for the sea crossing then climbed to 17,000 feet before coasting in again over North Holland's Goeree-Overflakkee Island. Then it was a case of flying a series of short legs designed to take us clear of the most heavily defended areas; the key word being designed. And even then these were merely the flak installations on the way. For our actual destination was a Ruhr Valley every bit as lively as crews from the year before had described it; a red-carpeted expanse of vertically-directed hate. Not only that, but on this particular night the defences had the benefit of gin-clear skies!

Approaching Gelsenkirchen we saw another aircraft, just ahead, coned, hit, and transformed into a fireball. But, 'Their rotten bloody luck!' was all that consciously came to mind. Then, the overall good-weather pattern aside, just before we reached the aiming point, low cloud moved in. We had expected Oboe-directed, yellow markers but were forced, instead, to bomb from 18,000 feet on cloud-diffused red and green markers. Something of a hotchpotch, perhaps, but a typical enough effort for the period, and one from which two of our squadron aircraft did not return.

The squadron supplied sixteen aircraft for a similar raid just days later, this time on the railway marshalling yards at Vitry-le-François, a hundred miles east of Paris. As we approached there was some patchy medium cloud but good visibility; certainly the flak found conditions suitable enough. We began dropping from 6,000 feet and our crew were fortunate in getting our load away. After that, however, the bombing grew so scattered that we heard the controller call a halt and order the remainder home with their bombs.

Of the 107 aircraft involved, just two were lost. Both, however, were from our squadron.

The bombing campaign was well into its maturity, nevertheless new techniques were still being tried out. The wind between dropping height and the ground had long been recognized as significant, and on 3 August 1944 we were actually supplied with a near-the-spot wind as we ran in. This had been gathered by aircraft sent ahead of the main force, the result of their findings being transmitted to the raid controller, then relayed to the main force. On that occasion the technique was novel, but a short while later we would be used as wind finders ourselves. Yet the novelty of having an accurate bombing wind paled in contrast to the accuracy of the flak which, within seconds, sent two Lancasters spinning down over the target.

Many raids took just three or four hours, but others, like the one we carried out on Nevers, some 120 miles south of Paris, took us seven and a half. Our target was the railway yards, our load seven 1,000-pounders and eight 500-pounders. The yards had been well marked by Pathfinders before we arrived so all 100 bombers dropped from 4,500 feet, later photo-recce results showing total obliteration around the aiming point. What made the raid noteworthy for most of us, though, was that for the whole seven hours there was an almost total lack of flak. Far from comforting, however, this was so far from the norm as to be distinctly unsettling.

Throughout May and early June our crew had rarely been off the battle order so we especially welcomed being sent on leave. The break lasted from 30 June to 13 July 1944 but the moment we returned, it was back to the grindstone. Only what we now found ourselves doing was practising flying in close formation!

Looking back, all I can say is that ops were one thing, close-formation flying quite another. I have already said that my temperament pretty well took ops in its stride. But close formation! I thought even less of the notion when, during one practice, an aircraft caught in slipstream rolled into another, with only one crew member surviving the collision.

At least there was a reason, it transpired, for the sudden devotion to formation flying. It seemed that, although the Allied armies had now gathered sufficient resources within the Normandy Beachhead, they were still having difficulty in beginning a meaningful advance. A thousand-bomber raid on Caen, designed to aid the army, had resulted in so much rubble that, in effect, it had held up the advance even more.

It was decided, therefore, that an even vaster air armada would be employed to pulverise German resistance along the proposed break-out route to the east. It was to be a joint operation. Approximately a thousand RAF bombers were to head the attack, closely followed by the same number of American bombers.

Caen, blocked by rubble

In all, including fighters and markers and the like, some 4,000 aircraft were to take part.

On the appointed day, 18 July 1944, our crew arrived over our specific target – the Mondeville Steel Works, at that time a virtual fortress – at sunrise. Running in wingtip to wingtip with other Lancasters we bombed at 9,000 feet through a sky literally filled with flak. Later, we learnt, as the bombing developed, so the flak had dwindled, so that as the last American bombers cleared the target the only gunfire had been from Allied artillery that throughout the assault had never stopped pounding the target areas.

We had long gone by then, of course, breaking formation and diving for the ground the moment we had obtained our aiming-point photo, so transmitting, it could be, any nervousness on board to the livestock that scattered beneath us as we hedge-hopped all the way back to the Channel coast.

No such relief just a week later when, having successfully raided Stuttgart, we were seriously caught by flak over France. Perce pulled out a stop or two, and with me at his shoulder, nursed us back over the Channel and into the first airfield we came to. Only to find that our undercarriage was among the items damaged, so that we carried out a most spectacular ground loop before coming to rest. We were all fine. But the poor old aircraft was out of commission for a fair time.

That was the thing about ops, you never knew what was going to happen. Towards the end of July 1944 we raided St Cyr, the French military college – their Sandhurst – at that time a very sizeable German military complex. As always we were flying in a loose gaggle with each aircraft following its own flight path. As always, we were keeping a good lookout all around, but especially above; the last thing anyone wanted to see on the run-in being the open bomb doors of a Lancaster immediately above you! Only on this occasion, just moments after Barry Turnbull had called, 'Bombs gone!' both I and Harry Hebb, our rear gunner, saw our load take away the rear turret of the Lancaster below us. Needless, to say – I hope – it was a terrifying thing to see.

That there were other collateral tragedies was shown just days later when we were among two hundred bombers to raid Givors railway junction, near Lyons. Shortly after we had cleared the target there was a violent mid-air explosion as two Lancasters collided; an accident that accounted for fourteen of the thirty-five crew members who failed to return.

That, though, would have been regarded by the statisticians as a very low loss rate. Later, when we once more raided Stuttgart, this time with nearly five hundred bombers, German fighters were active, many of them using upward-firing cannon, so that, in conjunction with flak, we lost twenty-nine aircraft! Over two hundred aircrew!

Our bomb, like this one, might have missed, instead, it took the rear turret off

And then it was back to the long-awaited break-out, this all-arms operation being codenamed Totalise. It was just a month since D-Day with Falaise as key to the whole plan. Our part was to provide hitherto unheard-of night-time close support by attacking in the area of Secqueville la Campaigne. Because of the risky nature of the enterprise it was arranged that the normal Pathfinder Force flares would be supplemented by coloured marker shells carefully laid down by the artillery.

Over 1,000 aircraft were employed, with us in the van. Flying at 6,000 feet in clear weather we dropped relatively early in the raid but already bomb smoke and the dust ground up by the advancing armoured columns was causing problems. A human touch after we had turned for home was to hear the master bomber – normally so phlegmatic – getting frustrated as incoming bombers showed their reluctance to break off the attack. But, of course, Allied soldiers were being hazarded. And the attack had to be called off. Even so the raid caused over three hundred casualties among friendly troops.

But it was not all doom and gloom on ops. On one occasion we had suffered a certain amount of damage, which attracted the attention of a Spitfire. Concerned, he then flew on our wingtip the whole way home, exchanging hand signals with me – standing in the astrodome – as we went. Arguably even more concerned – or concerning, rather – was the mental state in which we left an American Fortress crew who appeared on our port side in the course of one ultra-quiet daylight return trip.

For devilment, the Yank feathered his starboard-outer engine, then cavorted up and down at a distance of several wingspans. Perce inclined his head, but then gave me the nod. I promptly stopped and feathered our own starboard outer. Moments later the Yank feathered a second engine. But, we noted, this time the matching engine on his other wing, the port outer.

We duly followed suit, but deliberately stopped our starboard inner, leaving us with two engines out on the same side. For some miles we flew on with nothing more happening. Then, at a further nod from Perce, I reached over and feathered our port outer, leaving us on just one engine. At which the Fortress huffily turned away and began to dwindle in the distance, clouds of smoke dispersing in his slipstream as he lamely restarted his motors. Pointedly we waited until even his rear gunner could no longer see us. Then like a pair of paperhangers on piecework we put things right in our own house, and sedately began a let-down into Metheringham, home and beauty.

By this time we had flown thirty-seven sorties and, despite aborts and recalls, had completed twenty-nine of our required thirty-four operations. Though, for fear of tempting providence, we might try to push the awareness from our minds, the end of our tour was moving inexorably closer.

This nearing-the-end-of-tour phase saw many crews reacting to the stress they were under, with morale dipping markedly. I would like to claim that the chaps in my crew were different. But viewing the matter from so many years of detachment, I don't suppose I can. Or at best, only by conceding that that was honestly how it appeared to me, back then, in the days of my youth.

First, though, we had a very welcome leave. And a particularly significant one for me in that I entered into a deeper relationship with Ruth, a girl who, until then, had long been merely a friend.

But only too soon we were back in the thick of things, and with the battle order now favouring Germany over France, we fairly pelted through the balance of our ops, reaching our thirty-four and being temporarily screened. On standing down, I had flown 123 hours by day and 177 by night; a total of just three hundred hours.

For me there was only a short respite before, on 10 October 1944, I began my new job as an instructor on Stirlings at No. 1660 Heavy Conversion Unit at RAF Swinderby, near Newark. The flying I then embarked upon was significantly different from flying ops, not that non-operational flying didn't have its stresses and strains. And training fledgling crews to operate a heavy bomber as unwieldy as the Stirling had many of them.

With the Stirling's nose rearing twenty-three feet up in the air, and a tailwheel dragging the ground far behind it, judging the touchdown attitude, let alone the distance from the tarmac, could be a real problem for the inexperienced pilot. And having struck the runway, the beast had to be kept straight!

Then there were all the pitfalls associated with deliberately stopping engines in flight, exercises throughout which the staff instructors had to be at instant readiness to deal with the situation when the trainee pilot or engineer began to feather one engine and ended up by inadvertently stopping both the intended engine and another one. To say nothing of the deliberate failing of two, and even three engines, as some Stirling pilot-instructors insisted upon doing.

Then there were the joys of having the pilot-instructor recover when the trainee had allowed a corkscrew evasion-manoeuvre to get away from him and develop into a full-blooded nose-down spiral dive; the seemingly interminable time before recovery – even without a bomb bay full of bombs – affording every crew member some sense of what it must have been like for those unfortunates we had seen so many of plunging to perdition during operations.

I have to admit, however, to being the cause of one such upset myself. It happened at a time when Ruth and I had actually begun 'seeing' each other. In the course of an early morning training sortie – whether by accident or design – we found ourselves over Sandiacre, near Nottingham, where I knew Ruth would be awaiting the bus for work. The staff pilot was game, so he set up a circle over the bus stop, flying tighter and tighter. The inevitable happened. With both of us gazing downwards the turns got so tight that the Stirling – lumbering great beast though it was – began to flick. Suddenly, while realizing the situation we had got ourselves into, I also saw that, although the pilot had the stick hard over, he had run out of control. He clearly had his hands fuller than full, so I reached over and supplemented his efforts by winding on some trim. Fortunately this gave the poor old airflow just the impetus it needed and we began to recover.

I never did find out whether Ruth knew that it was us overhead playing silly buggers, or whether our show caused her to miss her bus. But we made our way sedately back to base, vowing to leave low-level aerobatics to the fighter people in future.

In retrospect, viewing the operational flying I had done, and setting alongside it the training flying I was to do for the next year and a half, I would say that white-knuckle times during the training might well have outweighed those encountered during ops!

As it was, with the war finishing on 8 May 1945, and with Japan packing it in on 15 August 1945, I never was recalled for a second operational tour. On the handling unit we did mount one intensely moving trip from Swinderby: a round tour with an itinerary including Calais, Ostend, Knokke, Zeebrugge, Eindhoven, Düsseldorf, Cologne, Essen and Bochum; a seven-hour revisiting of so many of our aerial battlefields. Apart from that, however, the rest of my flying was restricted to the Swinderby area.

So it was that when I accepted demob in 1946 I had flown a total of 567 hours; 329 by day, and 238 by night.

Tour of former targets, Krupps, Essen

Even so, nowhere near all the personnel who supported the fliers

I say, accepted demob, for it was not without regret that I left the RAF. Indeed, Ruth has always maintained that if she had not decided it was time I married, I would have stayed in the Service. Certainly, I have long spoken of the RAF as my university.

Even now things come back to me that never found their way into my flying logbook, such as flak damaging our undercarriage, and our jolting to a halt upon the long, wide runway at Carnaby, one of the emergency landing fields on the east coast.

I recall with fondness too, the way our groundcrews – with our security in mind – never asked about the intended target beforehand. They could make intelligent guesses at where we were going, knowing the bomb load and the amount of fuel in the tanks, but only when the operation was safely completed did the target become a subject for discussion. Then they were all attention to learn where the fruit of their labours had taken us.

Then again, years later, I was at the National Remembrance Arboretum at Alrewas, near Lichfield, when, encountering a group of former searchlight operators, I mentioned how comforting it was, as we coasted in from ops, to have the searchlights welcome us back by sweeping their beams towards our base. The ladies were overjoyed! 'All these years,' one told me, suddenly tearful, 'and to find that the gesture was appreciated.'

Although I did not stay in the RAF I remained associated with the armed forces throughout a career in the Civil Service's engineering division, which saw me liaising with the RAF, the navy, and even the army – who let me drive a tank. Before I finished I had done over twenty-five years service and on retirement became entitled to the Imperial Service Medal, inscribed, as it is, 'For Faithful Service'.

There had been no such recognition for any of the crew I had flown to war with, for we had started ops too late to qualify for the Aircrew Europe Star. Instead, we were obliged to share the same France and Germany Star as that worn by our non-flying colleagues.

And the crew? Well, it was hard to keep touch. Yet how close we became during that tour we flew together. From our first op on 19 May 1944 to our thirty-fourth, on 11 September 1944, it was barely four months; just 115 days. But what months! And what days! What nights! Certainly, I look back upon them now with not a little sense of awe.

Bill and Ruth Dowman

Bill Dowman, 2012

4

Seeding the storm

Squadron Leader John Ernest Francis Mitchell, DFC, wireless operator/air gunner, then pilot

I had never known Mr Smedley, our headmaster at Eye Grammar, to be taken aback. When he asked at my leaving interview what I intended to do, however, and I replied without hesitation, 'I want to fly, sir,' it seemed to floor him. Probably he'd expected me to talk of university, for I'd been no slouch under his tutelage. And that might not have been so bad. What I had no intention of doing, though, was getting involved with the land.

Squadron Leader John Mitchell, DFC, 1956

The desire to fly, on the other hand, was something that had become ever more compelling. What we tended to see in the skies of Norfolk were airships. But I knew all about the record breakers and their machines, and far more about the wartime aces of the RFC – the Royal Flying Corps – about McCudden, Mannock, Bishop, and to me, the greatest of them all, Albert Ball, of Nottingham. And war fliers rather then civilian, for even in 1934 it was clear to those with eyes to see that another conflict was brewing.

I even knew the qualities Air Ministry looked for in an aspirant war flier: 'not exceptional, a good general education, a mechanical background advantageous, a fair working knowledge of maths and the application of simple formulae; more than keen to learn'. Apart from the 'not exceptional' – the very idea! – I more than fitted the bill.

The ensuing discussion went on for some time, but even then Mr Smedley was not happy.

'Think about it for a day or so, Mitchell,' he bade me, 'then come back.'

I dutifully did so. When, having finally satisfied himself that I was determined to pursue a flying career, he sent a recommendation to the local education committee. As a consequence, just weeks later, a letter – railway warrant enclosed – invited me to present myself at Victory House, Kingsway, in London.

The interviewers surprised me. I had expected them to be knowledgeable about aeroplanes. Instead, they seemed to inhabit some august intellectual level way above such things. Eventually, however, they descended from their Olympian heights to deliver their verdict.

At seventeen I was too young to become a pilot. Only here, as my face fell, they descended even further, to assure me that age was the only bar. Meanwhile, I could be taken on as either a wireless operator or an air gunner. Stifling my disappointment, I opted for the former. And a short time later reported to the Electrical and Wireless School at RAF Cranwell, near Sleaford, in Lincolnshire, where I was rigged out from cap to puttees, not forgetting boots that were initially reluctant to take the least shine, to begin my training.

It was clear that the government was among those aforementioned with eyes to see, for some months before it had decided upon a vast expansion of the RAF. This meant the building of new airfields and the creation of new squadrons. It also meant a full-scale recruiting drive. And so it was that on 10 October 1934 I joined a Boy Entrant intake, doubled that year to nearly 600, for a nominal twelve months' course.

We were not the only trainees accommodated in the double-storied barrack blocks of Cranwell's East Camp. There were also signals officers on short courses, and air gunners who, after twelve weeks of instruction, were to take on an additional wireless-operating role. And there were Aircraft Apprentices, their entry too, swelled to some 600.

An East Camp barrack block, RAF Cranwell

Boy-Service 'wheel' (propeller) badge

The latter were boys like ourselves, from fifteen plus to eighteen who, also like us, wore the distinctive 'spoked-wheel' arm badge – in truth, a propeller. Only they had gained entry by competitive examination rather than education-committee recommendation and their three-year course would qualify them to maintain the RAF's communication equipment – as opposed to operating it, as was our destiny.

And then, of course, just across the road, but at an infinite remove from East Camp, was the gleaming new Royal Air Force College aloofly peopled by the future leaders of the King's Air Force.

Our year-long course saw us poring over wireless theory, disembowelling radios in workshops, achieving a mirror surface on those recalcitrant boots, and between times continuing our studies in English, maths, general subjects, and History of the Service – one of Albert Ball's machine guns was enshrined in a barrack-block hallway! We tapped away at morse keys, strained into headsets, memorized the most frequently used of the Q, X, and Z brevity codes – necessary with morse messages being so protracted – and even got the feel of airborne operating in the Wireless School's Wallaces, Wapitis, and Valentias.

Off duty, sports were highly rated, and I was able to indulge myself to the full in those which interested me. With the compulsory boxing bout over I shunned anything further in that line, similarly soccer and rugby, but was to the fore in

Vickers Valentia

cricket and tennis. Where golf and croquet were concerned, however, I found myself pretty much a loner.

We finished the course on 12 July 1935, and now competent at sending and receiving morse at 20 words a minute, I was able to replace the Boy-Service wheel with the Signals' arm badge, a hand clasping three electrical flashes.

On passing out my posting was to No. 58 Squadron, at Worthy Down, near Winchester, a major bomber station that was to achieve singular distinction some years later when, its Naval tenants having re-christened it HMS *Kestrel*, the traitor William Joyce, Lord Haw Haw, announced that it had been bombed and sunk!

I found the squadron operating Vickers Virginias, twin-engined biplane bombers which even to my eager eyes appeared distinctly venerable. Nor was the wireless equipment any more youthful. This was the transmitter/receiver combination known as the T1083/R1082, which was not only unreliable but difficult to operate, even altering frequency requiring a coil change in both transmitter and receiver.

The T1083/R1082 combination, unreliable and difficult to operate

One everyday problem was that to get any range at all a wire aerial had to be trailed from beneath the aircraft. The trick was to remember to retract this before landing for fear of garrotting some groundling. Except that the pilot would get engrossed in his own concerns, and forget to advise the wireless operator – me – when he was about to set down. Either that, or

Vickers Virginia

with the intercommunication system being so poor, his advisory wouldn't get through, leaving me to bawl, 'You've lost my bloody trailing aerial again,' even though my bloke was an officer.

Just the same, I counted myself luckier than a gunner colleague who felt a pattering on his helmet. And on turning, got a face full of pee, his desperate pilot, far forward of him, having stood on his seat to relieve himself into the air rush.

To a large extent, then, we were all learning, pilots and crew members alike. Although I doubt this showed when we flew our Virginias in tight formation over the jam-packed Hendon Air Display. In reality, however, it became even more the case a few months later when we began receiving the Handley Page Heyford, held to be very speedy, and the last word in design, with all-round protection that included a dustbin-like turret that could be lowered from the ventral – belly – position.

What the new aircraft also brought with it was a stepping-up of long-range navigational exercises, and of bombing and air-firing by both day and night. It quickly became evident too, that although trained as a dedicated wireless operator, I was still expected to fill in as a gunner: not the first evidence of the way the Service was being strained by the expansion.

For expansion necessarily meant a dilution of the experience embodied in both training school and squadron. And as these, in turn, lost their most capable men on posting – either to command or to bolster up new units – so their own experience level dropped. For example, new boy though I was, even I could tell that to have so many prangs – minor though most were – was not the way things should be. So many, indeed, that we never bothered logging them.

I was not in a position to know, of course, but not long after this the new Commander-in-Chief (C.-in-C.) of Bomber Command, Air Chief Marshal Sir Edgar Ludlow-Hewitt, would stir resentment in the very highest echelons by reporting upwards even more fundamental shortcomings.

The Handley Page Heyford

Foremost among these was the lack of a definite policy regarding the crewing of aircraft, only pilots being considered full-time fliers. Observers and gunners, the other two categories of flier, were drawn from volunteer airmen, highly-qualified tradesmen who, after a flying duty, would pocket their one or two shillings a day flying pay and return to their workshops. True, there were already moves afoot to employ full-time gunners, but like those we had trained alongside, these were then to double as wireless operators. Indeed, it was to be 1942 before gunnery and signals were to become completely divorced.

Navigation was another area of deep concern to the new C.-in-C. who cited that in the last two years 478 bombers had made precautionary landings because their pilots had lost their way. Certainly, in any sort of poor weather, determining our position continued to be a serious problem, my loop-aerial bearings notwithstanding! True again, observers began to depart for ten-week navigation courses. Even so – and also happily unknown to us – just two months before the outbreak of war the C.-in-C. would still have to warn the Air Council that Bomber Command was incapable of operating in anything but fair weather.

Blissfully ignorant then, of the true state of things, what we all knew was that, just like the war, newer and longer-range aircraft were only just over the horizon. And with that in mind we did not complain when pushed ever harder.

What did not improve, and totally disrupted continuity, was the number of times they had us upping sticks: another thing the new Commander was to view adversely! Our first uprooting came on 13 May 1936, when we re-located to Upper Heyford, near Bicester, in Oxfordshire. At least, though, this heralded the arrival of the Armstrong Whitworth Whitley, the monoplane bomber which, through Marks One to Five, was to see us well into the war.

True to form, however, my current bloke, a flight lieutenant at that, cost me four teeth on our first landing as the undercarriage, only half-extended, folded beneath us. I suppose he was busy congratulating himself on having remembered that he now had retractable wheels – many pilots didn't remember. But as the blood streamed from my mouth all he could offer was, 'I didn't realize the selector had to go so far.'

The Armstrong Whitworth Whitley, flying level, but at high speed

The Marconi T1154/R1155, with gaily coloured knobs, but technically sophisticated

From the wireless-operator's standpoint the major benefit brought by the Whitley was its state-of-the-art Marconi radio installation, the transmitter/receiver combination known as the T1154/R1155, very much easier to operate than the equipment we had struggled with before. It still incorporated a trailing aerial, but otherwise it was far more sophisticated than previous gears, the gaily coloured knobs of its transmitter belying its complexity.

Certainly, my dedicated training came into its own, and 'Send for Mitch' became the cry of the day, so that although still a newish-joiner I found myself acting as what I would soon become, the squadron's signals leader.

Upper Heyford, however, afforded us only a breathing space, for by the end of August 1936 we had moved again, this time to Driffield, near Bridlington, in Yorkshire. And in February 1937 we were heading south once more, to Boscombe Down, in Wiltshire.

Here, we did settle to some extent, although there was a bombing detachment at Aldergrove, in Northern Ireland, where we were permitted to drop live bombs into Loch Neagh, followed by a stint at West Freugh, near Stranraer, for gunnery. On that detachment, having by then done a gunnery course at Catfoss, near Hornsea, I was able to exercise my new-found skills from all our gun positions, front, dorsal (top of fuselage), and the ventral dustbin of our Whitley Mark Threes, firing 300 rounds from each, largely at sea markers. Another gunnery detachment took us to Pocklington, to the east of York. But on 20 June 1939 we were uprooted again, this time to Linton-on-Ouse, Yorkshire.

Such training detachments gave us a flavour of what our war task might be. But the results were not always that comforting. My own gunnery scores were consistently deemed satisfactory. But we did hear that whereas the previous year's averages for air firing had been an acceptable 20 per cent, this year, with fewer experienced instructors in the schools and competent gunners spread more thinly on the squadrons, averages were running closer to 0 per cent!

Equally concerning, we had noticed that even when we were permitted to drop live bombs – for there always seemed to be some rare wild bird or other that took precedence, or some influential landowner – a high proportion proved to be duds, or at best, ineffectual. In lieu of the real thing, however, we dropped practice bombs, or trained on the camera obscura.

The latter was an optical training aid that had us fly towards a building – identified by a flare at night – with a large hole cut in its roof. A lens would then project the approaching aircraft's image onto a table where instructors would assess the accuracy of the run-in. At his calculated release point the pilot would press the button, when either coloured smoke, or a parachute flare by

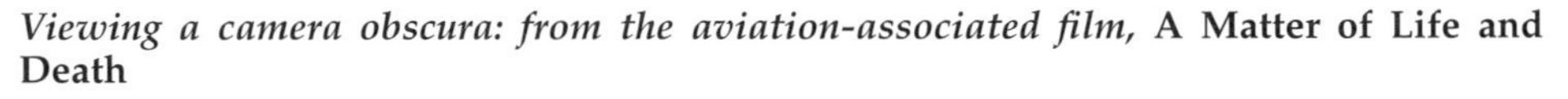
Viewing a camera obscura: from the aviation-associated film, **A Matter of Life and Death**

night, would enable the wind effect to be calculated and the likely striking point ascertained.

Other noteworthy exercises we flew at this time involved dropping very powerful flares, the forerunner, we were later to realize, of the Pathfinders' target markers. Arguably even more significant was the detailing of a squadron aircraft to patrol near the BBC's Daventry aerial, a sortie that led directly to the development of radar.

We were great moaners, of course. But even where the unsettling moves were concerned we conceded that some were dictated by extra construction work, most of our roosts having come into being under the expansion programme. For essentially, while we noticed shortcomings, we saw it as our part to master the equipment we'd be given, and leave others to worry about the rest.

Even so, though one might push shortcomings from the mind, the international situation could no longer be ignored. More particularly when, on 1 September 1939, Hitler's forces attacked Poland which, to the surprise of many, turned out to be our ally. But nobody on the squadron was surprised when, next day, we were dispatched to Leconfield, near Yorkshire's east coast. And that much nearer Hitler's Reich.

At 1115 hours on 3 September 1939 we listened to Chamberlain's fateful broadcast, and as darkness fell ours was among ten Whitleys laden with propaganda leaflets to get airborne for Germany, my logbook recording that the 'Anti-Nazis War' had begun.

Loading leaflets into a Whitley

On that first operational sortie I was flying with my regular pilot, Flying Officer 'Peggy' O'Neill, aboard a familiar Whitley, K8969. Even so it was the most surreal of experiences to be droning over a blacked-out Germany where millions of people were both ready and willing to kill us. Not only that, but to be doing so carrying nothing more lethal than propaganda leaflets. And leaflets

WARNUNG!

England an das deutsche Volk

Die Nazi-Regierung hat, trotz der Bemühungen der führenden Großmächte, die Welt in einen Krieg gestürzt.

Dieser Krieg ist ein Verbrechen. Das deutsche Volk muß zwischen dem Vorwand, den seine Regierung benutzt, um den Krieg vom Zaun zu brechen und den Grundsätzen, die England und Frankreich zur Verteidigung Polens zwingen, ganz klar unterscheiden.

Von Anfang an hat die englische Regierung erklärt, daß an der polnischen Frage nichts ist, was einen europäischen Krieg mit allen seinen tragischen Folgen rechtfertigen kann.

Fünf Monate nach dem Münchener Vertrag wurde die Selbstständigkeit der Tschechoslovakei brutal zertreten. Wenn Polen nicht auch von dem gleichen Schicksal erreicht werden soll, dann mußten wir darauf bestehen, daß friedliche Verhandlungsmethoden nicht durch Gewaltandrohungen unmöglich gemacht werden, daß die zu treffende Abmachung die Lebensrechte Polens gewährleistet und auch ehrlich gehalten wird. Ein Diktat konnten wir weder zulaßen noch annehmen.

Wenn Herr Hitler glaubte, die englische Regierung werde aus Angst vor dem Kriege die Polen im Stich lassen, so hat er sich schwer getäuscht. Erstens bricht England sein einmal gegebenes Wort nicht. Außerdem ist es aber Zeit, der brutalen Gewalt, die die Nazi-Regierung der Welt aufzwingen will, ein deutliches Halt zu bieten.

Mit diesem Krieg stellt sich der Reichskanzler gegen den unbeugsamen Willen der englischen Regierung, einen Willen, hinter dem nicht nur die gesamten Hilfsquellen und Mittel des englischen

One of five million leaflets dropped on 5 September 1939, two nights after our initial leaflet drop. Essentially: People of Germany, the Nazi regime has plunged you into a world war you cannot win. Too much is against you. The united free peoples will not relent in their fight

intended to do what – destroy the resolve of a nation already cock-a-hoop over its Polish *blitzkrieg*?

We could not know that Churchill had only grudgingly conceded that leaflets just might raise Germany to a 'higher morality' or that our future leader, 'Bomber' Harris, would declare that the only thing such 'idiotic and childish pamphlets' accomplished was to satisfy a requirement for toilet paper. Again, though, our job was to drop leaflets. So on we droned.

The route was to be wide-ranging across the Ruhr, specifically targeting both Essen and Düsseldorf before overflying the Maginot Line – France's much-vaunted defensive barrier – and turning for home. I suppose, at a certain level, we were on edge the whole seven and a half hours we were airborne, but training sustained us. In addition, besides feeding our leaflets from the dustbin turret, we had been set other tasks.

These included assessing the effectiveness of the German blackout. Was it broken by any well-lit areas, which would, therefore, be dummy – decoy – towns? Were the airfields active? What road, rail, or waterborne movements did we notice? Were searchlights evident? Was there any anti-aircraft fire? In fact, deciding upon the latter led to an animated on-board discussion until we concluded that what we had seen was some transient light flashing on low cloud. And just as well, for when we eventually got back to base, this was a point they really grilled us on.

Once more, of course, we were not to know that Higher Authority had accepted that the RAF was not yet up to bombing by either day or night, any lingering doubt being dispelled by the losses its early raiders sustained. What had pragmatically been decided, therefore, was that our nocturnal paper delivery was now being viewed as a means of building up an expertise in long-range navigation that might eventually allow Bomber Command to achieve most of its war aims through precision attacks by night.

Certainly, a little later, we all heard the broadcast Harris made, warning the Nazis of 'a cloud on their horizon ... presently no bigger than a hand's width, which would break as a storm over Germany'. And hearing it we realized that we, of course, were that cloud, the seeders of that storm, the attendant fosterers of its fury.

Unfortunately, the Whitley soon proved unsuitable to the task, early evidence of this being supplied on that first foray of ours when, having crossed the Maginot Line, an engine faltered, committing us to a descent. Fortunately, despite a pre-dawn mist, Peggy was able to put us down near Amiens. Nobody was hurt, but the aircraft was in a sad state. And so our first op finished in a French field, with a civil Dragon Rapide biplane being sent to pick us up.

The Whitley's engine trouble proved to be symptomatic. But so too, did the freezing of the dustbin turrets. These could provide belly defence, but whenever lowered they caused enormous drag. So when they froze in the down position they crippled the Whitley and came near crippling those of us who had to get them up again. Accordingly, at the end of October 1939 we, and our Whitleys, were taken off leaflet dropping and reassigned as convoy escorts for the English and Bristol Channels, and the Irish Sea.

This tasked diversion finished in early May 1940, when we moved back to Boscombe Down, by which time I had flown twelve patrols and a further fifty-three operational hours. More significantly, we had also received Mark Five Whitleys whose more dependable Rolls-Royce Merlin Ten engines finally enabled our crew to feature on the bombing battle order.

Ops then followed in quick succession. Initially, we raided objectives in Norway, bombing Oslo aerodrome on 17 May 1940 and landing after a 9 hour 15 minute flight. Results, however, proved disappointing, so we had to revisit the next night. After that we attacked Stavanger, a 7 hour 40 minute flight. And what fraught trips these were, often wave-hopping, following a snaking fiord with cliffs soaring high into the darkness above! But again, training paid off, and we doggedly pressed on, although from the outset we had little faith in the outcome of the Norwegian expeditionary venture itself.

Then too, the phoney war was over, and events to the west were moving swiftly. So it was that we faced about, being tasked to bomb the Albert Canal bridges at Maastricht – a day after the debacle of the Fairey Battles, and the suicidal gaining of two VCs – before passing on to raid, first, a bridge at Eindhoven, and then Schiphol aerodrome.

Following that we switched to the Ruhr, to Gelsenkirchen and Düsseldorf, returning after a night or two, this time pairing Gelsenkirchen with Duisburg, each sortie taking between six and seven hours. Only now, in an unsettling taste of things to come, I was obliged to record, 'Heavy ack-ack'.

At which juncture I should, perhaps, mention that the contemporary entries in my flying logbook do not specify the actual targets, but only 'Operations Norway', 'Operations France', and 'Operations Germany'. RAF crews, of course, are always restricted in this literary field, logbooks being official documents and scrutinized monthly by flight commanders. At that particular period, though, there was an extra dimension. For invasion was very much on the cards. 'You don't want some Gestapo thug reading that you bombed his Auntie Olga in Berlin,' we were told, 'so just make it "Operations Germany".' Which we did.

Even so, an incorrigible rebel, I kept a separate record of those early ops, entering the actual targets later in the war.

As the Germans advanced, so we were reassigned to the interdiction bombing of roads and railways. On 21 May 1940, for example, we attacked the rail junction at Jülich, dropping 4,000 pounds of bombs and coming away satisfied that we'd significantly disrupted communications, although achieving nothing like the destruction visited upon the same target a few years later.

Jülich, 1945, after Allied air raids

We also returned to the Ruhr, to Hamm, and again to Essen, dropping 10,000 and 14,000 pounds of bombs respectively.

After that, as the Battle of France intensified, we were tasked against more and more French targets, bombing railways, roads, and convoys at La Capelle, Amiens, and finally Abbeville. The situation was often fluid, and on at least one occasion I received a timely recall signal that stopped us bombing our own troops.

And on 11 June 1940 we did a special flight – purpose unspecified – to Guernsey, spending the night there before returning to Linton. We learnt two days later that the decision had been made to give up the Channel Islands without a fight!

France itself fell on 26 June 1940, after which we switched to German targets once again. Notably a seven-hour op to the Kiel Canal when I flew with a different crew, piloted by a Flight Lieutenant Thompson, on a sortie that moved me enough to wax lyrical and record in my logbook, 'Hell'ova Night'; an entry that dared the flight commander's ire when he signed the monthly summary!

An operational outing that I did not accord a similar accolade – though why, I cannot recall – was the next one I flew with Peggy O'Neill. We successfully raided a factory in Turin, but on returning over the Alps flew into rougher weather than any of us could have imagined. There was so much snow, ice, and turbulence that the engines started playing up, one temporarily cutting out altogether. Our co-pilot wanted to abandon, but Peggy gamely soldiered on, somehow retaining control of the machine, and eventually winning clear. But what a trip that was! Yet all I recorded was 'Operations Italy'.

By now ops had become a way of life, with fear its natural concomitant. For cringe down though we must as flak and bullets tore through the airframe, fear had to be lived with. Indeed, we received a master class on the subject from one particularly persistent fighter. Pass after pass, he made, riddling us from tail to nose on each, with Peggy desperately sacrificing height for any speed we could muster.

'He's determined to get us,' he gritted, as the wavetops prevented further descent. Only abruptly, the attacks stopped. For a breathless while we watched the fighter, holding off wide. Then, finally, concluding that he had run out of ammunition and was calling up support, we scurried for home, well aware that it had been our narrowest squeak yet!

Such things were wearing. But they had to be borne. For back then there were no set tours of operations. The squadron bosses, though, knew the score. And on 1 July 1941 I was posted away, off ops, to No. 19 Operational Training Unit, at Kinloss, near Inverness.

Since January 1940 all gunners had become full-time aircrew, and in theory, at least, sergeants, with the 'AG' brevet being introduced in the December. So I had become a reluctant wireless operator/air gunner, first a sergeant and then a flight sergeant. The instant-senior-NCO for aircrew, understandably enough, was not that popular with the regulars, 'You got promoted pretty swiftly, didn't you?' became a common jibe in the sergeants' mess. But you couldn't win, for when I received an overnight commission it was to be greeted in the officers' mess with, 'And where did you spring from?'

As for the commissioning, naturally I'd always known that I was upper-crust material, even so I was disturbed at being summoned by my commanding officer – not on this occasion, the Head, but the feeling could be similar when you put up as many little blacks as I habitually did! This time the interview was not protracted, just friendly, but still resulted in my travelling to London, only this time to Gieves of Savile Row, to be fitted for a new and shiny rig. 'And your bank account, sir?' 'Barclays – has been for years.' An NCO with a bank account! Upper crust, you see! Only there was still that elusive pilot's course …

At Kinloss, the task was to train Whitley crews for No. 6 Group using both the main airfield and its satellite at Forres – Balnageith. I was to spend four months here, and not uneventful months at that, for training had its share of excitement, not least on 3 September 1941 when I was in another crash, this one significant enough to be logged!

In mid-November 1941, however, I was sent to Enniskillen, in Northern Ireland, to deputize for the established station commander. The area was a political hotbed – I had to tote a revolver – so although the RAF had flying facilities at Aldergrove and Killadeas, and both a maintenance unit and a group headquarters at St Angelo, the predominant presence was army. As it was, my caretaker duties were not particularly onerous, the mess at Killadeas I frequented was sumptuous, and I got myself happily involved with some sailing craft I found on Loch Erne.

This detachment gave me a break from the routine of training, but it was to set a pattern I was to find increasingly irksome as the years went by. I was assured, of course, that each stores check or unit inquiry befitted me just that little bit more for higher command. As it did. So why did I invariably feel 'joe'd'?

Certainly, I had periodically applied to return to ops, my hopes soaring whenever signals arrived requesting aircrew for 'special-duties'. In August 1942 these were for the proposed Pathfinder Force, and in early 1943 for what we were eventually to discover was to be No. 617 Squadron. However, all such applications were blocked by my immediate boss. 'They want the best,' he would say. 'But I do too, Mitch. So you stay.'

Eventually, however, an Air Ministry posting arrived for me, rendering him powerless, and on 20 May 1943 – with every newspaper's front page screaming 'Dambusters!' – I was posted to No. 207 Squadron.

Killadeas, the erstwhile officers' mess (The Manor Hotel)

I found my new squadron at Langar, near Nottingham, still relieved to be rid of their Avro Manchesters – a disastrous machine – and happily settling with that queen of the skies, the Lancaster. As signals leader I might have chosen my own captain, but having accepted the first to be programmed with me, Flight Lieutenant Philip Brandon-Trye ('Brandy'), I never had cause to regret it. So, after just four hours of acclimatization flights, I began my second tour of ops.

Initially, we concentrated on the Ruhr, so that in short order I became re-acquainted with Düsseldorf and Bochum, although this time around such sorties took an hour or so less than on the Whitley, just over five hours. Yet how adversely so much else had changed! The defences in particular, had really got the hang of things now, with droves of searchlights and seemingly impenetrable box barrages on every run-up. Not to mention the radar-guided predicted flak! As for the night-fighters!

Seemingly impenetrable flak

I wasn't surprised, though – shocked, I'll allow, but not surprised – for two years back we'd prowled the night sky alone, whereas now our massed gaggles offered the defences score upon score of targets.

Shortly afterwards, on 20 June 1943, we bombed an industrial objective at Friedrichshafen, on Lake Constance, after which we overflew brilliantly-lit Switzerland – a wonderful, fairytale sight – to set down after nearly ten hours at Blida, on the northern coast of Algeria. And to show no favour to any Axis power, next day on the homeward trip we bombed La Spezia, the Italian naval base.

After that, though, it was Happy Valley again – the Ruhr – and to Gelsenkirchen, a place I had last visited in May 1940, over two years before, and on successive nights. So perhaps they bore a grudge. For as we ran in we were well and truly caught by flak, and then shot up by a whole procession of night-fighters.

Not nice! But the rear gunner, a commissioned lad, a Scot, from another crew, proved to be a good man to have along. As each fighter came in I was able to use the Monica rearward-looking radar to warn him, so that he was not only able to beat them off but, I fancy, to destroy at least one. Just the same, we were so badly damaged that we had to put down at Coltishall, near Norwich.

Though used to dealing with fighter aircraft, Coltishall's groundcrew chaps pulled their fingers out – when didn't they! – and patched us up, enabling us to return to Langar later that day. Our Lancaster, ED 627, had certainly done us proud. As for our guest rear gunner, he received a Distinguished Flying Cross for this spirited defence, and would later receive a bar to it for a similar exploit.

There were no such kudos for me, but I was well content with the way Monica had served us. Only I was already aware of Intelligence misgivings, and a few months later, when it was proven that the Germans were actually using Monica's pulses to both locate, and then home on us, it was with little reluctance that I saw it withdrawn from service.

Two days after our Gelsenkirchen outing, on 28 June 1943, 'Brandy' was promoted to acting squadron leader and left the squadron. Only to be killed in a training crash just weeks later while attending a senior officers' gunnery course. The news, I have to say, came as a distinct shock to the system. Death on ops, of course, one expected ...

For me, back at Langer, it was a-raiding as normal, initially to Mönchengladbach. And two nights later to the Big B, Berlin! It was my first visit, and 7 hours and 35 minutes simply packed with interest. But it was not my last visit, by any means, some taking a whole hour longer than others, and so, being packed with even more interest.

This initial Berlin outing, though, was our swan song from Langar, for in October 1943 we moved to newly-opened Spilsby, near Skegness, in Lincolnshire. The German capital loomed again, however, on 15 February 1944, and we penetrated just as deeply two nights later when we raided Leipzig, reaching base again after an eight-hour sortie.

At this point, however, our tasking was changed, and from April 1944 – shades of May 1940 – we were set to pounding communications networks. On 10 April this meant a wide-ranging series of strikes on Tours and Bourges, in central France, and on Antwerp. Then it was St-Valery-on-Caux, followed next night, by Paris.

It was clear to everyone that things were hotting up. Only at this point the boss handed me a signal. I knew what it was. But there was nothing to be said.

Berlin aiming-point photo

For by now I had flown 830 hours by day and 439 by night, the majority of the latter being operational. I had also completed 66 ops – over two tours' worth – and counting OTU callouts, an additional 15 operational maritime patrols. Further, on 18 January 1944 I had been gazetted with the Distinguished Flying Cross. But alongside all this I had also been part of a squadron which, by the war's end, would have lost 154 of its crews; at the very least 1,232 men.

Even so, I would love to have flown on D-Day, but it was not to be, and somewhat sadly shelving my flying logbooks for a while, I dutifully departed on posting as a signals-leader instructor, to No. 1661 Heavy Conversion Unit at Winthorpe, near Newark, in Nottinghamshire.

Distinguished Flying Cross

Neither of my operational tours had been all work and unremitting dicing with death, of course. There had been periodic leaves. And in off-duty times there had been favourite pubs, the Flying Horse and the Black Boy in Nottingham coming to mind. Then too, there had been sport. Lashings of it. Except that whenever called upon to fill a soccer or rugger slot I'd unfailingly responded, 'Not likely, they're too bloody dangerous.'

As for off-duty flying, in the past I had made a point of getting airborne whenever possible, so that nowadays the Types-Flown list in my logbooks read like a museum piece. They included not only the Virginias and Valentias I actually operated, but such erstwhile first-line types as Hawker Hinds and Harts, Wallaces, an Atlas, and the Navy's Fairey Seal – used by the RAF as a target tug. Then there were various Moths, and the Anson, which I had first encountered as a light bomber. Now, at Winthorpe, I used it for liaison visits. Otherwise I did little flying, the sheer pressure of my ground duties being too demanding.

Only suddenly, it was all over. And between June and August 1945 I was able to fly on three 'Cook's tours', taking in, among other old haunts, Hamm, Duisburg, Wesel, Münster, and Düsseldorf. Such flights, over such total devastation, were awesome. And sobering. On the other hand, both outbound and inbound, we

Cook's tour

would overfly so many of our own towns – not least Hull – blitzed unmercifully in those dark days when the Germans were riding high. When they had derided our leaflets, and refused to adopt Churchill's 'higher morality'!

Though the Service was shedding personnel wholesale, my retention seemed to be taken as read, and on 16 December 1946, after a spell with No. 1563 Heavy Conversion Unit at North Luffenham, near Oakham, in Rutland, I moved on to No. 91 Group Headquarters as a staff signals officer.

The headquarters was situated in Lincolnshire, at Morton Hall – subsequently a women's prison – very close to RAF Swinderby, my two-year stay giving me a deeper appreciation of the way the Service was run. But a headquarters was ideal too for getting things done, and as my tenure drew to a close, I resurrected the matter of my pilot's course. I was certainly not too young any more, not after fourteen years and a world war! So on 9 August 1948 I gleefully reported as a flight-lieutenant pupil pilot to No. 6 Flying Training School, at Ternhill, near Market Drayton, in Shropshire.

I suppose maturity – in 1946 I'd met and married Joan – allowed me to approach pilot training without fear of failure. And it clearly paid off. Starting on the delightful Tiger Moth biplane, I completed my course on the American Harvard, an excellent advanced trainer, being very demanding and only too ready to take control.

Indeed, the course couldn't have gone smoother, except that at the very end of it I suffered a slipped disk on dropping too clumsily into a Harvard cockpit. As it transpired, that took some months to heal, during which time I became the Flying Wing Adjutant and annoyingly, amidst all the paperwork, mislaid the logbook recording my pilot training.

Even so, having begun my aircrew career with a wireless-operator's arm flash, reluctantly enough supplementing this in late 1939 with an air gunners' 'AG' brevet; readily swapped in its turn, in January 1944, for a dedicated signallers' 'S' brevet; my chest finally bore the full wings so proudly worn in those old photographs by Bishop, Madden, McCudden, and Ball.

The operational phase of my pilot training, then, saw me opening a virginal logbook, but once more entering 'Lancaster' under 'type'. This time, however, I was to operate them from the sharp end, and for Coastal Command, starting at St Mawgan,

I'd met and married Joan …

A Shackleton on patrol

near Newquay, in Cornwall, where I was also checked out on the Avro Shackleton. This, like the Lancaster, was a spectacular aeroplane in its own right – a great, grey-painted roaring machine outside but with an interior hushed by jet-black drapes – which was eventually able to patrol for up to twenty-one hours: in every respect a far cry from the Virginia and Whitley! But aeroplanes are aeroplanes are aeroplanes. And for all that I held an above-average rating it was not that long before I was clambering out of a Shackleton whose tailwheel had collapsed after landing!

Aviation, though, has a multitude of tricks. So that, on joining my first maritime unit, No. 202 Squadron, at Aldergrove, it was to find that, alongside the Shackleton, they were operating the Handley Page Hastings, essentially a transport, and notoriously ungainly. As a new joiner I was to start off on these as a second pilot, which, at that time, meant raising and lowering the flaps – and watching. Not until I had built up enough hours on type would I be checked out on landing the beast. And I say beast advisedly, for I had watched other pilots at that stage skidding sideways, shredding tyres, and even sliding off the runway altogether.

As it was, my first Hastings sortie involved flying at 18,000 feet for some considerable time. Halfway through, however, my captain fell ill and passed out. And suddenly crew members were eyeing me from every corner. In the end, though, it worked out well, even to my landing away to expedite medical aid, with my squadron commander recommending me for an Air Force Cross, although having to settle for a green endorsement.

The green endorsement

Instances of avoidance, by exceptional flying skill and judgment, of loss of, or damage to aircraft or personnel

On the 26th August 1953, Flight Lieut Mitchell was second pilot in a Hastings aircraft on a special flight involving continuous flying at 18,000 feet.

During the flight, the first pilot, and caption, became ill and unable to control the aircraft. Flight Lieut Mitchell, although not qualified on Hastings and never having landed one before, successfully landed this aircraft without damage at a strange airfield.

By his presence of mind, initiative and judgment, he successfully averted what would otherwise have undoubtedly been a serious accident.

The Handley Page Hastings, a handful to land.

Our bread-and-butter task at both St Mawgan and Aldergrove was to exhaustively patrol the Atlantic. But in July 1954, after a spell back at St Mawgan – by then the School of Maritime Reconnaissance – and six months on No. 220 Squadron at nearby St Eval, I was posted overseas, to No. 224 Squadron in Gibraltar. And what a tour that was! No longer just skimming the Atlantic vasts, but landing in both Madeira and the Azores, with other flights ranging through Ceylon, India, Iraq, and Libya. Except that in October 1957 it was back to freezing-cold Britain with a decision to be made.

It was clear that the RAF had an interest in me, and indeed, even as I pursued my internal debate, they sent me to Worksop, to No. 4 Flying Training School, for a jet familiarization course. I had twenty hours on the single-engined, twin-boomed Vampire. What a mind-blowing experience, from the simplistic engine control to the swiftness – and unbelievable smoothness – of jet flight! Flight, moreover, with never, ever, a mag drop!

It was a great interlude! But still my problem niggled. I was well aware that I had suffered a sea change, possibly from seeing so much of it. For although further advancement in the RAF, and even a new career in civil aviation, was offered, neither attracted me.

To a large extent it was the RAF's ground jobs that put me off, the rationale remaining the same; indeed, more so since I had become a squadron leader. For what interested the RAF now was not my flying skills but my command and administrative abilities. Yet being hived off to an admin job had always made me feel put upon.

Of far greater moment though, Joan and I had never had the opportunity of setting up a real home together. And that really weighed. But – to give up flying?

Then again, since 1934 I had flown 1,400 hours as crew, a good proportion of it on wartime operations, and 1,600 hours as a pilot, almost all on operational patrols. Only ... wasn't it true that for some time now the zest had gone?

And that, when it finally found expression, I recognized as the crux. Accordingly, on 4 November 1957, I submitted my resignation.

Getting used to civilian life took some time. Eventually, however, unable to find a niche at any level I found acceptable, I sought advice from a golfing acquaintance who persuaded me to try my hand at vehicle sales. Initially this meant my matching commercial and agricultural vehicles to the needs of prospective customers. And it all went very well, so that within a matter of months I had developed a lucrative, countrywide chain of client contacts, only to remain fundamentally unsettled. Until I confessed to my boss that I didn't like my image as a flash-Harry motor salesman. He was enormously amused yet puzzled also.

'But,' he reasoned, 'everything hinges on the company sales director.'

Director! *Company Sales Director!* Ah! And suddenly all doubt vanished. Indeed, I rather think my golf improved too.

Above all, I finally had a real family home; essentially, for the first time since meeting my wife, Joan, back in Nottingham, in 1946. Joan Mitchell, or as she had been then, Joan Ball, daughter of former RFC-cum-RAF pilot Cyril Ball, and niece of my boyhood hero, Albert Ball, VC.

John Mitchell, DFC, 2012

5

A certain sense of satisfaction

Warrant Officer Bill Newhouse, navigator

During poet Rupert Brooke's sojourn in Germany in 1911 he wrote home, 'I am [now] wildly in favour of the [Royal Navy's] nineteen new Dreadnoughts. German culture must never, never, prevail.' Conversely, when future-humanist Leonard Cheshire visited Germany in 1935, with Hitlerism approaching its zenith, he returned home, it is said, without the experience having any profound effect upon him, observing only, 'They do seem to have a lot of tanks.'

Aircrew Cadet Bill Newhouse, 1941

As a young teacher I had visited Germany the year before Cheshire and had found that everyone appeared to be in uniform, whether Brown-shirt (SA), black-garbed SS, or Hitler Youth. I had also found that air-raid shelters abounded and that the existence of labour camps for political prisoners was accepted as a commonplace. It is gratifying, therefore, to know that I was of a mind with Cheshire and not necessarily lacking perspicacity, for I too viewed the overt militarism as merely the German way of doing things.

In 1939, when war loomed, I was teaching general subjects in my home town of Accrington, in Lancashire. At that time teaching was a reserved occupation but when the rules changed, because the RAF needed aircrews, I applied to become a pilot. At the selection board, however, it was suggested that being twenty-nine, and with a teaching background, I was too highly qualified to be wasted as a pilot. 'After all,' the chairman said, 'pilots only drive the aeroplane, so they're ten a penny. What we've an increasing need for is people to tell them where to drive to.' And so I accepted training as a navigator.

On 29 March 1941 I reported to No. 7 Aircrew Selection Centre at Babbacombe, near Torquay, moving then to No. 11 Initial Training Wing (ITW) at Scarborough. The ITW course kept us pretty well occupied, combining square-bashing, physical training and general service training with subjects common to all aircrew, a whole raft of them; aircraft recognition, principles of flight, basic navigation, maths, morse code, anti-gas precautions, engines, armament, hygiene and sanitation, RAF law, administration, organization and discipline; meteorology and signals.

We soon decided that the authorities had chosen Scarborough because of its two levels, so that we would do one session on the beach, the next on the promenades far above, being doubled between the two by officious drill corporals.

It was an easy way, of course, of getting us fit. Then again the food was good; indeed, as aircrew we always ate well; whereas other airmen might have one egg a week we had three! And the Scarborough girls! Wow! It was summer, of course, and we were free after lectures, when the freshly blancoed, white aircrew flashes in our forage caps acted like magnets. Mind you, the girls weren't slow; they may not have known about the eggs, but they were very well aware that even trainee aircrew got more pay than ordinary airmen!

The next training phase meant voyaging from Gourock, on the Firth of Clyde, to Hamilton, Nova Scotia, travelling aboard HMS *Worcestershire*, a pre-war liner-turned-armed merchant cruiser. The crossing took six days and while it was an unstressful voyage, it was so hot below decks that I slept on top the whole way across. Clearly my mind was on my creature comforts at that time for my fondest memory on arriving in Hamilton remains the steak supper we were greeted with: no shortages on that side of the Atlantic!

We then began a three-day train journey, calling at Montreal then, in succession, Toronto – where we visited the Niagara Falls – Cincinnati, Chattanooga, and Atlanta. Between the major population centres we appreciatively took in the scenery, sleeping the nights through in bunk beds. Again, the food was better, and far more plentiful, than anything we could remember.

The train eventually dropped us at Miami, Florida, after which we were transported to the suburb of Coral Gables, and the campus of Miami University where the navigation course was to be run by Pan American Airlines using American Air Force instructors. The campus facilities, we quickly found, were excellent, not least the single rooms we enjoyed, as were the American tropical uniforms – with khaki shirts and slacks – which we exchanged for the civvies we had arrived in.

The five and a half month course was tightly presented, but as I had taught arithmetic, algebra, geometry and trigonometry for several years, I found no problem with it, enjoying equally the introduction to astro-navigation; indeed, back then I could identify as many as fifty stars and constellation groups!

I was fortunate enough too, to find myself equally at home in the airborne exercises. True, we were aware that in Florida we were flying over vast open

Consolidated Commodore flying boat

areas with every township well lit and easily identifiable, with virtually every day bringing guaranteed good weather. Even so it was not until we got back to Britain that we realized just how different flying conditions in Europe would be.

The aircraft we trained in were Consolidated Commodores, twin-engined flying boats that had started life as luxurious Pan Am transports; the first airliners to have padded seats, we were told, and still quite comfortable despite their spartan conversion to navigational trainers. In them we were able to achieve thirty hours of flying by day and twenty by night.

My overall exam results, my logbook reveals, were Theory 91 per cent, Plotting 95 per cent, Met 83 per cent, Flying Exercises 85 per cent, with the Chief Instructor of Pan American Airlines assessing me as 'Average flying, above-average ground'. And so, by a stroke of a Pan Am pen, I became an RAF sergeant navigator!

Off duty, Miami had proved another world from the UK, with lights blazing throughout the twenty-four hours, establishments that never shut their doors, and with the amenities of close-by Miami Beach opened to us by special arrangement. The people themselves could hardly have been more hospitable and we were frequently invited to parties, the girls, in particular, making much of us. In fact, we even had a royal visitor, for the Duke of Windsor, then serving as the Governor of the Bahamas, came to call. But that was only the start of my intimacy with royalty for later, back in the UK, my squadron would be visited by both the King and the Queen!

Visit of the Duke of Windsor, Miami, Florida, September 1941. Me, on the right, only just getting into the shot

We had arrived in Miami in mid-August 1941, to an America at peace. Nor had anything changed by 3 December 1941, when we said farewell. In the interim, of course, there had been tensions, as reflected in their press. But just four days later Japan attacked Pearl Harbor and plunged America into war.

The homeward crossing was again from Hamilton, Nova Scotia, but this time in the SS *Letitia*, docking at Liverpool on Christmas Eve. A period of leave followed, but on reporting for duty again, I found, I had a decision to make: by the look of it whether to opt for Bomber Command, or Coastal.

Navigating in Bomber Command meant running an air plot out to Germany, getting as near as possible to the target, then air-plotting back once more. It would be interspersed, admittedly, with moments – if not hours – of terror, but essentially, just sitting there at a plotting table. Coastal-Command navigating, in like manner, meant running an air plot over thousands of square miles of empty ocean for up to twelve hours at a time, then air-plotting back to base again, the monotony broken only by servings of coffee and doorstep-sized Spam sandwiches. Even when the ocean was not entirely empty it meant hours of calculating and then flying searches to find the location of whatever it was that the apparent-emptiness held; creeping-line-ahead searches, and square searches. Again, just sitting there, if with rather less chance of being terror struck.

But there was an alternative, I found. Namely, to fly with Fighter Command, the job being to look for, intercept, and shoot down German aeroplanes. Real Biggles stuff! I put my name down right away, and on 23 January 1942 commenced training as a navigator/radar at No. 3 Radio School, at Prestwick, in Ayrshire.

During the month-long course we were introduced to the still highly-secret Airborne Interception (AI) radar. This was equipment carried on an aircraft that would show a target aeroplane as a blip. Initially the navigator/radar had two, three-inch radar scopes, although later there would be just one.

The nav would direct the pilot to change heading until the blip was in the centre of one tube, at the same time having him change height until the blip was centred on the other. With the blip centred on both scopes he would advise the pilot as the range decreased. The pilot would crane forwards until the time came when he could see the target. Then came the critical step of identifying the quarry. If it proved to be an enemy aircraft, an attack would be delivered. If a friendly aircraft, then the contact would be put down to experience, and the chase broken off.

Air Interception Radar Mk 10

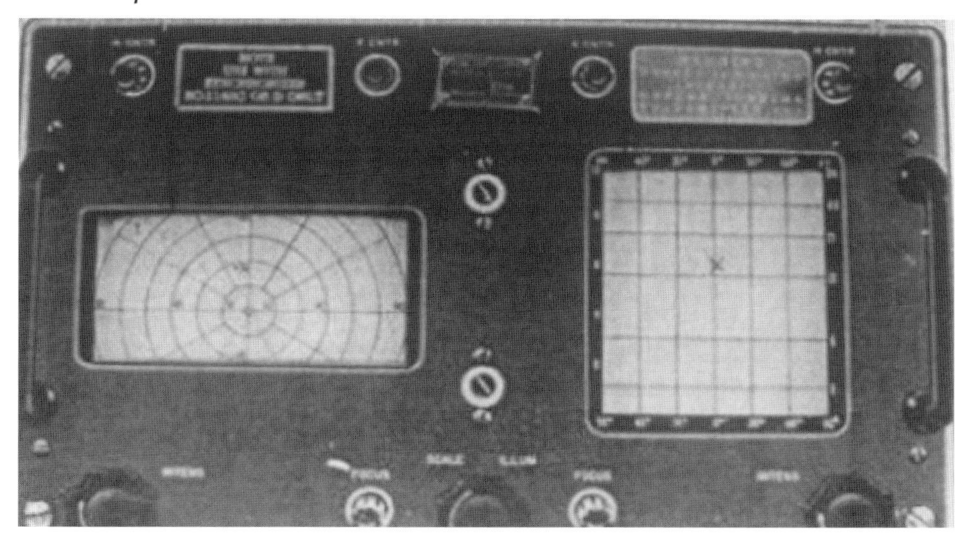

AI earlier version

We did little flying at Prestwick, and that in Ansons, Oxfords, and Blenheims; just enough, in fact, to allow us to see how the equipment worked. Or, as often as not, failed to work. Our airborne operating experience was consolidated, however, during a three-week attachment to the resident No. 96 Squadron, a night-fighter unit belonging to No. 9 Group. Here too, as we honed our AI skills, we began to discover the enormous difference between flying – and in particular, navigating – in the States, and doing so in Europe.

By day all was clutter here, with so many built-up areas linked by webs of railway lines that map reading became a real problem. This was a problem exacerbated at night by a blackout that was so effective that even large cities barely gave off a glow. We also began to come to grips with temperate-zone weather!

Our final training posting was to No. 60 Operational Training Unit (OTU) at East Fortune, in East Lothian, where we passed to the control of No. 81 Group, Fighter Command. Here I joined up with a Sergeant Pilot Irving. We came together socially, as it were, chatting in an organized get-together in the sergeants' mess and deciding that we could probably work as a team. As indeed we did, flying together for some four months. We would only split up when he was commissioned and then posted, but though we did so with regret his first name, to my chagrin, has long vanished.

We flew Beaufighters, clearly far more effective as a fighting machine than the outmoded Blenheims but requiring us to speed up our operating procedures no end. The Beaufighter Mark Six was also very satisfactorily armed, with four cannon and six machine guns. True, the weapons were all under the control of the pilot, except that whenever they went wrong it fell to me to get my fingers oily sorting the darned things out.

Many of the exercises we flew involved pairing up with another aircraft and practising interceptions. At first the other machine would fly steadily but as the pilot-nav intercepting team grew more competent so the one currently playing at target would throw in more and more violent evasive manoeuvres.

Then again we carried out 'Canopy' exercises, which involved us flying a patrol line from which we could be rapidly directed to anywhere within the sector. We also flew in co-operation with the searchlights, them trying to cone us, and us doing our best to escape the beams.

The flying was intensive, but far too often the sorties were wasted, either when the weather proved unsuitable or, more frequently, when our radar became unserviceable. Even so, on being posted in June 1942 my airborne time had increased by forty hours' day and twenty hours' night.

Next came No. 1457 Station Flight at Northolt, near London, where we converted to the Douglas Boston – and its fighter variant, the Havoc – and were introduced to the unlikely-sounding Turbinlite concept of night-fighting.

The Turbinlite, we discovered, was a 2,700 million candlepower searchlight, the precursor of the better known Leigh Light. At Northolt it was mounted in

The Leigh airborne searchlight, a development of the Turbinlite

A Boston illuminated by Leigh light

the nose of our aircraft, its lead-acid battery pack leaving no space for the standard fit of either cannon or machine guns. Having no armament, therefore, the Turbinlite aircraft would be accompanied by a single-seater fighter; in our case a Hurricane.

The Turbinlite carrier would use AI to home onto the target, switching on the light when the target came within its range. The fighter, until this time flying loose formation, would then surge ahead alongside the beam, identify the target, and if it was an enemy, commence an attack.

It should be mentioned that we would switch the light on for no more than twenty seconds, just long enough to guide our friendly fighter; any longer and we might well have become the target for another night-intruder.

We were to spend less than a month at Northolt, then we were moved down to Predannack, in Cornwall, for a further month. But from then on our life became peripatetic in the extreme. Eventually we took root at Middle Wallop, remaining there from September 1942 until late February 1943. During our stay we were first attached to No. 1458 Station Flight and then to No. 125 (Newfoundland) Squadron. Not long after our arrival, however, all Turbinlite flights metamorphosed into squadrons, No. 1458 Flight becoming No. 537 Squadron.

Prior to this the Hurricane playmates had come from any convenient fighter squadron but now they became part of the Turbinlite squadrons, the system continuing in operation until improvements in the AI system, and the arrival

A Boston on patrol

of the Mosquito, rendered it obsolete. Our crew continued operating the system until January 1943, after which we moved in quick succession to Fairwood Common, west of Swansea; Middle Wallop in Hampshire; Defford in Worcestershire; and finally to Bradwell Bay in Essex where we once more worked with No. 96 Squadron.

Although we rarely enough made contact with the enemy we did suffer losses. I remember being held off in the circuit and watching as one of our colleagues, a pilot called Cook, came in with his battle-damaged aircraft, only to hit a parked aircraft in the process, writing off both the – previously – stationary one and his own. On that occasion, fortunately, nobody was more than slightly injured.

It was shortly after this, in mid-June 1943, that my pilot was commissioned and moved on. I was then posted to No. 54 (Mosquito) Operational Training Unit at Charterhall, in Berwickshire, where I crewed-up with the man I consider to be my permanent pilot, Sergeant John Duffy of the Royal Australian Air Force. Gelling immediately, Johnny and I converted to the de Havilland Mosquito, the 'Wooden Wonder', that magnificent machine that was so fast and

De Havilland Mosquito, with quick-recognition Invasion stripes

manoeuvrable, so powerful and versatile, that it made every preceding fighter or fighter-bomber seem like a dray horse in comparison.

Part of our training flying on this magnificent steed we did at Charterhall, the rest at its satellite, Winfield, just west of Berwick. On an early sortie we took it up to 29,000 feet where, although it still handled like a fighter – its service ceiling was 36,000 feet – it was clear that the air was so much thinner than at our normal operating heights! On that occasion, I remember, we finished by diving down at top speed, then slowing right up to examine the machine's stalling characteristics: a stomach-churning procedure if ever there was one! But fast or slow, high up or low down, what a magnificent aeroplane! What a superlative gun platform!

Regrettably, having AI fitted to the Mosquito did not solve our technical troubles. Like all aircrews we swore by the groundcrews who kept us in the air. But as sortie followed sortie during which the guns would not fire, the undercarriage would not come up, and the radar would not work, swear-by tended to become swear-about. As for our feelings when an engine cowling became unfastened in flight and was torn off by the airflow to strike the tailplane!

Whenever the guns agreed to work we practised firing air-to-air and air-to-ground, and when the AI worked we never missed the chance of carrying out interceptions on opportunity targets, even when the sortie did not call for it.

Having completed the course, we were then assigned to No. 264 Squadron, part of No. 9 Group, Fighter Command, back at Fairwood Common, Swansea; although not that much later we moved to Hurn, near Bournemouth, our night-fighting task being to cover Southern England and the approaches to what were eventually to become the invasion beaches.

On occasion we were also diverted northwards to cover other sectors, notably in December 1943 to Church Fenton, in North Yorkshire, where we stayed for five months and were accommodated in unheated tents, for all that the ground was snow covered for much of the time! This purgatory lasted until May 1944. Then came a move to Hartford Bridge – soon to become Blackbushe – in Surrey, where we stayed for two months while patrolling the South Coast once more. But all these moves were little more than administrative changes of the squadron base, for the job took our individually-operating aircraft and crews even further and wider.

Just the same, wherever we operated from, the daily – or rather nightly – grind was to fly standing patrols while at the beck and call of whichever ground-controlled interception station (GCI) was directing operations in that sector. Then again, with the GCI installation itself being mobile, and with its convoy taking just a matter of days to relocate to pastures new, they, like us, could rove in the way of desert caravans, and did so, particularly after D-Day. Our main control station, however – codenamed 'Starlight' – was Sopley, near Christchurch. This was the centre we worked under when operating from Hurn, Middle Wallop and later, Tangmere, our working pattern at that time being two nights on, two off, and a period of leave every six weeks.

While patrolling, the message we would listen for was, 'We have trade in the area.' The GCI controller would then give us a heading to fly and a rough height. Once on heading and approaching the height we would take over with our airborne sets, finding the contact, then refining its location until the pilot made firm visual contact, when he would transmit the 'Tally ho!' sighting call. At this point, with the Mosquito night-fighter's armament, its speed of 380 mph, and improved AI radar, we had no need for searchlights and tame-dog Hurricanes. We still had our problems, however.

For some of the time we continued to fly the inherently wasteful standing patrols but increasingly we would wait on the ground until the ground controller saw a contact and scrambled us. The latter practice conserved both aircraft hours and fuel, but both scrambling and standing patrols had their place in the scheme of things.

On occasion we would act as a practice target for other AI-equipped aircraft. And then there would be the wasted sorties when, whether we were to chase or be chased, our playmate did not turn up and we were left to stooge about aimlessly until we were recalled.

Far more often, however, we would get airborne, only to have our AI go unserviceable. More frustrating still was the occasion when, having identified a German, but in thick, cloudy conditions in which we needed radar to make the kill, Johnny opened up with our guns, only to have the recoil shock the AI into giving up the ghost. Indeed, my flying logbook is studded with the entry, DNCO – duty not carried out – reflecting that some technical snag had caused the AI to fail. Invariably this led to a disconsolate turn for base, preceded by the near-snarl to control, 'My weapon is bent'; the use of 'weapon' instead of 'radar' indicating that the airborne-radar's existence was still being treated as top secret.

Besides the AI task, however, we were employed upon a variety of others; not least carrying out 'Bullseye' decoy sorties where we would fly part-way to the enemy coast with the aim of diverting their fighters from a real raid. Then again, when enemy fighters began to get too troublesome for our bombers, we would be sent to mingle with the outbound bomber stream, the job being to pick out any intruders that had managed to insinuate themselves.

On one occasion we got very excited at picking up such an intruder, especially as it led us a merry chase, pulling out every evasive measure in the book. Just the same, with me giving a running commentary and Johnny following my every instruction, we eventually made visual contact, only for Johnny – with his finger firmly taking up first pressure, as it were, on the firing button – to recognize it as a fellow Mosquito.

But frustration came in so many forms. There was the occasion when we were homed towards a blip heading for the bomber stream. We were just on the verge of declaring AI contact when the bombers let go a flood of 'Window', the aluminium-foil strips that were aimed at disrupting the German radars. What the strips did this time was snow-up – clutter – the AI screen and blot out our quarry, rendering us powerless while allowing the intruder to fly on and carry out his depredations among our bombers.

Frustrating in a different sense was when, after a protracted chase, we were within seconds of opening up on a pair of enemy aircraft, only for a Hawker Tempest to cross in front of us and in short order shoot down both of them.

We eventually had our day, however, for on 3 June 1944, ten miles south-east of Bayeux, Johnny confirmed that what we had been pursuing was a Ju188. This was a high-performance, medium bomber, the more advanced version of the Ju88. A few short bursts and it disintegrated, leaving me, at least, with what I afterwards expressed as, 'a certain sense of satisfaction'. The sortie during which we made this kill had taken us three hours and fifteen minutes.

Then, on the night of the 5 June 1944, we stumbled upon the very biggest event to date: D-Day! We had been carrying out a routine Channel patrol and had turned for home when we unexpectedly found ourselves face-on to wave after wave of glider-towing bombers, all heading towards the Cherbourg Peninsula! Not only that but, in a departure from the norm, each of them had its navigation lights on, the powers that be, we concluded, having decided that German night-fighters were less of a risk than collision.

Junkers Ju188

Strafing enemy installations

After this our role changed somewhat, and for a while we were fully occupied in carrying out fighter-bomber sweeps behind the invasion beachhead. These were both exciting and productive but they exposed us to all manner of anti-aircraft and small-arms fire. In fact, for the first fortnight or so we were subjected to, not just German flak, but that of the Royal Navy, the British and American armies and even the Free French, once they got going. After that, however, a degree of order was imposed and we were routed to the beachhead via Littlehampton and a safe cross-Channel corridor, so circumventing most of the misidentifications.

Not that any such widely-promulgated arrangement stopped hard-pressed friendly units or ships opening up on us. Nor, of course, did it protect us from American fighter aircraft who, as a breed, were notoriously trigger happy. Indeed, we were always warned when they were to be in the neighbourhood, 'Your friends are flying.'

By the nature of things, then, anti-aircraft fire remained an everyday problem, indeed on 8 June we were so severely damaged by light flak that although we managed to re-cross the Channel we had to put down in a field.

Another sortie that has to stick in the mind was when we had made a low pass over a German airfield and pulled away to watch as another of our aircraft – flown by a Flying Officer Brook – made short work of at least one enemy machine parked in the ground. We'd hardly had time to grin, however, when flak struck our starboard engine, causing it to burst into flames. Sitting beside Johnny – in both the Boston and the Beaufighter my position had been some way back, but on the Mosquito we sat shoulder to shoulder – I watched as he carried out the fire drill, and moments later breathed again as the flames died away. Then he took us back to base, touching down after a 2 hour 50 minute flight, making a careful but thoroughly competent job of what was his first 'for real' landing on one engine.

There were other 'near-miss' occasions too. As when we were patrolling to the north-east of Cherbourg and met a German head-on – my logbook records, 'Met *Hun* head on': Biggles again! We turned after him, closing to 3,000 yards, descending as we did so from 8,000 feet to 900 feet. Only to run into the Allied flak coming up at him! We even fired off the colours of the day but the brown jobs were too intent on protecting themselves from him, and in the end we had to break off the attack. Virtually the same occurred just a day or so later when fish-head – Royal Naval – gunfire actually damaged our tailplane and forced us to return to base.

That we had got off lightly was brought home to us a little later when we saw two enemy aircraft blown out of the sky. Not that we gave the incident overmuch thought at the time, for again we were heading disconsolately back to Ford, both our AI and its scanner having decided to stop working just as we had reached our operating area.

Though unserviceable equipment infuriated us, anti-aircraft fire remained the bane of our existence, notably on 2 July 1944 when we intercepted a hostile aircraft, only to have ground fire, whether friendly or enemy, force us to break away so that we returned to base after a 2 hour and 45 minute waste of time. And only a day later, pursuing a very hopeful contact, we found ourselves coned by searchlights that brought up the very heaviest concentration of flak and once again forced us to throw away the chase and dive out of trouble.

Then again, on 6 July 1944, a month after D-Day, we found ourselves threading through severe electrical storms that shielded us from the flak but prevented us making any radar contacts at all. By the very next night, however, the weather pattern had changed to give such brilliant moonlight that searchlights were hardly needed, and even so we were well and truly coned.

In fact, that was an altogether disastrous night. The moon aside, double summer time ensured that it was virtually light until midnight. So light, indeed, that we mapread back to the French coast; only to be hit by flak as we crossed it. Our starboard engine packed up, then the port one began to stutter. Then, to really make our day, a red fire-warning light began to glare at us from the instrument panel. We prepared to bale out, but Johnny managed to drift us over the water to a south-coast airfield where the aircraft was found to be absolutely riddled with holes.

We left it there, awaiting a decision on its future while we got ourselves back to base. Not to receive kudos for Johnny's magnificent piece of flying but to face a blistering reprimand from the CO for ever getting ourselves into such a predicament in the first place!

After that we had a brief respite, leaving the area of the invasion beachhead and spending our nights patrolling London, chasing after Doodlebugs, the unmanned V-1 pulse-jet Flying Bombs. We were helped in this by GCI and our own AI but for most part we sighted on their flaring jet nozzles and employed the Mark One Eyeball from there on.

We were to have another brush with the enemy's modern technology on 12 September 1944 when we were directed onto a contact just north-east of Brussels, only to find him far too fast for us; almost certainly, Intelligence concluded, one of the new, pilot-manned jet-propelled fighters!

Messerschmitt Me262 jet fighter

Back in July 1944, though, we had soon been recalled to the bread and butter work around the beachhead, with flak setting our port engine on fire on the very first night of our return, although Johnny yet again got us safely home. And on 11 August 1944 the two of us actually landed in Normandy!

We had positioned from Hurn to operate from airstrip B4 at Bény-sur-Mer, Banville. On arrival we found it so busy that we had to circle to allow four other aircraft to land, even though by then, only just over a month after D-Day, there were something like two dozen Allied airstrips operating. Indeed, the first of these, B1, at Asnelle, just north-east of Bayeux, had been completed as early as D-Day plus one!

Destined to become of particular note to our squadron were strips B6 at Coulombs and B8 at Picauville. Most of the new landing grounds had been carved out by hurriedly-working engineers but some were former German bases, which provided me with some fascinating memorabilia in the shape of enemy documents. As it was, we operated from Banville for a month before moving on to another French strip, at Carpiquet, where we stayed for a further three weeks.

One of the hastily-fabricated post-D-Day airstrips

Towards the end of August 1944 Johnny and I took advantage of some spare time and hitched lifts to recently-liberated Gay Paree, enjoying a day of so of Parisian life. There were, however, a couple of occasions when we were eyed rather frostily, having been taken for Germans on account of our RAF blue-grey uniforms, which were not too dissimilar, people obviously thought, from German field grey.

But back in Normandy too, we had been not a little surprised to find a local resentment of the Allied presence. We might not have expected kisses and bunches of flowers, not a full month after the invasion, but to encounter rank hostility hurt.

The sordid reason, it emerged, was that the invasion had upset the local apple cart, for the Germans, having been resident in the area for up to four years, had become accepted, some not only marrying, but even acquiring property. Then again, the invasion had brought recriminations, with the 'Jerry bags', as the German-sympathizing Frenchwomen were styled, having their hair shorn by partisans and forced to suffer other indignities. Our discomfiture, it was clear, was small beer in what was a harrowingly divisive time for the region.

Another source of local discontent was the collateral damage attendant upon the invasion. On 3 July 1944 I noted, 'Caen ablaze'. And this was some days before the 'thousand-bomber' raid that heralded Operation Charnwood and eventually, if rather too tardily, levered the Germans from the city but came

The shaming of women who had consorted with Germans

close to obliterating it in the process. Then again, on both 3 July and 9 July 1944, I recorded, 'Le Havre still in flames'. But of more immediate concern to us, the logbook note about Caen actually read, 'Caen ablaze; coned, hit by flak'.

At intervals we were moved back to Hurn, and from there dispatched north to Middle Wallop to renew our acquaintance with the Doodle-bugs. Formerly, patrolling London, we had been mere novices at the game. And even now, ranging the south coast, we were often hard pressed to actually get to grips with them. GCI, as always, helped enormously, but having got into the area our best guide was still the flare from their jet tubes. Yet even on closing with them great care had to be taken, otherwise, when they blew up, their debris was only too likely to take us with them. And no, as a hunting pair Johnny and I did not attempt to emulate the Spitfires and the new Meteor jets and engage in tipping the Flying Bombs over with our wingtips!

Spitfire about to upset the underwing airflow and topple a V-1 Flying Bomb

Experienced though we now were, we were constantly learning. But still the technical gremlins bugged us. On one occasion we had to return to base when our electrical equipment surged, every amp we owned going wild. On another sortie our main fuse blew! Yet another trip had to be aborted when both the voice radio – through which we communicated with our GCI station – and our internal intercom system broke down.

It was rather different, however, when, owing nothing whatsoever to flak or enemy interference, our port engine failed, leaving Johnny to get us home. Practice makes perfect, they say, and he touched down leaving barely a slick of tyre rubber. Shortly afterwards he was commissioned, but, unlike my previous pilot, stayed on the squadron.

When operating from the continent we were already, in effect, an integral part of the Second Tactical Air Force and later, although slightly after our time, squadron aircraft based at Twente, in Holland, would actually carry out patrols over Berlin. But at the end of 1944 Johnny and I were screened from further operations.

By that time there seemed little chance of being called back for another tour, so we went our separate ways. Johnny returned to Australia and I lost track of him; indeed, it was only by chance, in 2008, that I heard that he had died just a few months before.

Back in 1944, however, when I came to leave the squadron, there was no grand parting ceremony, my departure being a mundane processing of my clearance chit, the begging of a lift by gharri to the railway station, then catching the train to my new posting. All of which was fine by me. But I had thought that Johnny, before he had been shipped home, might have got some recognition. For all those engine-out landings, at least, if not for the joint effort that had ended with us downing the Ju188. But it was not to be.

At least we had the Aircrew Europe Star to show that we had spent our war actually carrying the fight to the enemy; unlike so many of our flying colleagues who were left sharing the France and Germany Star with worthy non-fliers from all three services! It never seemed important at the time, but it has rankled with many since, and although there has been British retrospective recognition, persistent calls to honour aircrew service have so far come to nothing. Though one still hopes ... For my part, with ops finally behind me, my logbook recorded 580 flying hours, 330 by day and 250 by night.

My new posting was to No. 62 Operational Training Unit at Ouston, Northumberland, as a navigational instructor. Here, we flew the students in Ansons and Wellingtons, both of which I found very comfortable machines after so many months of bucking around in unsprung fighters. On the other hand, they were not only lamentably lacking in zest but bedevilled by AI snags that lost us far too many sorties.

As things wound down I did detachments to several other airfields, not least to Twinwoods Farm, in Bedford, the fateful departure point for bandleader Glenn Miller.

I suppose, after the intense flying I had become used to, anything else had to be an anti-climax, and in December 1946 I dutifully reported to Uxbridge, handed in my kit, received my civvy suit, about-turned, and quietly closed the door behind me.

I returned to teaching, obtained a post at Draycott, in Derbyshire, and eventually retired at sixty-five in the post I had long held as headmaster.

In earlier days I went to a few reunions, and more latterly I attended meetings of the Notts and Derby Branch of the Aircrew Association. But in the last five years since my wife, Mifanwy died, I have tended to stay at home more. My daughter comes and does for me, while my son, although living in Northamptonshire visits virtually every weekend. Thanks to them, and to a few cronies who keep me company in the local club, life is never that lonely. Just the same, the mind increasingly tends to return to those excitement-packed years on the Beaufighter, and the even more satisfactory time on the dear old Mosquito.

People who bother to interest themselves in those days ask what I felt about daily putting my life at risk. Discounting youthfulness – though even then I was somewhat older than most aircrew – I can only think I must have had just the right constitution for the job, for I never recall being in the least bit scared. In flight I would always be too busy peering into the scope and trying to solve the essentially mathematical puzzle the would-be elusive target blip was setting me. Then again, off duty, when one might have expected stress to bite, I was able to shrug it off. By no means a born warrior, then, but enough of one, I suppose, for the working day.

Bill Newhouse, 2012

6

What the heck's a met flight?

Flight Sergeant Ernest Winfield, wireless operator/air gunner

Becoming a Coastal Command wireless operator/air gunner in 1940 was, I discovered, both a complicated and protracted business. Having been accepted, I had done my initial service training at Morecombe, only to find that there was a backlog of trainee aircrew, resulting in a delay before I was called forward to Yatesbury, the wireless school in Wiltshire, to do the first of my technical courses.

Even then, once I had qualified for my wireless arm flash, it was to find that another backlog had developed, this time in the gunnery field. To fill in the time, therefore, I was given a holding posting to No. 10 Squadron, at Leeming, in the Vale of York. They would have welcomed a ground wireless mechanic but had no use for an only partially trained air-wireless operator. As it was, I was employed in station headquarters.

Sergeant Ernest Winfield, 1942

After some while the backlog cleared and I continued my training proper, a progression that took me up to No. 1 Air Gunnery School at Pembrey, in South Wales, and after that to No. 3 Radio School at Prestwick, in Ayrshire, where I learnt to operate the Air-to-Surface-Vessel radar (ASV).

It was mid 1942, therefore, getting on for two years down the line, before I became a qualified wireless operator/air gunner. Even then, being destined for Coastal Command, there was another course to do, my final training posting being to No. 1 (Coastal) Operational Training Unit (OTU) at Silloth, in Westmoreland, where trainees were introduced to the Lockheed Hudson. This course took until November 1942 but when it ended I was, at last, ready to fly on operations.

Air-gunnery training: from front, Vickers K, a Vickers, and a Browning

During the OTU course I had crewed up with the men I was to fly with, our captain, Sergeant Pilot Charlie Glover; Flying Officer Maurice Buttler (two Ts!), our navigator and meteorological observer; and another wireless operator/air gunner, Sergeant Roy Gilbert.

Both being wireless operators, Roy and I had undergone similar training, finishing by studying the two American wireless sets – the Bendix and the Westinghouse – that were the standard maker's fit on the Hudson. As wireless

Lockheed Hudson on patrol

sets they were all very well but to check them before take-off called for the engines to be powered up to over 2,500 revs.

This requirement had led me – a mere trainee wireless operator – to fall out with one of the staff pilots who, initially, refused to advance his throttles so far, being unhappy with the way the aircraft bounced about at such high revs. But raw though I was I had insisted, arguing that if the set proved to be unserviceable once we were airborne the sortie would have been wasted, and all for failing to do the pre-flight checks properly!

Fortunately, this proved to be a one-off spat, for the Hudsons we actually used on operations had no such requirement, having been fitted with the standard RAF transmitter/receiver, the Marconi T1154/R1155.

As it was, when flying as a crew Roy and I would split the duties, one of us operating in the turret on the way out, then switching to the wireless duty on the way back, so keeping ourselves up to the mark at both specialities.

At the end of the course the crews got their postings, ours being among those told off for St Eval, in Cornwall, which was fine. After all, didn't they call Cornwall the English Riviera? But when we looked down the list and saw the unit, No. 1404 Met Flight, we were at a loss, with a concerted cry arising of, 'What the heck's a met flight?'

On arrival at St Eval we soon found out. In the case of No. 1404 Flight it meant a unit tasked to patrol the Bay of Biscay and send back weather reports. The rule of the game was equally simple: get off, get the gen, and transmit it back. That was it.

The trips were always of the order of seven to eight hours, the outbound leg being spent gathering the met, the return leg in encoding it and passing it back to base by W/T (morse). All very well, except that such transmissions enabled enemy direction-finding stations to take bearings on us.

To obtain the met information we carried special instruments, although they lay outside my field of expertise, among them a radio altimeter – whose signals bounced off whatever lay below and told us our exact height above it, unlike the ordinary pressure altimeter – and also equipment to enable Maurice, our navigator, to get atmospheric pressure readings. Using these aids, the general pattern of our flights would be to set a course down the whole length of the Bay of Biscay at between 1,500 and 2,000 feet – which also happened to be the best height for sighting submarines – periodically dipping down to 500 feet to obtain the barometric pressure. Then, towards the end of the leg, we would descend to 50 feet – visually, and very carefully, of course – obtain a near-sea-level pressure reading, then turn for home, climbing steadily to a pressure-level equivalent of 20,000 feet. Mind you, I say 20,000 feet easily enough but getting up to anything approaching that was no mean achievement in a Hudson!

As you'll gather, keeping track of our position while taking all these observations kept Maurice pretty busy. In the end, though, as we began our climb to height he would feed all the met readings he had obtained into the psycho device, so converting the plain language into a daily-changed mix of 5-symbol groups of figures and numbers..

Met information being the unit's reason for existence, our messages were prefixed with the high-priority indicator O-P; high priority because, with no ground-station reports from the area to otherwise illuminate the met-men's crystal balls, meteorological information was a treasured commodity. And coded, because we did not want the Germans getting the benefit of our observations! Another priority prefix at our disposal was O-A: 'We are being attacked by enemy aircraft'. But this was one we kept in mind, while hoping never to employ it.

Once we were at height it would be the turn of either Roy or me to get busy at the morse key and transmit the information back to Group. The volume of material to be transmitted was invariably of the order of two hundred coded groups. First time out, red-hot-keen as we were, we gaily rattled off the whole two hundred without a pause. Then sat back with a glow of satisfaction at a job well and smartly done, anticipating nothing more than the 'All correctly received' acknowledgement. Only to have the ground station come back with, 'IMI all after group thirty' – repeat everything after the thirtieth group! After which salutary lesson we would split the message up, sending just twenty groups at a time, then seeking an acknowledgement before sending the next twenty. This was much slower, but far less frustrating for all concerned.

On that first day, having 'arrived' at St Eval, we had discovered that we were one of three new crews posted in. Of the crews we were replacing, one had been lost from St Eval, another had been operating from Gibraltar when they failed to return from a patrol, but the third, more happily, represented a crew and a Hudson who were being rested together, the crew having successfully completed their operational tour and the aircraft having run out of airframe hours.

After a day or so the first of the replacements went off on patrol. Eight hours later, when they landed, the rest of us new chums were all agog to find out about the way these operational met flights actually panned out. On the face of it flying down over the Bay and back with nothing but sea all the way did not sound all that exciting. Even boring, perhaps.

'We met a Ju88,' Sergeant-Pilot Tiebeck said dourly.

And that's virtually all any of them had to say. Except that when we went to look at their aircraft it brought to mind a colander; there were holes everywhere. They had met a Junkers Ju88 with a vengeance! Not so boring, then!

'But how did you let it get so close?' we asked the gunner, wonderingly.

'Thought it was a bloody Beaufighter,' he snarled.

And only when we rushed away to treble-check the aircraft-recognition silhouettes of the two did we see how similar they were.

Junkers Ju88

Bristol Beaufighter

Our commanding officer, Flight Lieutenant Hugh Eccles, proved to be a man of stern temperament and strict principles. On landing from our own maiden operation we were cock-a-hoop with ourselves. Hugh came in, eyed us coldly, then let fling. Eventually, having quaked under his tirade for what seemed like ages, we discovered that our crime – eight tiring hours before – had been to get airborne two minutes late!

Nor was there any winning with him. On a subsequent occasion the weather over the airfield was so bad that we had felt it politic to hold at the end of the runway to allow the torrential rain to die down a little before taking off. When we returned he ignored the delay but laid into us just the same, 'When you lot finally decided to get airborne you held so low over the road that you damned nearly took me and my bike with you.'

His strictest tenet, however, was that if he told us to fly, then we flew without question. The corollary being that, whoop it up as we might when nominally off duty, it was incumbent upon us to keep ourselves fit to get airborne regardless of when the call came.

He was hard, of course, but supportive – indeed to a fault, one might say. As an example: coming back from a flight in late December 1942 bad weather had forced us to divert into Chivenor, on the north coast of Devon. On arriving back at St Eval the next day we found – not altogether to our surprise – that we had been volunteered to do a sortie on Christmas Day. When it came to take-off time, however, Maurice was a bit below par, having over-indulged himself in the officers' mess the night before. We arranged, therefore, that, throughout the flight, I would do his plotting for him.

At the due time we got onto the runway, only to have the tower start flashing red lights at us. This was puzzling, for we could detect nothing wrong with our aircraft, so Charlie, as captain, determined to ignore the lights and get under way on schedule. Then they came up on R/T (voice radio) and we could no longer avoid acknowledging that we were forbidden to take off. And so we taxied back to dispersal and, with it being the festive season, stood down.

After a while, and predictably enough, Hugh walked in to wish the rest of his merry lads a Happy Christmas. Only to instantly take stock, and seeing us in the throng, to glower, 'But by this time you lot should have been halfway down the Bay.'

Festive pints in hand we explained that the tower had cancelled the sortie on the grounds that the weather had become unworkable; at which he really hit the roof. He got onto the telephone and, junior though he was, proceeded to lay down the law to the far more senior officer at the end of the line, telling him that nobody on the station had the power to countermand his orders, that only Group had that authority. Stopping in mid-tirade to glare at us, he barked, 'Get yourselves into the air, and on your way.' Then he continued his ranting on the phone. And so – with no more red lights – we got airborne, successfully carrying out the sortie.

During these patrols there was always the chance of being intercepted by German aircraft – as had happened to Sergeant Tiebeck's crew on their first op. Such hostile marauders might sight us visually or home (or be homed) onto our transmissions. And being lengthy transmissions, as I have indicated, this gave the various detecting stations plenty of time to take cross-bearings on us and fix our position.

But our main enemy in the storm-generating Bay of Biscay was always the weather. This not only gave us a rough passage but also made it only too easy for us to lose track of our position. Certainly, weather was the cause of several of our aircraft and crews failing to return to base.

New boys though we had been, we quickly settled into the routine, carrying out eight operational patrols satisfactorily. And the ninth started out like all those that had gone before it.

It was 25 February 1943. We were not on an everyday sortie, but on a very-long-range one, with a jerry-built extra fuel tank installed to enable us to extend our patrolling time. The main difference with these patrols was that we would end up getting sea-level readings at both the southern and northern extensions of our patrol. Descending to the south of the Bay had been no problem for there had been plenty of gaps in the cloud, but as we approached the northerly descent point the general murkiness had long been floored with unbroken stratus. Not that this was any problem either, for no enemy long-range patrol aircraft could possibly find us in such poor visibility, not even if it should home towards our transmissions. Nor was navigation bothering us, even as we approached the thorny, flak-sown areas of Ushant (D'Ouessant) and Brest, for Maurice had been able to use Gee to keep track of our whereabouts while obtaining his met readings.

As midday approached, however, we were obliged to descend, gap or no gap. Even so, it was all plain sailing. We'd get that final low-level pressure reading, change heading off Ushant, and climb for home. Maurice reckoned that we should be some way off Brest and miles clear of any high terrain, so Charlie eased back the throttles. It was all going so well ...

Gee lattice chart: approaching Ushant (D'Ouessant), navigating by Gee. It was all going so well ...

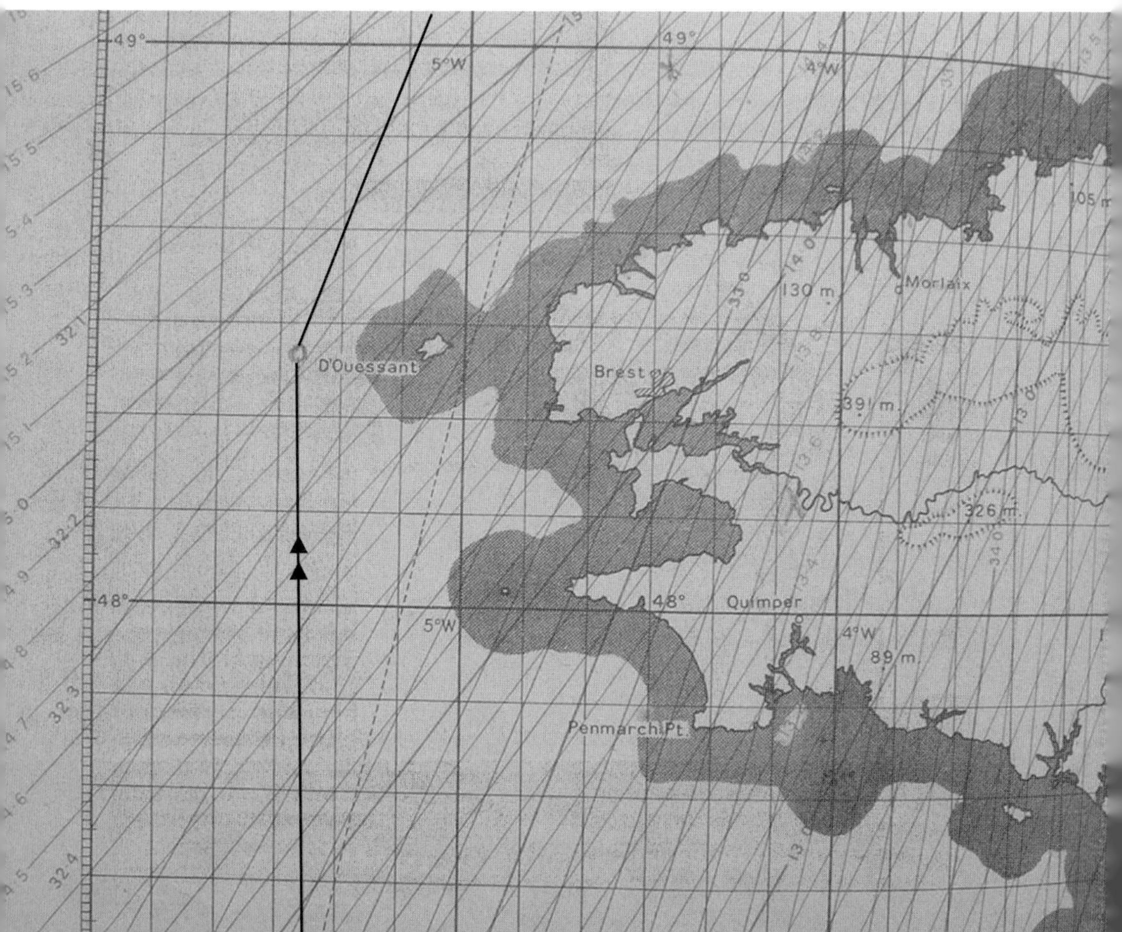

I was in the turret when we began the let-down, my eyes joining those already alertly looking for that first shredding of the clouds. Such blind descents always seemed to take forever, but we eventually began to see the waves at just two hundred feet on the radio altimeter. Only, watchful as we were, hostile eyes were equally so. For although we had broken cloud just where Maurice had predicted, well clear of the Brest approaches, Fate had arranged that we should have done so directly overhead a German coastal convoy! And a wide-awake one at that.

After so many hours of droning flight, things happened with lightning rapidity. Being in the turret I was facing the tail when Maurice shouted, 'Watch those ships, Charlie!' With which Charlie flung us into a right turn – and tracers began flashing past my shoulder!

Everything changed on the instant! Stationed atop the fuselage in the turret I was in the best position to make an assessment of the damage we had suffered. Looking back there were bullet holes in the tail, then looking forward I saw flames coming from the port engine.

'Charlie,' I yelled, 'port engine's on fire. Use the extinguisher.'

He must have stabbed the button instantly, for a second later the fire went out. Relieved, I turned to inspect the right-hand side of the aircraft, seeing no sign of damage. Only on turning back to the port side I discovered that the fire had not only re-ignited itself but worsened immeasurably, the flames flaring rearwards to totally envelop the tail.

There was clearly nothing to be done. We were still diving, on an easterly heading now, towards the coast. The enemy coast! And not that far off! Nor that far below! But my immediate problem was to get free of the turret. In itself, no easy matter! We used to say that there was no way an unconscious gunner could be extracted from the Hudson's turret in the air. For a start there was only space for a single helper, and he would have had to approach the task by reaching upwards above head height. But then entering the turret in the first place was a business in itself.

You got in facing the tail. Then dropped into the seat. Next, you lowered the firing table across your knees. After which you were ready to fight. And what a good fighting position it was! Interlacing the fingers of both hands and further steadying yourself against turbulence with your elbows, you operated the trigger with a thumb. But as for getting out of the turret again! All that to be done in the reverse! And done, in this extremity, in double-quick time!

I got the table up and was all ready to exit the turret when I found my harness snagged! Just what I needed! Struggling free, I jumped down – to find the fuselage a mass of flames. Not least, blazing about the parachute rack! Not that parachutes were going to be of any use at this altitude.

'This is it, Ernie,' I told myself, 'there's just no way out.'

Maurice suddenly appeared, lunged at the main door, pulled not one, but both, the toggles – the one releasing the door hinges as well as the one that freed the dinghy – and kicked the door clear.

Then we hit the ground. And I passed out.

What I learnt later was that Charlie had been struggling to put the Hudson down on the beach. At the last moment, however, he had been forced to pull the nose up to clear an obstruction. After that he had shoved the stick forward again, striking far harder, I imagine, than he would have chosen to. Had we been carrying ordnance, whether bombs or depth charges, all might have been well. Instead, our bomb bay contained that flimsy supplementary fuel tank, still with a hundred gallons of highly-inflammable petrol in it. The tank took the full brunt of the impact and instantly exploded in a welter of flame.

Only many years later would we discover the precise sequence of events after that, and learn how it was that we had not been burnt alive.

At the time, I regained consciousness to find myself lying on a table in a fisherman's cottage. Roy, I realized, was facing me across the room.

'Where are we?' I asked him.

'France,' he said.

I thought about that, although everything was still pretty fuzzy. Unknown to me I'd already been dosed with morphine and was in that state where one goes in and out of consciousness.

'Then I suppose,' I said glumly, thinking ahead, 'it's the long walk down to Spain.'

There was no answer.

Into the silence, I asked, 'Got a cigarette?'

One appeared over my shoulder.

'Light?'

A match flared, and I had my light: from a good-natured fairy, perhaps? (I was a Gilbert and Sullivan devotee!)

It would indeed, I reflected, be a long trek, living off the land, and evading capture all the way down to Spain. But others had done it. No reason, therefore, why we shouldn't! Inhaling gratefully, I turned my head. To face the biggest bloody German you could wish for.

Initially, they took us to Brest. It seemed a long way, and the pain from my burns was pretty awful. But during waking periods I began to catch up. My fellow wireless op, Roy, had been thrown clear of the aircraft but had snagged his wrist, nearly severing it. Maurice was badly burned on his face, hands, and knees. I had a damaged hip and knee and a burnt face, although my burn was nowhere near in the same class as Maurice's.

It was some time before I missed Charlie. He had not been strapped in, it seemed. On impact, therefore, he had been thrown into the instrument panel and suffered a fractured skull. He died thirty-six hours after we arrived at Brest.

As I came around more completely I discovered that we had been taken to the German naval hospital in the docks. Talking it over it struck us that this was a prime target for the RAF. Let's hope, we told each other, that they move us before the lads come to pay a visit. In fact, we stayed there for three weeks, and the docks were never raided.

What we did get, though, were two Hitler-youth types inhabiting our room, clearly posted there to note anything we said. One was fine, but the other was a typical Nazi. Although I suppose when you've been brought up on nothing but propaganda it's no wonder if you strut.

Roy and I showed a steady improvement but at the end of the three weeks, when we were moved, Maurice was still in such a poor state that he was kept there. Which brings me to concede that during our hospitalizations the Germans treated us on at least equal terms with their own wounded.

Leaving Brest we were moved to Paris, to the *Luftwaffen Lazarette*, the German air force hospital. Then, eight weeks after the crash, and no longer in need of specialized treatment, Roy and I were moved to Germany, to Oberursel, just north of Frankfurt, to the Dulag Luft Interrogation Centre.

This was a daunting place where they kept us in individual cells each of which had just one window, far too high to see out of, and far too high to reach. However, I don't think they were particularly interested in us; after all, it had been nearly two months since we'd been brought down. Just the same, throughout our three-day stay they tried to give the impression that they knew all about us. There was no ill treatment, but the various interrogators did, on occasion, play the bad guy, good guy routine on us.

When we were moved from there it was by train. The other groups being shifted on had been allocated rations but because Roy and I were added at the last minute nothing had been provided for us. We had no idea how long we would be travelling for, so we kicked up a fuss. And in the end we were given some sort of cake.

Dulag Luft Interrogation Centre, Oberursel

In fact, we spent three days on the train, trying to find some comfort despite the most basic and unyielding of wooden seats, pausing at Annahof, but eventually de-training at Lamsdorf, in Silesia (later, Łambinowice, Poland).

Stalag Eight B Prisoner of War (POW) Camp, our ultimate destination, it turned out, was a walk of about a kilometre from the railway station and as we had spent so long in hospital, to say nothing of the train journey, I found it very hard going. Indeed, some distance before we got there I fell down. I got up again, if with a struggle, but then collapsed completely and had to be carried the rest of the way. Whether to Spain, or from Lamsdorf, it was clear that walkies of any sort weren't for me!

Stalag Eight B was essentially a prisoner of war camp for army POWs and had a population of some 10,000, although many of these were accommodated outside on semi-permanent working parties. We were sent to a compound set aside for RAF aircrew.

It transpired that some months earlier the original Luftwaffe camp at Sagan, Stalag Luft Three – the Wooden Horse place – had become so overcrowded that a thousand of the prisoners, mostly NCO aircrew, had been transferred to Lamsdorf. It seemed likely, however, that the thousand in question had been judiciously selected, for when we arrived the RAF compound was generally regarded as a bad boys' area.

Not that the aircrew compound was the only 'special' one, for there was another that we called the Dieppe Compound, set aside for Canadians, many of them commandos. Being what have since become known as special forces – and viewed, therefore, as likely escapers – the Canadians were not allowed out on working parties, the same restriction applying to aircrew. Consequently, the

Roll call at Stalag 8B, Lamsdorf

main occupation for both groups was to be as awkward as possible. We would cause the maximum amount of bother without going too far and precipitating real trouble. But certainly, we never volunteered for anything.

It would tax the patience to describe the two years I stayed in Lamsdorf. Since those days the routine and innate boredom of POW life has become familiar through films and print. Suffice to say that although life was not easy at Lamsdorf it was a well-established camp, which meant that we got regular Red Cross parcels as well as other amenities.

After two years, however, rumours began to reach us of POWs from camps even further to the east being marched westwards as the Soviets advanced. Much later we would learn that the argument successfully advanced at his 1947 trial by the officer responsible for all POW camps, *Generalleutnant* Gottlob Berger, was that the Geneva Convention required the removal of POWs from a potential combat zone. When a planned rail evacuation had been forestalled by the swiftness of the Russian advance Hitler had decided upon the forced-march solution. General Berger had protested, but had been ordered to comply.

Easterly though Lamsdorf was, however, we had been complacent, considering it out of the question that the Germans would be able to set the ten thousand of us on the march. Our hosts, however, had already worked out how to do it. The evacuation was on, we were told, but if any man escaped from the column, a hundred others would be shot.

In the event, I never heard of this or any similar reprisals, but the threat was enough to convince the group I found myself with. When orders came, therefore, we all prepared ourselves as best we could, making up packs of provisions and getting together the sort of kit we thought we might need.

Next day, on 10 February 1945, exactly two years after the crash, we set off in a great column stretching miles, on what was to become a nightmare march that was to start in the coldest winter remembered, last for nearly three months, and take us some five hundred miles in a generally westerly direction. There had been no good-natured fairy to give me a light in the fisherman's hut, but clearly one of the ill-natured sort had marked me down for some long walk or other!

As early as the first day on the road men were throwing away kit they had considered essential the night before but could now no longer carry. Along the borders of the columns the guards were backed by dogs and any slackening of the pace was discouraged. It was a really rough time from the outset. And as the days went on it got rougher.

For a start, the weather was atrocious, freezing hellishly, and for all that we had tried to prepare ourselves, the kit we had was totally inadequate. The guards did their best to get us into farms or other shelters overnight but it was often impossible. On the first night I made the mistake of taking my boots off, to find that the leather had turned rock hard by next morning. After that I slept fully dressed. Just the same, it was not long before the boots actually froze, after which I was in agony with my feet. My main concern, though, was the outer two fingers of each hand, which I feared I would lose from frostbite.

Many men dropped out on the way, although most of these were collected by the carts that brought up the rear. The guards threatened laggards, and although I never saw it happen, it was known that in other columns, and conceivably, in parts of ours, some of these unfortunates were shot. What certainly happened, though, was that some, having been POWs for several years, were simply not fit enough to endure such hardships and died of exhaustion, malnutrition, and dysentery.

Nor were regular meal facilities provided for the POWs who, to a large extent, had to be self-sustaining, filching from the fields what the often-starving Polish populace had left.

Again, it would be some years before we learnt the magnitude of the toll taken by marches that involved some 80,000 prisoners, and even then estimates would vary. Safest to say that the indictment levelled against General Berger was that the forced marches resulted 'in great privation and death to many thousands of prisoners'.

For our part, after eleven days, and getting on for two hundred miles, we arrived at Görlitz, on the River Neisse, and some fifty miles east of Dresden. That is, Görlitz, and Stalag Eight A, where we were absurdly glad to see buildings after spending so many nights in the open. But Görlitz, though still in Silesia, proved to be a very different proposition from Lamsdorf, being a far newer establishment and lacking the administrative sophistication of the older camp.

Then, after all too short a time, it was back on the road again. And now conditions really began to deteriorate. However, I do remember arriving in a village square where there was a soup kitchen. On this occasion there was no check on us so we went round and round and round again, the soup gradually getting thinner as our stay there lengthened, although whether that was due to the cooks watering it down or to the steadily falling snow doing it for them we could not say.

The westward march went on, until eventually the stage was reached where both sides realized that the POWs could no longer carry on. The Germans insisted that we were still within the Russian pincer, but eventually a compromise was reached and we were turned aside into some wooden huts that had been abandoned by some working party or other. Here, two Polish girls spent a considerable time massaging my damaged fingers. Only, as things were done then, they did it with snow! The digits finished up badly blistered, nevertheless I still hold that the girls saved my fingers for me.

Then it was on again, until we eventually reached Stalag Eleven B, at Fallingbostel, in North-West Germany.

POWs at Fallingbostel, Stalag Eleven B

Once there, the Germans were happy enough to allow the army POWs to stay but insisted upon the RAF contingent taking to the road again. Except that by now we were beyond doing so. Promptly, then, we dumped all our RAF kit and scrounged army bits and pieces from the others, presenting ourselves as 'all army together', at which the projected segregation initiative petered out.

There was one tragedy we avoided. We had heard that Red Cross lorries were scouring the countryside for the various POW columns, mostly without success. But one managed to make contact. However, as the POWs were sprawled by the roadside enjoying the food and hot drinks, RAF fighter-bombers came over and strafed them, causing many casualties.

Then, on 16 April 1945, following a series of highly unsettling off-and-on rumours, and with gunfire edging closer until it was all around us, we were unexpectedly liberated by the 51st Highland Division. The fighting troops, having seen to our immediate needs, then took stock of our condition. Next, they turned to the other compounds of the camp, in some of which, not all that long before, several thousand Russians POWs had been allowed to perish of neglect. After which our liberating Jocks, checking their weapons before moving on, vowed to a man, 'No more Gerry prisoners.'

Just hours after that we were escorted back from the front line to an advanced dressing station. My immediate need was to get treatment for what had started as a sore on my foot then spread as an infection up to my knee. Unfortunately, the orderlies in the column had had nothing to treat it with and although the liberating medics did their best, the effects of it have stayed with me ever since. At the time, additionally, I was classified as a bad case of malnutrition – instead of my normal ten and a half stone I was weighed in at just six!

I rather think we confounded the army cooks, for we refused anything sweet, insisting upon meat and veg, our bodies, instinctively knowing that we needed building up. Then again the cooks were used to preparing and serving just three or four meals a day whereas we would wolf down anything savoury they put in front of us, then immediately hare off to the nearest slit-trench latrine. Only minutes later to be back swelling the meal queue once more.

Having been held for two days in the area of the advanced dressing station we were transported back to a nearby airfield to prepare for repatriation. It was evident that the airfield had been fought over just days before because there were crashed and burnt-out German aircraft all over the place. Nor, from we saw, had the organization got that much better since. Indeed, we watched spell-bound as one particular Stirling made five separate attempts to set down, only to be balked on each occasion by Dakotas that would pop up from all directions.

The repatriation arrangement, we found, was that ex-POWs were being given priority according to the date on which they had been shot down. As it happened, I had palled up with a lad who had been shot down some months before I had. Making the most of the confusion, therefore, we passed ourselves off as crew buddies, and I moved a fair way up the list.

Not that we were able to take full advantage of the subterfuge, for finally replete with food and drink and having enjoyed hours of sleep despite the only accommodation being unheated bell tents, we arrived back at the airfield too late for the earliest lift. Just the same, we eventually got away, and after a refuelling stop in Brussels, found ourselves back in dear old Blighty.

I then spent some considerable time in RAF Hospital Cosford, Shropshire, having my leg and the burns injuries on my face treated. This involved week after week of leave between procedures. In fact, it was true to say that I got thoroughly sick of sick leave. Just the same, I delayed my demob for as long as I could, not knowing what I wanted to do with my future. Before the war I had served my time as a joiner but by this time I had been earning my living in the RAF for far longer than I had in civvy street.

I did various resettlement courses, each of which added a bit of skill here, another there. But the breakthrough came just before my demob when, in 1946, a Nottingham employment agency advised me that there was a vacancy for a surveyor in a local firm. On one of my courses I had learnt the finesse of using a dumpy level – the tripod device surveyors employ – but the more sophisticated theodolite was still a mystery to me. But nothing ventured ... Besides, my second name being James, dad often called me Jammy Jimmy. So, living up to that, I talked myself into the job, and indeed kept it, until, after a year or two, works politics intervened and I moved on, turning to another firm, Geo Wilkins,

Back in dear old Blighty, WAAFs greet returning POWs

instead. Some time after that I was sent to join one of their subcontractors, George Rolinoff, who, during the war, had been involved in constructing the PLUTO fuel line across the Channel to the invasion beaches. And here I settled for some time.

By now the die was cast. So I buckled down, gaining qualifications and gathering experience so that when I finally retired I had long since been wearing the hats of both a chartered and a building surveyor. Of greater importance than all this, however, is that shortly after my return from Germany I had become re-acquainted with Joan, a schoolfriend. We had then started courting and on 24 November 1945 had begun what was to be, to date, a happy sixty-six years of marriage.

From the earliest days, naturally, Joan heard tales of my POW stint, and in the course of time we joined a group revisiting the former POW camp at Görlitz, a visit during which we were made much of by former members of the Polish Home Army, the wartime Resistance movement. Our hosts had not expected wives to be among the party and were initially quite discomfited because, it seems, it is the custom in Poland to greet a lady with a flower, and they had been caught unprepared. In which context, when we later passed through Warsaw, still in ruins, with reconstruction only just starting, we were told that the first businesses to re-open were the flower shops!

The three of us who had survived the crash maintained contact after the war. Roy, with his badly-damaged wrist, could no longer follow his pre-war trade as a butcher and became a civil servant. Maurice, for his part, because of his severe burns, had endured a long period of treatment. The Germans had done what they could, but then, on repatriation, he had become one of Sir Archibald McIndoe's guinea pigs, and was eventually able to return to his steel-foundry work in Sheffield. As it happened, it was Maurice who first made his way back to Cameret-sur-Mer, in Brittany, the scene of our crash.

A year later, Joan and I followed, when the mayor was able to tell me what had happened when our Hudson had first leapfrogged, and then pancaked, before exploding in flames.

The fire, it seemed, had been so intense that the Germans had formed a cordon, judging that nobody could be saved. Two Frenchmen, however, had ignored their threats, even disregarding weapons raised against them. Breaking through the cordon they had actually entered the wreckage, first extracting Charlie, and then both me and Maurice. Roy, thrown clear of the flames beforehand, had already been receiving attention.

By the time we learnt this, the older of our two rescuers, a retired gendarme, had died. The younger man, however, Joe LeRoi, was still very much alive. We, of course, made as much of Joe as we could, but at a personal level there is only limited scope for showing one's appreciation, heartfelt though it is.

So, with Maurice pushing at all levels, the three of us began to pursue various leads towards getting some form of official recognition for Joe's selfless heroism. Heroism, moreover, carried out under the threat of summary execution for disobeying the order of an occupying power! Sad to say, our efforts, pressed as they were, came to nothing.

Or rather, to nothing but a touch of the banal. The only person Maurice could find to take an interest in Joe's case was television celebrity Esther Rantzen who, in 1988, was hosting a programme called *Hearts of Gold*. Her show celebrated

Joe LeRoi's courage recognized, albeit unofficially

people who had performed 'unsung acts of outstanding kindness or courage'. She had Joe brought over to England, and staged an edition of the show at the RAF Museum at Hendon. The venue aside, the nearest we managed to get to official recognition was that Joe's Golden Heart Award was presented by 'a senior RAF figure'.

The years have rolled by since then, but I often think of the irony of my despondent supposition in that fishing hut at Cameret-sur-Mer: 'Then I suppose it's the long walk down to Spain.' Had I only known that exactly two years to the day we would be facing an even more protracted walk, this one from Poland into Germany, and in the depths of winter at that! Nor is it only in conscious thought that it comes to mind, for during a protracted hospitalization from 2008 the nurses told me I relived the trauma nightly. That ill-natured fairy, then, may well have the last laugh yet!

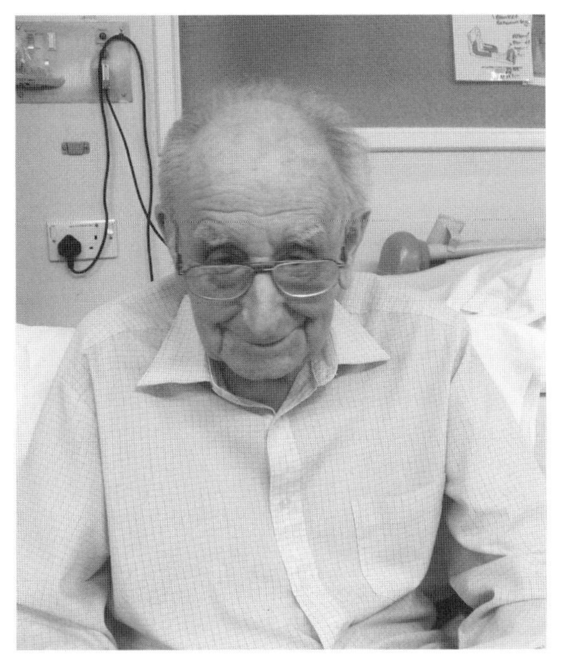

Ernest Winfield, 2011

7

I paid 'em back

Flight Sergeant John Marsden, wireless operator/ air gunner

Sergeant John Marsden, 1944

I sometimes think my life would have been empty had it not been for aeroplanes and the fascination they held for me. I started building aero-models before I was a teenager and then immersed myself in aviation magazines, and in particular, in the aircraft-recognition books that came out just before the war.

As it happened, I was still at school when war was declared but shortly afterwards I was taken on as a laboratory assistant in the physics department of Nottingham University. Being airminded I was the obvious choice when the university authorities had to appoint a member of staff to do ARP (air-raid precaution) duties on the roof. I don't suppose we were all that organized, and on the majority of nights sky-watching turned out to be a thankless and pretty boring task. But it was not to stay that way.

On the night it changed for me the local siren sounded when I was at my post. Despite the warning, however, nothing seemed to be happening in the immediate area. True, there was a raid going on some distance away, but it was too far off for me to make out any details. Then, nosing downwards from a moonlit cloud almost directly overhead, appeared what I recognized instantly as a Junkers Ju88.

I suppose there was nothing else to catch the pilot's eye but this lone figure in a white laboratory suit, presently gathering itself to sprint for cover. All I knew was that suddenly there were bullets chipping concrete and sending up sparks all about me. How he missed me, I'll never know! But even as I bolted I gritted, 'You just wait, you bastards, I'll pay you back!'

Air Raid Precautions: a rather more organized watcher, with both rattle and bell

Not for a moment did I intend this as an idle threat. Nor did I forget it once my nerves had calmed. But before I could do anything towards bringing it to fruition I had to wait until I was old enough to join the RAF. That came in 1942 when, having put in my application, I was called to a centre in Birmingham for three days of aptitude tests. There were lots of maths questions, and many more practical exercises. Although the thing that sticks in my mind – particularly these days – was a section from the medical, itself the stiffest examination of the type that had ever come my way.

For this test I had to take a deep breath then keep a U-tube of mercury up to a certain level: the 'forty-millimetre test', they called it. That really taxed the lungs, and it is a sad reflection that although I managed it then I certainly couldn't do it now. Not even with my NHS oxygen bottle close to hand!

Understandably enough the session during which I felt most at ease was an aircraft-recognition test where the shapes flashed on for just a second or so. I did particularly well on this.

In all, though, I found the whole three days very demanding, so I was more than pleased to be assessed in the very highest category and found suitable for pilot, navigator, or bomb aimer. There was no doubt in my mind which of the three I wanted and without hesitation I chose to train as a pilot; meaning, of

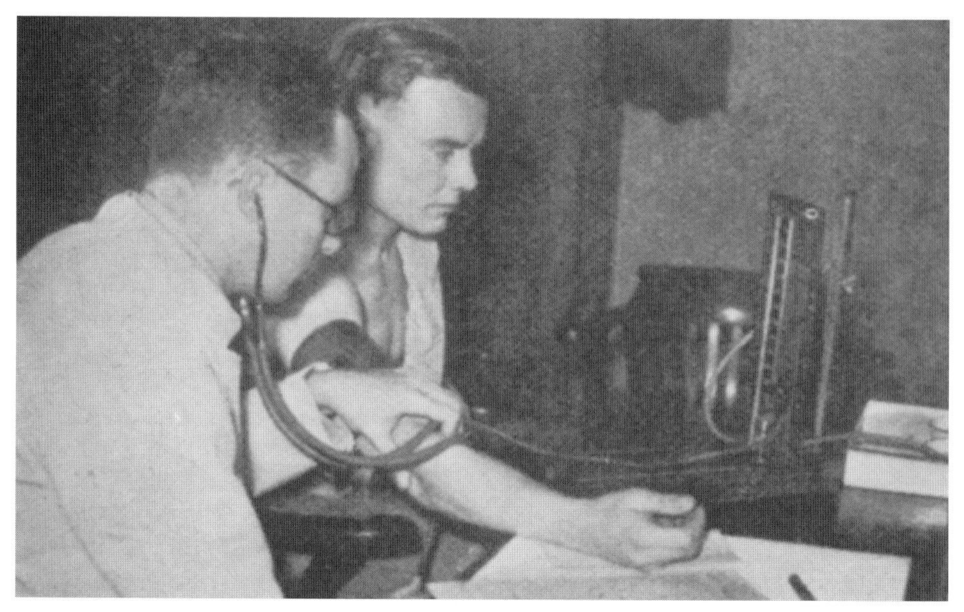

Blood pressure test

course, a Spitfire pilot, for they, after all, were the ones who shot down Ju88s! I was photographed, signed all the relevant papers, then went home to await a course at an Initial Training Wing, the posting, when it came, taking me first to Scarborough then to Blackpool.

I was photographed ...

Among things that stand out from that period is a dinghy drill they laid on. An inverted dinghy had been positioned some fair way out to sea. We were required to dive in, swim out to it, and right it. Having done that we had to invert it again for the next chap, then swim back. This was all very straightforward, except that as the first chap dived in so the sea around him turned blood red! Quite literally. It transpired that his thigh had been ripped open by a submerged hawser. He was pulled out and taken off for treatment. Then the next chap was told to dive in. 'Not me,' he retorted. And that was it. He was chopped on the spot, sent back to the unit he had come from, or to a re-allocation centre, who knows! There was no question of a second chance; the trainers clearly had 'lack of moral fibre' very much in mind.

We lost another fellow on the course too, physically, that is. For not a few failed in other respects. We were doing an assault course that required us to swing on a rope and clear a horizontally-suspended tree trunk. Once over it we had to let go and drop to the ground. This chap misjudged his swing, failed to lift his feet, and struck the log full on, breaking both his legs. We never saw him again, either.

Later, I was somewhat taken aback myself, if in a more pleasant way. One near-unendurable afternoon I was running around like a wild thing stabbing at sandbags with a rifle and bayonet, yelling and shrieking as bid. Inwardly I was wondering if I would ever get onto a flying course or whether I really was destined to end up plastered in the trench mud I had heard so much about. Suddenly, on being hailed from behind, I turned to see my father, resplendent in his Royal Naval rig! Present at the Battle of Jutland, he had been recalled for the duration of this war and, being in the area, he had come to see how his little lad was faring in the sky. I was given permission to fall out and join him, gladly setting aside my groundling's bayonet.

Though the initial training stages seemed interminable, even the subsequent course at Blackpool finally came to an end, our debut involvement being to take centre stage at the Wings for Victory Week parade. After that, with my general service training over, I was posted to No. 4 Elementary Flying Training School (EFTS) at Brough, near Hull, to begin my pilot's course.

I must say that at Brough I approached a state of bliss. From the very first day I was in my element; not least upon discovering that above airfields the sky is always so vast. Then again, in a prevailing atmosphere where everyone was keen to progress, I felt pilot's wings to be well within my grasp.

We started with grading school, during which each trainee was allocated up to fifteen hours of instruction on Tiger Moths to see if he was worth further training. My instructor was a real character; regular RAF, I believe. His name was Featherstone-Haugh, which he pronounced Fanshaw, his handlebar moustache quivering as he uttered the correction. Despite this one pedanticism, he was able to put me at my ease, and during our time together took me through all the

Grading School, de Havilland Tiger Moth

aerial evolutions I had so long merely dreamed about, from flying straight and level to rolling airily around the horizon, and even to spinning down from 8,000 to 2,000 feet before levelling out and landing. It was all perfectly great. All I ever thought it would be.

Then, one day, when I done a fair number of my allotted hours, but before I'd been sent solo, a stranger appeared and began to take up each of the pupils in turn. Eventually my name was called out.

'AC2 Marsden?' The man looked up from his clipboard, 'I'm a checker from Air Ministry and I'm going to fly with you.'

That was a surprise, but it was OK by me.

I saw him settled into the back seat, then, with him on the throttle, I got out and swung the prop. Settling myself into the front seat I did my after-start checks, and taxied out. At the take-off point I turned forty-five degrees, as required, did my pre-take-off checks, and getting a green from the control caravan, made for the stars.

Only to have him howl through the Gosport tube, 'What are you trying to do, kill us both?'

I gathered that he hadn't liked my spirited throttle opening, or the near-zoom climb I had attempted the moment the wheels left off their rumbling on the grass. And in that second I gathered too that all my piloting aspirations were at an end. Even so, the surfacing thought was, 'Well, 'fraidy cat, who cares!'

But clearly he did, for without another word he assumed control, turned back to the field, and landed. And after a flourish of his pen I found myself off the course.

I was enormously depressed. Nor did it make me feel the least bit better that of the thirty-plus pupils in my intake only three had got through the grading-school stage. I couldn't even find comfort, no matter how wry, in the reflection that even the three successful pupils had all learnt to fly before ever coming into the RAF! Two, having worked for Handley Page, had learnt with the company, while the father of the third owned a Tiger Moth and had taught him to fly.

But saddened as I was to lose out on the chance to become a pilot, I still look back upon my time at Brough as a happy one. In particular I remember the free and easy ways there; all of us clambering – rather gingerly placing our feet, perhaps – onto the wings of a Tiger Moth while someone taxied it across the airfield to the NAAFI wagon.

It comes back to me too, that there were Persian pupils being trained there. Why, I never did discover, although possibly from a hung-over contract with the Blackburn Aircraft Company whose airfield it had been. But the Persians seemed to do nothing but drive – or possibly, dive – Tiger Moths into the ground! That is, when they weren't landing on top of one another.

Ah yes! I really did enjoy flying the Tiger, although with its open cockpit one invariably froze. But nothing like the way I was to freeze in the rear turret of a Lancaster after the powers that be took out one of the perspex panels, supposedly to ensure that we saw enemy fighters more quickly. In much the

NAAFI break

same way as they removed the protective armour from behind the pilot in order to carry a bigger weight of bombs. But none of such refinements to discomfort would come until much later ...

Although I had originally been assessed as fit to train as either a navigator or bomb aimer as well as pilot, so many months down the line it became evident that the RAF's immediate need was for wireless operator/air gunners (WOp/AGs). Waiting for a navigator's or bomb-aimer's course, I was advised, would mean a long delay in re-starting training. I agreed, therefore, to remuster. And this really was my decision, for trainee aircrew being volunteers, I couldn't simply be detailed. The authorities were as good as their word, and within days I was posted to begin training in my new, dual, role.

An initial posting to Yatesbury ushered in a succession of wireless courses. As trainee pilots we had already been introduced to the morse code but then we had only been required to take and send at eight words a minute, and at rather less using signal lamps. Now, as trainee wireless operators, morse became our bread and butter and we had to learn to work at nearer twenty words a minute. There was also wireless theory to master and signals procedures to become familiar with.

The communications equipment we trained on, and would use in the air, was the Marconi transmitter/receiver combination the T1154/R1155. But apart from communications we also did a radar course at Madley, in Herefordshire, during which we were made familiar with Gee, the navigational radar, and with the mapping and bombing radar, H2S. The latter gave a picture of the ground, but at that period, certainly, the equipment wasn't that good, so that in the air the best we could ever get out of it was a coastline.

H2S display of the Scheldt Estuary, Rotterdam

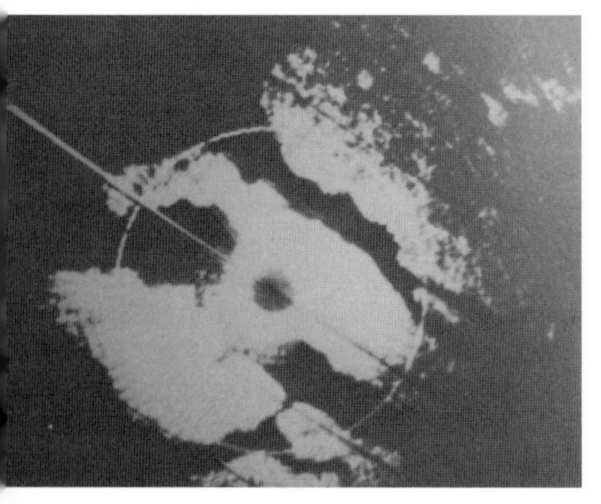

Chart of the Scheldt Estuary

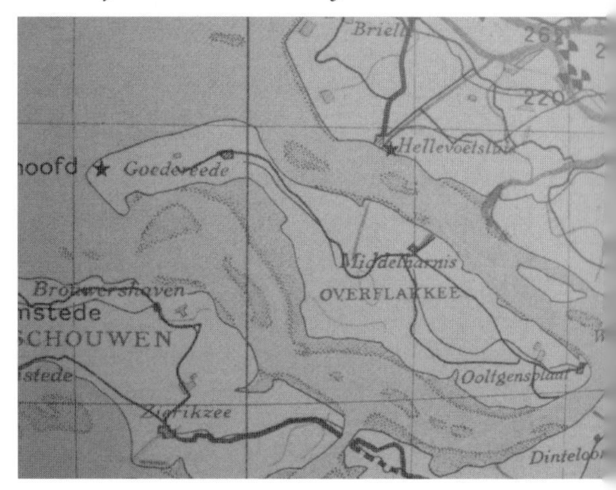

In fact, the most impressive thing I ever saw on radar back then was a ground-set that I viewed on the night of the first thousand-bomber raid, that on Cologne. As our crew had been stood down from ops that night I was able to watch the screen as the force assembled overhead before setting course for Germany. Standing there, our faces green-hued from the scope, seeing the phantom stream swarm and take shape, then make a beeline for the coast was something that smacked of the surreal, or of reality reflected by the camera-obscura gunnery trainer.

Equally unforgettable was that, on our particular course, we actually had to do a parachute jump from a balloon. Most trainee aircrew sat through lectures on the parachute and were told that landing was like jumping off a twelve-foot wall. Many jumped from a gym bench to practise the rolling finish recommended – demanded, by the instructors – after a parachute landing. We though, had this jump thrown in as well. But why just us, I never did discover.

When it came to it a few of us at a time were herded into a basket affair beneath this balloon – a barrage balloon adopted for the task – then lifted to eight hundred feet. Nothing about the business was fun, but once at height, with the very fiercest of parachute jump instructors at our backs, we had no option but to leap into the void.

The parachute

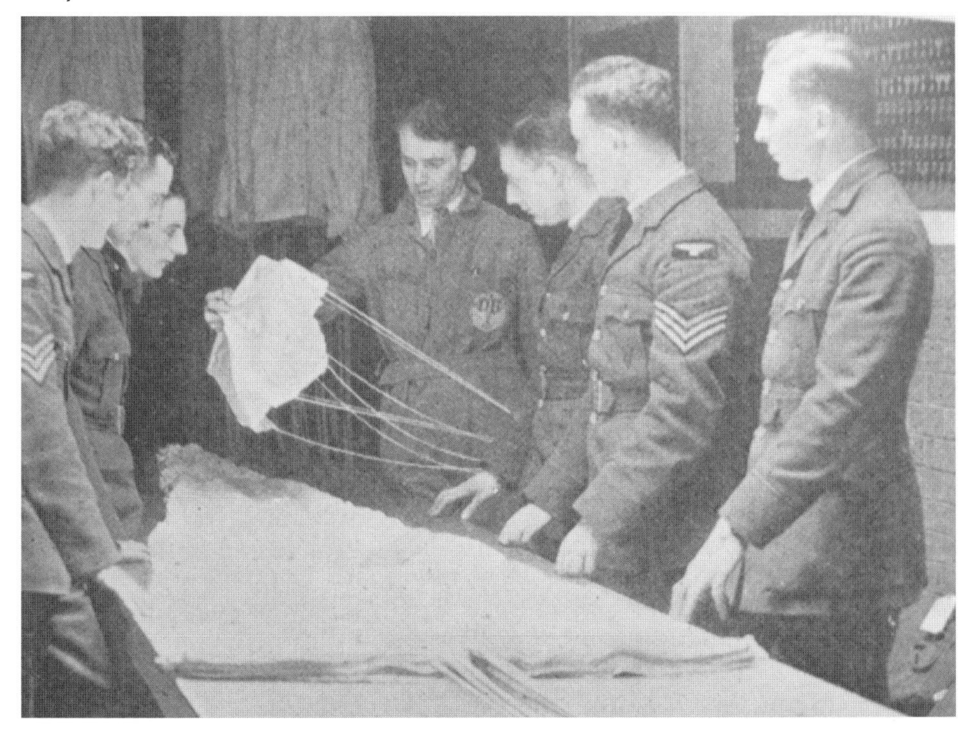

Aircrew who were forced to bale out of aircraft have told me that before the canopy opened it was like diving into a turbulent river. The drop from the balloon was far different, much more like the totally unchecked, vertically-falling sensation in a bad dream, with no airstream to cushion the descent. True, there was a certain amount of relief when the canopy snapped open. But having done the drop I swore that I would never do another, no matter how badly shot up the aircraft was. Fortunately, perhaps, I was never put to the test.

What mostly comes to mind from training days, however, are the lighter times, away from the circuit diagrams, the headphones, and the morse keys. For example, the highlight of my time at Madley (No. 4 Radio School) remains our visit to the local harvest festival. A few of us went along and were greeted by the pastor with, 'Nice to see some of you Raff lads, you know you need some religion.' Once inside though, we found an undreamed of abundance of fruit – even pineapples! – and knowing no better, and thinking that this was what it was all there for, we began tucking in. The fruit went down well, but our innocent setting-to and scoffing it, not so well. Certainly, the pastor was rather more brusque as we were shepherded out.

Then, at other training stations, there were the even sillier moments, such as when, peeved at a girl having stood me up at a dance, I took myself to the bar where for ten bob you could have a drink of every spirit on the shelves. I took advantage of this, and when throwing-out time came I was way out of my mind. Just the same, convinced that I was well capable, I put three pints on a tray and carried them off to the billet with me.

This was all very fine, except that a peculiarity of this particular station was that among the units sharing it were two prisoner of war (POW) camps. Indeed, because accommodation was so limited, our billet was actually inside the German compound. In the crazy system obtaining, therefore, to get to my billet I had to unlock the gate with a personal-issue key, enter the POW site, then lock the gate carefully behind me.

But there was another hazard in the shape of a stream that bisected the domestic site. In my owl-like state I spent some time solemnly looking for the bridge, but finally, being unable to find it, simply waded through. In which condition I actually made it to my billet, put the tray – with the three pints still reasonably intact – on the flat-topped stove, and then passed out. I woke in the morning to the outraged howls of my fellows and a room that reeked of boiled-off beer, as the others, before getting their heads down prior to my return, had stoked the stove to a cherry-red heat to ensure that it lasted the night.

But then, to be locked in a compound with a whole crowd of Germans was weird in itself, even if contemplated when truly sober. Certainly, I have to admit to some sleepless tossing and turning as I wondered what would happen if the Germans in the next huts took it into their heads to rise up. Not that there was any doubt, for locked inside with them as we were our single hut load wouldn't have stood a chance.

The other POW compound contained Italians, but they were a different kettle of fish altogether, so much so that we used to take some of them drinking in the local pub.

The training itself was comprehensive, but there were other chores that never sat too well, one of these being night-time sentry duty. My most unnerving experience was to hear a rattling as I patrolled the far side of a hangar and became convinced that it was German paratroopers leopard-crawling my way! Summoning all my courage, I edged around the corner, and shone a torch beam into the darkness. To reveal a tortoise making hard – and unbelievably noisy – work of negotiating a pile of loose stones.

Unusually, being trainees, we were armed for these night forays. And not with broom handles or the like, but with Sten sub-machine guns! All very Samurai-like. However, on examining the weapon before setting off on the first of my stints, I found a piece of paper glued to the magazine instructing, 'This ammunition must not be used in any circumstances.'

Though initially mystifying, the ban reflected an incident that had occurred a short time before our arrival. As we heard it, the sentry had come upon another airman and a WAAF making love. Somehow, in the ensuing confrontation, the Sten had gone off, killing the couple, after which the sentry was charged with murder. I never did hear the details, or learn whether it was any more than a tragic accident. But then WAAFs had already had a hard time of it during my service.

Back at EFTS, at Brough, for instance, the duty airman in the flight-control hut had been routinely preparing the Very pistols for use. His WAAF girl friend had come to the door with a mug of tea for him. Cowboy-style, he had pointed the signal pistol at her. Only to have it go off, the partly-ignited flare taking her full in the mouth ... The would-be cowboy was charged with manslaughter. But the poor girl had stood no chance.

Wireless and radar training at Madley had been followed by gunnery training at No. 1482 Bomber and Gunnery Flight at RAF Swanton Morley in Norfolk. I felt relatively well at home during this phase, for having had an airgun as a boy I was used to shooting at anything that moved. So when they started us off with shotguns I proved to be a dab hand. In fact, having returned a 100 per cent score, I was chosen as the intake's champion in the Group competition. When it came to competing against other people, however, I wasn't that keen, and dropped two points, coming in second, which didn't best please our instructor.

Then again, having learnt from the cradle, as it were, about leading a target and deflection shooting, and having made myself familiar with aircraft recognition, I found the air-gunnery course nowhere near as taxing as what had gone before, so that when it came to turret work I was once more his prize pupil.

Gunnery practice, turret firing on the butts

There was a final radio course at Cranwell, in Lincolnshire, and at last – it was now 1943 – I found myself fully-qualified aircrew.

Before a place on an operational training unit came up, however, I was given a short holding posting to a unit flying the twin-engined Manchesters; although the term 'flying' seems somewhat misplaced, these rather less than successful predecessors of the Lancaster being only too fond of facing their crews with a puttering descent on a single engine.

Avro Manchester, an unhappy design

Fortunately my posting to an operational training unit was not long in coming, upon which I found myself introduced to the Wellington. The introduction began benignly enough but towards the end of the course our trainee crew was detailed to take a repaired Wellington on a night-flying test. In its first-line days this poor old thing had been badly shot up, indeed judging by the number of dope-sprayed patches it must have been holed all over! Now it had been fitted with a new starboard engine.

Taking off we got up to about nine hundred feet, still over the runway, when the new engine cut dead. The skipper put the nose down but was too late to connect with the tarmac. Instead, we touched on the grass, then careered through hedges, over a main road and a field or two – not least across one full of corn, badly upsetting the farmer – before coming to rest in a duck pond.

We had made very hard contact with the ground, but my face made even harder contact with the knobs of the Marconi transmitter. These were red, yellow, and blue, but on impact I saw a whole palette of colours! Indeed, I was still nursing myself, and dazedly trying to locate my parachute, when the skipper told me to get out. I did so through the upper hatch, then walked along the fuselage towards the tail before jumping to the ground.

With blood all over my face I was taken to station sick quarters where my cuts and bruises were cleaned up. My first visitor was the chief signals officer.

'Well, you're lucky,' he told me.

'Lucky?' I still felt as if my cheekbones had been caved in.

'Yes,' he said, 'had the kite been bombed-up the whole lot of you would've been blown to bits.'

Not really what I'd wanted to hear!

Having said goodbye to the Wellington, our crew did another course, learning to fly the Halifax. But this was more to give the pilot experience in four-engined aircraft, for once he was checked out we moved to the Lancaster Finishing School at RAF Syerston, near Newark. And finally, we were posted to No. 3 Group, and No. 115 Squadron, initially stationed at Little Snoring, near Fakenham, in Norfolk, although we moved to Witchford, near Ely, in Cambridgeshire in November 1943.

This was when I began to do the job all the training had been for. Ops began with a vengeance, the posted battle order unrelentingly featuring our crew. We had anticipated being in the forefront of things for many a long month. But it soon lost its novelty. After even a week or two I remember we'd get back from ops and collapse on our beds, exclaiming, 'Thank God that's over!'

Then, almost before we knew it, the corporal would be throwing open the door and shouting, 'You're on again tonight, chaps.' Setting off a disgruntled howl of, 'Oh, no, not again!'

There was very little remission. Even a badly damaged aircraft did not necessarily offer much respite. Not the way our groundcrews worked! However, I did witness an alternative way of going about things.

This was when we found ourselves overnighting at an American base. As we were walking towards our assigned accommodation, this Marauder came past, very low, and with a gaping hole in its fuselage. By the time we got to the next corner it was upended in a ditch with Yanks around it like ants, getting bits off it for souvenirs. We couldn't help laughing. Had it been a damaged Lanc back at Witchford the lads would have had it patched up and off on ops again the same night. Not the Yanks, though. They had so much of everything they didn't have to bother, so when an aircraft was that badly shot up, it seemed, they simply wheeled out a new one.

They were equally free with their hospitality. But their ways were so different from ours. They had unlimited food, and all of the best. Only they had the weirdest way of serving it. Everything was dished up on a single tray that had different compartments so that you might have a main course right next to a sweet. And the combinations they had on offer! I remember there were potatoes cooked in syrup! And a luscious-looking steamed pudding that turned out to be so hard that you couldn't get your teeth into it. To say nothing of peanut butter. Just the same they were all so friendly and enthusiastic.

But jaunts like that aside, we soon began to realize to what extent we had become the playthings of Fate. This first came home to me one night when we were over the Ruhr and I leant forwards the better to hear an incoming wireless transmission from the raid leader. At which instant a cannon shell smashed through the fuselage just where my head would have been.

Perhaps because of such uncertainties the most sceptical of us seemed to take to some superstitious practice or other. Virtually all rear gunners, for example, would pee on the tail wheel before boarding. For my part I carried a rabbit's paw; I'd have my aircrew whistle on the left of my battledress blouse, and the good-luck paw on the right.

But I don't suppose, in truth, everyone felt that way. Indeed, I had found cause to ponder that point some months earlier on encountering Guy Gibson – my sole brush with celebrity.

He was, he told me, about to drop a new type of one-million candlepower flare. Or perhaps that was only part of it, for whatever the new device, his Lanc's bomb-bay had been extended to accommodate it. It was just that, fraught as this trial-undertaking clearly was, he seemed delighted at the prospect and not in the least fazed. But then I don't suppose men like him could be counted as any sort of norm.

Most of the trips our crew did were to German targets, the Ruhr seeming to act upon us like a magnet. But we did a fair number to France too, not least when a nominal thousand bombers were sent to attack Caen. The aim was to clear the way so that the Allied armies could break out of the invasion bridgehead and begin making ground eastwards. The sky was simply full of aircraft, and the opposition was far heavier than we might have expected. Certainly, the town was really plastered. Although this, it seems, wasn't that clever, for the Germans simply holed up in the rubble and had to be winkled out piecemeal, the additional delay and carnage defeating the whole object of the raid. On top of this, aircraft losses were high.

But, of course, even without interference by the enemy, losses were inevitable when so many bombers were packed into a single piece of sky. Certainly, the most loathsome thing to me was the sight of other bombers blowing up, whether through collision or through direct enemy action. Whenever it happened all I could think of was, there's another seven poor chaps gone west. And then, some hours later, there would be all those empty chairs in the dining hall ...

Not a Lancaster, but a Halifax, sans nose, after a mid-air collision

As a twin-roled member of aircrew I always arranged that during ops I would do about half the trips on the wireless set and half in the turret. Although my main station was at the set, therefore, the arrangement was that I'd take over in the tail turret if anything happened to the rear gunner. So getting into and out of that turret became second nature.

How chagrining then, to visit RAF Waddington during an altogether different era and find that having finally got into the rear turret it took me a good twenty minutes – I swear – to get out of it again. I remember too, with equal chagrin, that the Battle of Britain Flight's Lancaster had been parked some distance from our tent and that the flight lieutenant detailed to escort me had set off at such a pace that although the tips of my walking sticks must have been glowing from friction I could hardly keep him in sight.

I found it easier, though, to get behind the wireless set and to sit there a while as the memories came flooding back ... Then again, visiting Elvington Air Museum, I had a go on their simulated gun set-up, and managed to shoot down three enemy aircraft. I suppose it's like riding a bicycle ...

I did, in fact, let fly at several German fighters during my tour of ops, and indeed, may well have hit one, for it peeled off with smoke coming out of it. But feeling that our other gunner had probably pumped more lead towards it than I had I didn't put in a claim. In fact, I don't think any of us felt very strongly about that sort of thing, just so long as the fighter buzzed off and we got away with the encounter it was fine by us.

Ops were undoubtedly a great strain for everyone; I'd like to think that even people like Guy Gibson would admit to that. Fortunately, I had a few interests that stopped me brooding too much when we were on the ground. For instance, I was a great gadget maker, so I took two carbon rods from a battery, wound up some wire, and fashioned myself a hot-drinks maker. It was not up to the appearance of a commercial Teasmade, perhaps, and working off a different principle, yet very efficient nonetheless. Another pastime, however, paid far higher dividends.

As I mentioned before, aero-modelling had been a passion I had embraced in boyhood and had kept up ever since. Now, helped by my wireless training, I embarked upon building a series of models that were controlled by radio. I even had a friend who could get me the then virtually-unobtainable balsa wood!

One day I was flying my pride and joy, a machine I called *The Bee's Knees*, when I saw two girls approaching. One was so beautiful, and so obviously taken with *The Bee's Knees* that, on the instant, I decided I was going to marry her. And so I did. Indeed, we were to be married for fifty-six years!

There was just one snag, at the very beginning. As her father was commissioned, indeed a squadron leader, I had to formally ask his permission to marry her. Fortunately, he acquiesced, although I did stipulate that we would not actually marry until I had come off operations at the end of my tour.

And long in coming though it so often seemed, I finally clocked up my thirty ops and was stood down for a rest.

It was clear to everyone that the war was coming to a close. Or, at least, it was clear to everyone on the Allied side. That others might see it differently was brought home to me as I travelled south on leave. In fact, we were just passing RAF Hendon when I happened to look up. My initial thought was, 'A white telegraph pole?' But what had caught my eye was still very high, and coming vertically downwards at an unbelievable speed. Instants later there was an enormous explosion. And I realized that I had seen the final moments of a V-2 rocket!

The first V-2 rocket to fall on Britain

But rockets, and the last flurry of Doodlebug arrivals aside, my own war certainly seemed to be reaching its end. I was posted to the staff of the Central Navigation School at Shawbury, in Shropshire, a unit modelled on the lines of the long-established Central Flying School for pilots. During our course the various trainee-aircrew members supported the already experienced navigator students as they polished their skills, the aim of the school being to improve the accuracy of navigation and, thereby, of bombing. Off duty around the bar I used to tell my WOp/AG trainees that my job was to teach them how to put their lives at risk, just as I'd been taught to put mine. It seemed to give them a laugh. Poor lambs!

The aircraft we used were Wellingtons and Stirlings and the flying was undoubtedly full of interest to the post-graduate – as one might term them – navigators who had been recalled from ops to do the course. For the instructors, though, it palled somewhat. Certainly, it lacked the zest of operations. Not that there was any hope of getting recalled for another tour by that time. Just the same, it wasn't a bad posting, and in the local area RAF personnel were fêted and allowed to pay for nothing. But that aside, without the buzz of ops, I began to find Service life itself becoming irksome.

Then came VE night, which I spent in Bedford; and that really was a wonderful do, not least because there were all manner of food and drink stalls, and again, nobody in service uniform was permitted to pay for anything.

VE night jollifications

Our old target, Cologne

Before throwing aside my flying kit for good, however, I was to take a final Halifax flight on a tour of former German targets. A real eye opener that! Especially looking down upon Cologne – which we had visited nocturnally on three occasions – and marvelling that for all the destruction round about it the cathedral spires were still standing.

In the Far East the war was still on, but even applying to go out there proved to offer no better chance of getting back on ops, although I persisted in applying. In the end, however, as even the Japanese War came to a close, I went to see the CO.

'I'm totally fed up with the Raff now,' I told him. 'Can't you just get me out?'

He did his best, authorizing me to enter a college in Doncaster. I tried to study, but found it hard to concentrate, and soon gave it up. The reality was, I suppose, that I had no idea what it was I wanted to do. Eventually, however, in 1946, my demob came through, and still undecided as to my future, I made my way back home.

I had told my CO how fed-up with the RAF I had become. And I truly had. So much so, that on finding myself a civvy I threw away everything to do with the last few years. Into the bin went my flying logbook, even my uniform, although there might have been an excuse for that, seeing that after a few weeks of mum's home cooking it no longer fitted. Mind you, since then I've seen the prices people pay for uniforms. At least I didn't dump my flying-cum-escape boots, but actually sold them for thirty bob!

Money was a problem, of course, but didn't loom too large, for I'd been getting fifteen shillings a day as aircrew and I'd about £100 in the bank.

I looked into all manner of jobs, but none appealed. At length, utterly disillusioned, I met another ex-flier who said he was going to catch the first train out of Nottingham and simply see what happened. I determined to accompany him and just an hour or so later, having collected some kit from home and said a hurried cheerio to everyone, I joined him at the station.

The first train happened to stop at Spalding, in Lincolnshire. We duly got out, and by following up a newspaper advertisement, secured jobs on a farm. However, after six weeks I tired of life as a farmer's boy, especially as the farmer in question kept loading us with more, and even more tasks without the incentive of additional pay. And so, leaving my companion to soldier on, I returned to Nottingham.

And a timely return it was, for the very next day someone steered me towards a job in the Rolls-Royce test establishment at nearby Hucknall.

This, it turned out, meant working on as many as fifty disparate aircraft, the first task every morning being to drag a trolley accumulator to each of them and run up the radios. But there was also a roving element, which on one occasion took me to Luqa, Malta, where I supported some British European Airways pilots who were converting to the Ambassador.

Not that I was able to do much supporting of one batch who got airborne but, being unable to locate the alternator switches, ran out of electrics, lost all their comms and nav aids, and had to get back to the island using battery power.

But on the same detachment I was obliged to delve deep myself, when a warning was received that a bomb had been placed on 'one of the aircraft' at Luqa. Eventually, I discovered a device in the wheel well of the then-top-secret V-bomber we had with us. What the background to that was, I never did find out, but at the time the initially-unexplained Comet crashes had put everyone on tenterhooks.

I stayed at Hucknall until 1956, after which I moved the family to Melbourne, Australia, where I specialized in guided missiles. But eventually, for all its foul weather, Britain drew us back.

The years were kind, above all in allowing me to enjoy a long and happy marriage. Only now, alone, my mind more frequently turns back to those years before my wife and I met. Oft-times my thoughts fleetingly turn to the ninety-one Lancasters lost from Witchford. But only fleetingly, for even at this remove that is far too painful to dwell on. So I sternly force my thoughts to revisit once more the young lad I was, in my white overalls, on that Nottingham roof. And I hug to my consciousness the vow I made as I scampered for cover with that Ju88's bullets chipping at my heels, '*You just wait, you bastards, I'll pay you back*!'

As I said, it had never been intended as an idle threat. Nor did it prove to be. For the memories also come back of each and every one of those thirty operational flights, and of the loads we carried. And should I need any additional aide-memoire, I have the retinal images of that final Cook's tour of the Ruhr.

Oh yes, it may have taken some time. But I certainly paid 'em back all right. And paid 'em back in bloody spades!

John Marsden, 2009

8

Aren't we lucky?

Warrant Officer Eric Cope, wireless operator/ air gunner

Sergeant Eric Cope, 1944, evasion photo, in civvies

Whenever my wartime navigator, Trevor Clarke, and I find ourselves together, one of us will eventually muse, 'Aren't we lucky?' And if Trevor gets it in first, my reaction, whether spoken or silent, is 'And I owe my life to you.' For being a brilliant mathematician Trevor slipped easily into the navigating role, his expertise meaning that whereas many crews really didn't have a clue on ops, he always kept our aircraft tight within the bomber stream, never leaving us floundering and lacking what security the pack offered.

Close though Trevor and I became, it was to be two years into my RAF service before we met each other, for when I applied to join up, at Wilmslow, in 1940, they had a glut of aircrew trainees. I had told the initial recruiters that I wanted to be a wireless operator, knowing in my heart that I didn't want the responsibility of being a pilot. When I reported to Blackpool for my medical and assessment, therefore, they suggested that until the aircrew blockage cleared I might serve as a ground wireless operator. Having accepted this I commenced training at Cardington where radio theory loomed large and the morse code loomed, if anything, even larger. Just the same, with application, I managed to assimilate the theory and also to achieve a very respectable morse-receiving speed of twenty-four words a minute, four words a minute, indeed, more than the requirement.

Once qualified I found myself on a draft for the Middle East. We travelled out by troopship, sailing in convoy; and a large convoy at that, with at least two aircraft carriers and a host of destroyer escorts.

The first port of call was Durban – a city with lights blazing at night! – where, during our time ashore a very pleasant and hospitable lady took our group under her wing. Not only that, but on both entering and leaving Durban harbour we were serenaded from the dockside by the now-legendary Lady in White, contralto Perla Siedle Gibson, who sang in every troopship with old favourites, then sang them out again: a memorable and very moving experience!

Our next landfall was Bombay – Mumbai, these days – where we were marched all around the bay in the sweltering heat to a transit camp where they kept us for two weeks. Two weeks, after which we were only too grateful to be loaded aboard the SS *Neuralia*, a vessel whose peacetime job had been to take schoolboys from the United Kingdom to Scandinavia – 'British Cruises for British Boys'. In May 1945 she would fall foul of an Allied mine, but in 1941 she delivered us safely enough to the head of the Persian Gulf.

The 1995 statue of Durban's Lady in White, contralto Perla Siedle Gibson

The whole outbound trip took an unbelievable thirteen weeks, but eventually we landed at Abadan, the major port and oil terminal of Persia – or Iran, whichever they were choosing to call it that week.

Even then it was to be some time before my particular party found ourselves settled, for after a week in nearby Khorramshahr we were sent upcountry by lorry – each of us donning the then-obligatory sola topi; to us, the solar topee – to set up a wireless station at Hamedân, the oldest city in Persia and reputedly in the world. The site selected was the Shah of Persia's shooting lodge but, being in the mountains, and Hamedân being not only the oldest but also the coldest town in Persia, we found ourselves snowed out.

Boarding our lorries once again, and still wearing our sun hats, we headed down from the mountains, only this time bound for Iraq, and specifically for RAF Habbaniyah, some way west of Baghdad.

With Iraq being under a British mandate, and the decision having been made that the least costly way to police that mandate – in ground casualties, at least –

was with air power, RAF Habbaniyah had been established in 1934 and was the biggest-ever RAF station. True, the aircraft we saw there tended to be rather old-fashioned compared with those we had grown used to at home, with bombers, in particular, capable of only some seventy miles an hour! But we had no complaints about the camp itself. It had everything. Good billets, wonderful facilities for every activity you could think of, great food, several NAAFI canteens and cinemas, while even us lowly airmen had servants!

And perhaps it was just as well that the station had so much to offer during our off-duty hours, for our shifts in the radio cabin were hectic to say the least. We were responsible for the signals traffic to Bombay in one direction and Jerusalem in the other, traffic that we would then pass onwards to the UK. Nor did we get a moment's rest during our time at the set, being constantly badgered by the other stations, invariably manned by professional operators, to 'Send faster'. For our part, we only too often found ourselves pleading, 'QRS' (send slower), and 'IMI' (please repeat).

My sojourn lasted two years. But one day, quite literally out of the blue, I was told, 'Your aircrew application has come through. So pack your kit, you're off to Blighty tomorrow.'

Having reported to Lake Habbaniyah, I found myself on the Imperial Airways flying boat *Carpentaria*. This initially touched down on the Dead Sea and finally on the Nile at Cairo, the crew treating us like any of their passengers, in first-class style.

This was not at all the treatment we got, though, once we had disembarked, for a very officious sergeant marched us right across a sticky and dusty, clamorous, and traffic-snarled Cairo, with a grunted 'Don't ask me' as his only response to all our queries about where we were going and how far it was.

In fact, we finished up at a transit camp where we were held, not, as it seemed, for ever, but certainly for a wearying couple of weeks before they moved us onwards again, this time to Port Said to board the SS *Mauretania*.

Imperial Airways flying boat

Two years before, outbound from the UK, we had steamed at the speed of the slowest vessel in the convoy. Now, after calling in at Cape Town – which, in contrast to Durban, we found industrialized, but friendly enough – we virtually sped back, with *Mauretania* making the very most of her service speed of 23 knots while curving widely into the Atlantic to avoid U-boats and enemy aircraft. Just the same, Liverpool seemed a long while in coming, so that having disembarked I was more than ready for home, and for a period of disembarkation leave that went all too quickly.

On reporting for re-assessment after that leave, I was at once asked if I was, indeed, still interested in aircrew. Of course, I was! And once embarked upon training, being already well versed in wireless theory and procedures, and with my morse well above the standard required for air operating, I did not find the transition from ground to airborne wireless operating all that onerous. Indeed, my major concern was to remember to reel in the trailing aerial before landing, for losing it meant a one pound fine: no mean sum, even to a trainee on the lofty pay of a leading-aircraftman.

I began my aircrew training proper at RAF Madley, near Hereford, where we carried out air-operating exercises on twin-engined Dominie biplanes – rigged out as flying classrooms – and two-seater Proctors. In the main the pilots were Polish, resting from operations, madcaps all, who would fling the aircraft around without thinking of the trailing aerial and certainly not of the trainees desperately trying to tune in radios and tap out morse messages behind them. They were incapable too, it seemed, of appreciating that while they wanted to fly as low as possible we needed adequate terrain clearance for our signals.

Unlike his ground counterpart the air wireless operator had a dual function as a gunner. The next training stage, therefore, meant a posting to No. 10 Air Gunnery School at Walney Island, Barrow-in-Furness, where I began to learn about machine guns, not least in the intriguingly clever Dome ground trainer, which presented the trainee with very realistic model enemy (and friendly!) aircraft.

For airborne gunnery trainees would often fly in pairs, when a feature of our firing exercises was that the tips of one pupil's rounds would be painted red, and his partner's blue, so that holes on the drogue would be rimmed with colour, allowing the score to be broken down. A side effect was that the pupils themselves would come down smothered in paint. I remember too the seemingly excessive care insisted upon in avoiding the mixing of live and dead ammunition, so that after each exercise the discharged cartridge cases, though now clearly shorter, lacking the bullet, still had to be posted through a specially profiled slot in the lid of the disposal box. We could only presume that there had been accidents enough to make this necessary, certainly never attributing the procedure to the mere Service bureaucracy it might well have been.

The Dome air-gunnery trainer

At the end of the day, though, having fired off our course to the required standard, we were then sent to No. 4 Observers' Advanced Flying School at Hereford, a unit we left wearing sergeant's stripes and brevets. And as I proudly sewed these up, I realized a little wryly that it was May 1944, and a full four years since I had first applied to fly!

My penultimate training posting was to No. 19 Operational Training Unit (OTU) at RAF Kinloss, in Scotland. One of the first things we did here was form ourselves into crews. However, in our case there was something of a hiccup.

The pilot I gravitated towards was a Flight Lieutenant Nick Doyle, a very experienced pilot for the day with over two thousand flying hours. True, most of his hours had been accumulated while instructing on light aircraft, but after an initial spat when we began our conversion training– which I'll return to in a moment – he turned out to be a fine heavy-bomber pilot.

He quickly gathered the basis of a crew around him but, try as we might, none of us could find a navigator floating loose. So it was that, when the session finished, we were left on the shelf. In fact, the delay turned out to be to our advantage for just days later Trevor Clarke became available, and we got him!

Our good fortune, as only too often happens – and more especially, perhaps, in wartime –, came at someone else's expense. This was because, as they neared the end of the course, the pilots were sent to observe the conduct of an actual bombing operation. The pilot Trev had originally crewed up with had been detailed for such a flight but the aircraft had been shot down. So it was that we inherited Trev. Lucky for us, as I have said. As I have also said, lucky for me!

The type we used on the OTU course was the Whitley, outmoded as a first-line bomber long before. In flight it was characterized by its nose-down sit, or attitude, an attitude that became extreme in what passed, on the Whitley, for rapid flight. Conversely, when standing on the ground it was markedly high-nosed, most certainly so when compared with the diminutive trainers Nick had become used to: which occasioned the initial spat! I happened to be at his shoulder when he first took his seat. He looked out, shook his head, and then said somewhat uneasily, 'It's like looking out of an attic window.'

We duly got airborne, and all seemed to go fine for him, until the screen pilot told him to go in and land. Nick began his approach but then showed obvious signs of unease, finally declaring, 'I'm not going to make it.' The screen pilot tried to cajole him, but Nick was adamant. 'No, if I try it, I'll end up killing the bloody lot of us.' The screen pilot urged him yet lower but at the last moment had to lift us over the trees himself. And that was our first flight as a crew.

Nick immediately asked for an interview with the commanding officer, telling this dignitary that the Whitley was beyond his capabilities. The CO listened, then insisted that the whole crew take the weekend off before having another go on the Monday. Nick only grudgingly assented, but when it came to landing off Monday's sortie he made his approach and touched down like silk. The screen pilot leant back with a satisfied grin. But Nick simply growled, 'I still don't like it.'

Fortunately for Nick, which meant, as always, for all of us, we then moved onto No. 1652 Heavy Conversion Unit at Marston Moor, where we converted to the Halifax, which he took to like the proverbial duck to whatever. In fact, on the course we flew both the Halifax Mk 4, with the Rolls-Royce Merlin engines, and the Mk 3, with the Bristol Radial engines, which were much better machines. In earlier days, instability problems had earned the type a poor reputation, but

Handley Page Halifax

these had long been solved, and though it would never achieve the popularity of the Lancaster, it was a good machine to have around you.

The Marston course saw us truly come together as a crew. But although many operational crews might have been homogeneous I cannot quite say that for ours.

Pilot Officer Ernie – his surname escapes me – our second pilot, was very county. Not so Sergeant Ken Wright, our bomb aimer. Whether or not Ken was a washed-out trainee pilot I never did discover but we regarded him as our second pilot in case of need rather than the nominal candidate, the flight engineer, who had been put through sessions on the Link Flight-Trainer – the flight simulator of the day. Fortunately, however, the need never arose, so we never had occasion to choose between them. But Ken, anyway, was essentially down to earth, and I – as the wireless operator-cum-air gunner, although now a lofty flight sergeant! – was the same.

Then there was a very disparate pair: Sergeant Ernest Lawson, our flight engineer, who had been a London policeman, and was never out of the copperly-officious mould; and mid-upper gunner Sergeant Charlie Bush. Charlie was an out-and-out East-End cockney. He was a former lorry driver and was constantly ready to take umbrage at any imagined slight, particularly from the ex-policeman, even in flight reacting angrily when he thought Lawson had accused him, for example, of 'fievin' a piece of flying clothing, incipient outbursts that Nick never failed to nip in the bud.

Left to right: Sergeant Ken Wright, bomb aimer, and second pilot; Sergeant Harry Van Dem Boss, DFM, rear gunner; Flight Sergeant Eric Cope, wireless operator/air gunner; Flight Lieutenant Nick Doyle, pilot; Sergeant Charlie Bush, mid-upper gunner, sporting the top hat!; Sergeant Ernest Lawson, flight engineer (subsequently commissioned); Flight Lieutenant Trevor Clarke, navigator

Charlie, being a cockney, went out of his way to be seen as a character. Betting mad, he later took to wearing a top hat on ops. But amusing though he could be he was not the sort you'd take to for choice, and indeed when I encountered him after the war – by chance, at a race-meeting, I fancy – I remember balking at inviting him home with me. And nobody could call me a snob!

The top hat, in fact, became something of a talisman with us. Our allotted aircraft being 'C' for Charlie, we got one of the groundcrew (always a multi-talented bunch: what couldn't they do!) to paint us a mascot: a top hat, cane, and a bottle of champagne. *Champagne Charlie* duly stood us in good stead. How sad a day it was when we flew her on her final flight! Not to the Ruhr yet again, or even to Berlin, but to a breaker's yard in Scotland! Fortunately, though, that was long way into the future.

When the crew first formed, our rear turret was manned by a flight lieutenant named Scanlon; being an Irishman he naturally answered to Paddy. He was tall and good looking, with a moustache, an easy manner, and a wealth of tall tales. But he always seemed to be involved in something shady; he was the archetypical spiv, or wide-boy. Then, one day, he simply disappeared. I asked Nick what had become of him but I never did get a satisfactory answer. Nor did I ever discover whether even Nick really knew what had happened to him.

Scanlon's replacement was a gunner who settled immediately. He was Sergeant Harry Van Dem Boss, from East Anglia's Little Holland district who, even before joining us, had been awarded a Distinguished Flying Medal for shooting down an enemy fighter.

Among the memorabilia I retain from OTU days are the passport-sized photographs we had taken of us in civilian clothes – or jacket, at least – and wearing civilian ties. Designed for the convenience of the Resistance in furnishing us with documents, these were packed in a wallet with other pieces of escape-and-evasion equipment.

Silk escape map, Berlin area

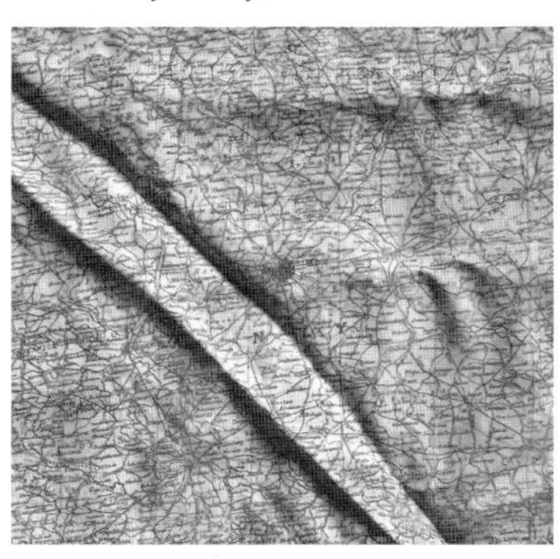

Tunic-button evasion compass

Finally, however, with all the preliminaries completed at last, we were posted, to No. 4 Group, Bomber Command, and to No. 51 Squadron, at Snaith, near Goole, in Yorkshire.

As a crew we were destined to complete twenty-five operations, yet although each can be recreated from my logbook, bringing with it, despite the passage of the years, all the strains and tensions of those days, only the occasional sorties stand out. Not surprisingly, perhaps, these are the ones I made an especial note of at the time.

For example, for a raid on Düsseldorf on 2 November 1944 we briefed at 1400 hours and took off at 1745 hours to make a time-over-target of 2100 hours. 'No cloud over target,' I recorded. Following that with, 'Plenty of flak, searchlights, and fighter flares, with one Ju88 seen. Many fires and bombs bursting'.

Then again there was the raid on Wanne Eickel oil refinery, near Essen, on 2 February 1945, which I recorded as a 'nasty trip, with plenty of predicted flak' – for those straying from the stream, that was. And then, 'moonlight on the way back ...'

Such terse notes instantly recreate the mental picture of me leaving my set and standing over the flare chute, shovelling out radar-distracting 'Window' twice a minute; moving forward then to eye the box barrage directly in our path, the dictates of the fixed run-in to the target allowing Nick no effective deviation. The notes also recreate the soaring tracer, and those ominous fighter flares; the harsh breathing on the intercom from Ken Wright's open mic as, face down in his bomb-aimer's station, he monotones his instructions to Nick. And they bring back, like a bad taste, the tension bordering on the unbearable.

Then too, they resurrect the return flight, no less menacing. And a vignette, of a light-bathed silhouette as it might be seen from beyond the confines of the fuselage, by a wraith – or a night-fighter – with our Halifax so vulnerable in the moonglow ... But instantly reality interposes. And one can breathe again. For we are still here, so very many years later, and able too to re-read those near-forgotten logbook notes: how lucky we are, indeed!

The few raid maps I have retained, additionally recording our briefing times and the colours of the day, show that, having assembled, we often routed south from Snaith, to pass over Reading. They show also that from then on we would fly surprisingly tortuous routes to and from the target in order to avoid the areas of flak and fighter concentrations conjectured by Intelligence; and which they sometimes got right.

And once again, looking at the heading changes called for, and considering the sparsity of navigational aids available – the flights being at night and over blacked-out lands that proffered few pinpoints – I yet again pay tribute to Trevor's skill at keeping us on track; which meant, additionally, keeping us as one-of-a-multitude in the bomber stream.

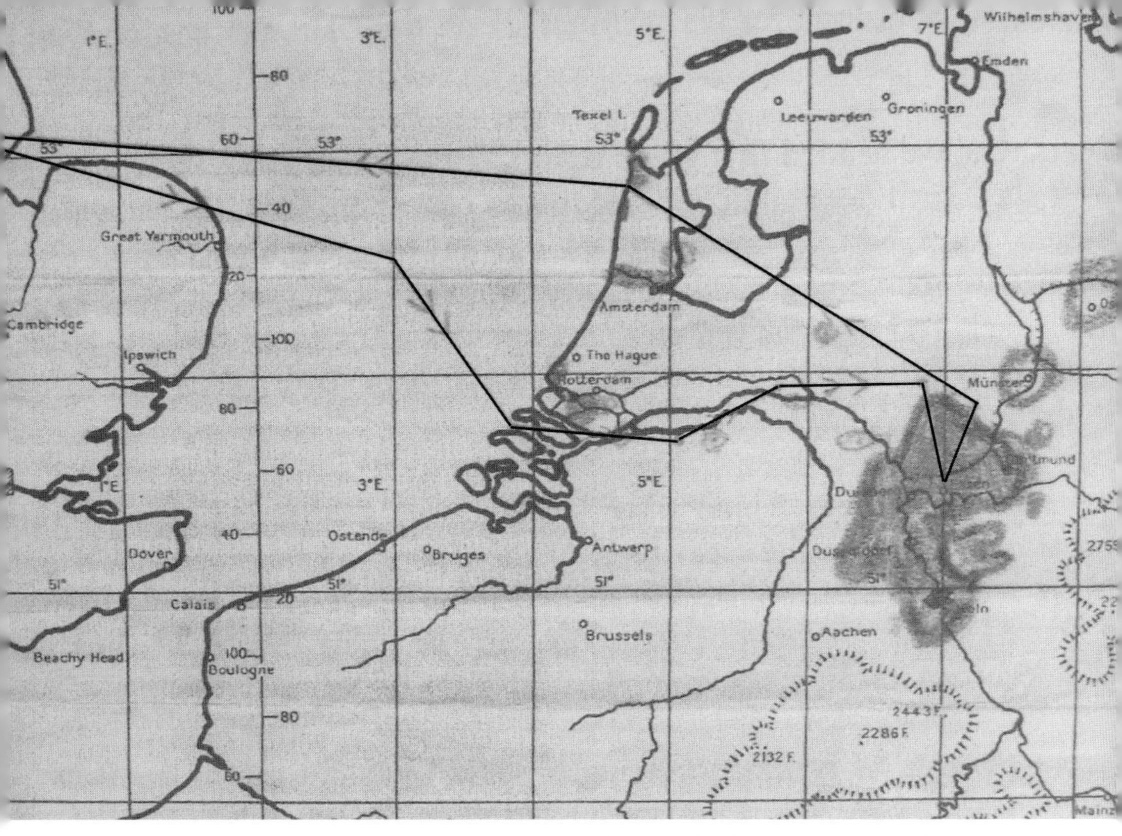

Captain's raid map of a Ruhr target, Wanne Eickel, north of Essen, avoiding hot spots

Not, of course, that being one of many in any herd is an absolute guarantee against Fate, but at the time it gave us a feeling of security from which we could draw comfort, and that was all important.

As a small enough footnote, although there may have been no cloud over the target when we raided Wanne Eickel, and although we had moonlit skies for the return across the Channel, such conditions were little surety for the weather over the British mainland. For, on that self-same night Snaith went out in poor visibility, and so, tired and on edge though we were, it was necessary for us to turnabout and divert. In this case, to Marston Moor, where Nick made a fair landing, after which we took pot luck with accommodation and returned to the relative comfort of Snaith the next day.

Although, as I have indicated, the seven of us were quite disparate as individuals, nonetheless we tended to do things as a crew, among others communally buying an Austin Coupe to take us to the local pubs. Not that Trev would always be free to accompany us, for often enough, as we went out junketing, so he would be preparing a piece of homework, for having gained a BSc in – I fancy – maths before joining up he was now qualifying as a chartered accountant.

Our last crew op, and my twenty-fifth, turned out to be the one we flew on 25 March 1945, a sortie to Lower Saxony, to bomb Osnabrück. A day or so after that, however, Nick was hit by a car, and finished up in hospital. But the pressure on crews was lessening by the day, so, lacking a captain, we were effectively taken off the flying programme. After that I busied myself visiting Nick and indeed, going to fetch him when he was discharged from hospital.

Then, on 25 May 1945, the squadron flew its final operation of the war. It had operated from Snaith since 1942, since when, despite never having had an establishment of more than, I believe, sixteen bombers at any one time, it had lost 148 aircraft. Now it was moved to Leconfield, passing, along with the administrative and operational control of that airfield, from Bomber to Transport Command.

In our new role we continued to operate Halifaxes, but also Stirlings, both of which had been converted to enable them to carry out long-range flights with both passengers and freight. It was a marked change, even the tasks themselves being more varied than those we had been engaged upon. And with few – if any – people shooting at us!

My logbook records two flights from RAF St Mawgan, in Cornwall, to Karachi. On these our first port of call was to the former Italian base in Libya, Castel Benita – to later generations, RAF Idris, and since 1968, Tripoli Idris International Airport. From here the route passed through Lydda (Tel Aviv), and RAF Shaibah (Basra, Iraq), then down the Persian Gulf and onwards to RAF Mauripur (No. 48 Staging Post, Karachi). Yes, the Empire was still alive and kicking at that time!

Other Indian-Continent flights took me from Leconfield down to Istres (Marseilles), then via Malta, Almazah (Cairo), Shaibah, Mauripur, Palam (Delhi), and finally to Dum Dum (Calcutta). This route was one that got particularly busy during India's approach to independence when we would fly out King's Messengers and other officials, some with briefcases chained to their wrists.

During this period my appointment to warrant officer came through, but even so I was not tempted to stay in the Service beyond my release date, whenever that turned out to be.

In the course of time we lost our Halifaxes and Stirlings and in March 1946 found ourselves members of No. 246 Squadron, converting to Avro Yorks. Having been checked out, I flew a further three trips to India, this time from Lyneham, but again routeing through Cairo. Then, on 30 June 1946, my turn for demob came, and suddenly I had a future to find.

In fact, I opted for the Nottinghamshire Fire Service, and in the course of an active career became a Deputy Station Chief Fire Officer.

Long before reaching that position, however, I had met Vera, who had spent her war as a driver in the ATS. Early in our courting days we had discovered that while I had spent VE night in Little Holland, near Clacton, watching as Harry Van Dem Boss capered before a gaily lit Christmas tree, Vera had celebrated in Brussels. 'All very nice,' as she always had it, 'but far too many

WARRANT

The Right Honourable the SECRETARY OF STATE FOR AIR

To **Eric Mawer Cope**

By virtue of the Authority to me, by the King's Most Excellent Majesty in this behalf given. I do hereby Constitute and Appoint you to be a Warrant Officer in His Majesty's Royal Air Force *from the* Thirtieth *day of* November 1945, *and to continue in the said Office during the pleasure of the Right Honourable the Secretary of State for Air. You are therefore carefully and diligently to discharge your Duty as such by doing and performing all manner of things thereunto belonging, as required by the Established Regulations of the Service, and you are to observe and follow such Orders and Directions as you shall receive from your Commanding, or any other, your superior Officer, according to the Rules and Discipline of War*

GIVEN *under my Hand and Seal this* Thirtieth *day of* December 1945

Appointment to warrant officer

Yanks.' And thank goodness that was how she saw it, for it was the highlight of my life when, just a little later, she agreed to marry me.

The crew, of course, had gone their separate ways. Just the same, demob was not entirely the end for us, for there were occasions when some of us met up again.

One such was when we visited the Yorkshire Air Museum at Elvington. Having thoroughly toured the site we entered the souvenir shop. As we did so I failed to notice how Nick and the others hung back. Then, looking around the memorabilia and souvenirs I could hardly believe it when I saw, on a shelf, what had to be Charlie Bush's top hat! We had originally come upon it, as I well knew, in the snug of a pub we frequented in Lincoln. Then, after a visit or two, we had persuaded the landlady to give it to us as a mascot, initially using it as a repository for our in-flight sandwiches. Then Charlie took to wearing it ops. But to find it here! All these years later!

I pressed the lady behind the gift-shop counter for confirmation that it was indeed the hat Charlie had sported, only to have her profess to know nothing of its history. Then, after a while, I saw the others grinning, after which she lost her straight face too. I finally realized that I had been set up, that some weeks earlier Nick had discovered that the hat been presented to the museum for permanent display, and hadn't told me, while he and the rest of them had gleefully awaited my reaction. And how they enjoyed it! There were smiles all around.

But then, we've such a lot to smile about: twenty-five ops without a scratch, and so much more besides. Not least, full and productive lives to look back upon.

How lucky we are, indeed!

Eric Cope, 2012

9

A glorified office lad

Flight Lieutenant Ron 'Bram' Bramley, AE, wireless operator/air gunner

While growing up in Nottingham a fair deal of my early-teenage, off-school time was spent cycling out to the aerodrome at Hucknall and watching the Westland Wallaces of No. 504 City of Nottingham (Auxiliary) Squadron wheeling about the sky. When schooldays finished and it came to getting a job, however, I joined the local printing firm of Thomas Forman's Ltd, working in the calendar office until I was seventeen after which, ambitious to learn more about the trade, I moved on to the print division.

Flight Lieutenant Ron (Bram) Bramley, AE, 1945

By then, of course, the international sky was darkening and a year later, in 1937, I applied to join the RAF Volunteer Reserve (RAFVR). On reporting to Redhill Lodge, in the Arnold district of the city, I was disappointed to find that the area already had its quota of pilots. Instead, they offered to train me as an observer, as navigators were then styled, but I found myself more attracted to the role of wireless operator/air gunner (WOp/AG). Having attested, therefore, to undertake five years of Volunteer-Reserve service I was given an RAFVR badge and a number, 751478.

The Service number, I discovered, impersonal as it might have seemed, had a built-in significance. Overall it identified me as a member of the RAFVR, as opposed to the regular RAF. Delving further, the 751 component denoted wireless operator – had I trained as an observer it would have been 741 – while the 478-element showed that I had enlisted in the Nottingham area.

During training there was little square-bashing, and that only half-hearted, much more emphasis being placed upon night-school classes in morse and radio theory at the RAFVR Centre in Nottingham's city centre. Then, at weekends, we reported to the National Flying Service's airfield at Tollerton where I had my first flight, an air-experience flip in a Hawker Hart piloted by a civilian pilot – undoubtedly Civil Air Guard by then – who was attached to the RAFVR for carrying out such flights.

On Sunday 3 September 1939, when war broke out, my group was immediately called up, issued with uniforms at Nottingham's Redhill Lodge, then sent home to wait. Three weeks later, after initially reporting to Tollerton, by then metamorphosed into No. 27 Elementary Reserve and Flying Training School, I was posted to No. 144 Squadron at RAF Hemswell, in Lincolnshire.

On joining the squadron all the trainee WOp/AGs were placed under the command of the armament officer and employed in such duties as night guard on the aircraft dispersal area. It was an uncomfortable sojourn but, while finding myself derisively regarded by the regulars as yet another 'phantom air gunner', I did fly in the squadron's Anson runabout and get a short flight in a Hampden bomber, occupying the lower air-gunner's station.

In the billet, however, I found myself more than a little embarrassed. This was because on joining up I had become an instant aircraftman first class (AC1), rising to the rank of leading aircraftman (LAC) the very next day. Now, at Hemswell, I was allocated a bedspace between a regular LAC with two good conduct stripes – inverted chevrons denoting at least eight years' service – and an AC1 with a single good conduct stripe, denoting at least three. Essentially ground tradesmen they had been part-time fliers for some years, getting one and sixpence a day flying pay, but only when they actually got airborne. Not only that, but both of them wore the air-gunner's brass-bullet insignia on their right sleeves and had already flown on ops.

The AC1, I remember, Gordon Comstay, was also from Nottingham. A little later he was shot down while raiding Heligoland Bight and became a prisoner of war, rising to warrant officer during his years of incarceration. However, although he returned to the city after his liberation it so happened that I never saw him again.

The Flying Bullet arm badge – cloth version shown here, but also in brass – which preceded the AG brevet. As shown, worn above the wireless flash, denoted a trained wireless operator/air gunner. Note too, the rank of corporal

Heligoland, an early RAF target

Our trainee-group's next move was to No. 2 Supplementary Wireless School at Prestwick, where, besides doing ground school, we flew in a twin-engined Fokker, the six pupils aboard busily sending morse messages, not to stations on the ground, but to each other! A brief holding detachment to Acklington, in Northumberland, followed, after which we reported to the Air Operating Section of the Cranwell-based No. 1 Wireless School. Here, once more in Lincolnshire, we completed our theoretical training alongside airmen destined to become wireless-cum-electrical mechanics, separating from them to do our airborne exercises.

For these we clambered aboard a Vickers Virginia, ten at a time. But we also flew in Westland Wallaces which, my flying logbook shows, were the self-same machines I had cycled out to watch at Hucknall back in 1935!

Having completed this course we were allowed to sew on our wireless arm flashes: a clenched handful of lightning darts. We then moved to No. 10 Bombing and Gunnery School at Dumfries, on the Solway Firth, flying in Handley Page Harrows to carry out air-to-ground firing at targets and air-to-air firing on

Brass flying bullet arm badge

air-towed drogues, a latter-day perusal of my logbook showing at least one gratifyingly high score on the normally elusive drogue!

Finally, with this course completed, we proudly eased the brass prongs of the coveted Flying Bullet through the serge of our right sleeves, attaching the emblem just above the wireless flash. Now we were no longer trainee aircrew, but actual aircrew, and trained in a dual category at that, capable of acting as both wireless operator and air gunner.

'Where do you wanted to be posted to?' asked the notice avuncularly. Then followed a whole host of choices. But my eye was drawn to the very bottom, to Coastal Command, and – I could see them in my mind's eye – to Short Sunderland Flying Boats.

'Well, lads,' I enthused to my half-dozen peers, 'who's for both eggs and bacon in flight and bunk beds?'

Apparently all of us were, for everyone applied for Coastal Command.

Well, we duly got Coastal Command, all six of us, but not the luxurious Sunderlands. Instead we joined No. 22 Torpedo-Bomber Squadron, which was stationed at North Coates, in Lincolnshire, and flying the twin-engined Bristol Beauforts, having converted from single-engined Vickers Vildebeest biplanes in December 1939.

Not what we had anticipated, but at least on 23 May 1940 – after tacit acceptance for some air gunners dating back to January 1939 – all airmen aircrew became sergeants. This, as may be imagined, went down even worse with the RAF regulars than had our instant-aircraftman promotions some months before.

Bristol Type 152 Beaufort

Domestic politics aside, however, and as regards crew composition, when flying the Vildebeest the squadron had operated with a first and second pilot and two WOp/AGs. Now, on the Beaufort, the former second pilots became captains in their own right, observers (navigators) appeared, and the two WOp/AGs were retained. On operations, then, the pilot would drop the torpedo, and the observer would adopt what had formerly been the second-pilot's dual role of navigator and bomb aimer, while the two WOp/AGs filled the wireless operator and turret gunner's stations respectively.

For armament in those early days our Beauforts carried a pilot-operated Browning machine gun in the wing and a single gas-operated, pan-fed Vickers machine gun in the dorsal – upper mid-fuselage – turret, both of 0.303 inch (7.7 mm) calibre. Between us, we WOp/AGs had total responsibility for the single Vickers. This meant that the one of us acting as gunner on a particular sortie not only selected and loaded the ammunition before flight – assembling a mix of ball, tracer, incendiary, armour-piercing, and high explosive – but fought the gun when airborne, then stripped and cleaned it after landing.

Eventually, in mid 1941, our turrets would be modified to take two belt-fed Brownings, the overall armament being supplemented by a Vickers projecting from each side hatch – either the port or the starboard gun to be fought as called for by the watchkeeping WOp/AG who would leave his wireless set in the case of a fighter attack.

Additionally, we were equipped with another belt-fed Browning in an under-belly blister that the observer could spray behind us as we went, operating it with his foot. This, in fact, proved very useful in keeping heads down, for we

Checking and sorting in-flight energy rations

quickly found that our best protection was to directly overfly the ships we attacked, giving us a moment during which their guns could not be brought to bear.

Overflying an attacked vessel

By choice, on ops, I would act as gunner, for the wireless operator had little to do, our sorties invariably being conducted under strict radio silence. So much so that even the transmission of 'hit' signals, and equally importantly, 'enemy vessels located' signals, were banned until we were within fifty miles of the British coast inbound, as indeed, were calls for homings, or as we knew them – from the morse brevity code –, QDMs.

Where the wireless sets themselves were concerned, the T1083/R1082s were laborious to operate, every change of frequency requiring a different coil to be fitted and tuned in. Granted, it all became much more straightforward when the Marconi T1154/R1155 was introduced. But only much later were we additionally equipped with VHF (Very High Frequency) voice sets, and then they gave lamentably short range.

Our speciality weapon, of course, was the torpedo. Dropping this required the aircraft to be flown level at a height of sixty feet on the run-up to the target. Once the weapon was launched it fell down on wires, a propeller to the rear keeping it stable. Then, with both wires and rear-stabilizer detached, it entered the sea. After that, a nose-mounted propeller would arm it once it had run some four hundred yards. The running depth could, if required, be altered in flight by reaching down to the torpedo but we normally had it set before take-off depending upon the target we expected to encounter; six feet for merchantmen, up to twelve feet for battleships.

Aerial torpedo being loaded

Setting aside the opposition (and how we'd have appreciated being able to do that!) care also had to be taken in the range at which the weapon was dropped; not before one thousand yards but no later than six hundred. Dropped further off than a thousand yards it was likely to be out of range. Dropped closer than six hundred yards it would still be too deep when it reached the target, not yet having come back to the selected running depth.

Apart from torpedoes we could also drop land and sea mines but although sea-mine sorties were designated 'Cucumbers', the only essential difference between the weapons was that the landmines descended on a parachute.

On joining the squadron I was fortunate in being crewed up with Pilot Officer 'Jimmy' Hyde. He was an Australian who had come to the RAF on a short-service commission and had already completed fifteen operational sorties while flying as second pilot to the squadron commander. My observer was Bill Prince, the dourest man I would ever meet: he never smiled. Not that he lacked a sense of humour, his most celebrated entry in the squadron 'line-book' – tall-story book – reading, 'I got to know the North Sea so well that in all our crossings I was never more than two waves out.' And I remember so well his laconic response to Jimmy's call for a homing to base from our regular hunting grounds, the Frisian Islands, 'Just head 270 degrees, Skipper.'

No. 22 Squadron's main task at that time was to send out a single aircraft on a 'Torpedo Rover' whenever enemy ships were reported by photo-reconnaissance machines. Loaded with a torpedo we'd go out to the area and search around, attacking if we found anything.

On one of my early Rovers, on 23 October 1940, our torpedo scored a direct hit on a 2,000-ton merchant ship. My logbook records that I also fired off fifty rounds and saw the crew take to the boats, although we were unable to dwell long enough to see the ship actually sink. Another early op was to Bremerhaven where we dropped landmines on the harbour installations and where I recorded 'Ack-Ack intense'. That op took us six hours, leaving us with just thirty minutes' fuel in hand.

Then again, what became known as the Battle of Britain was a particularly busy time for us, strafing and bombing the invasion barges gathering in the Channel ports and the supporting airfields, delivering four 500-pounders – carried in the bomb bay: normally used for the torpedo – and two 250-pounders,

Channel ports, German invasion barges

one under each wing. Among such sorties my logbook records that, during an attack on Cambrai airfield, the ack-ack was both intense and accurate.

On one occasion we even had a fighter escort, but just as shortage of fuel forced them to turn back so we were attacked by two Heinkel floatplanes; at which we turned back too, having no option but to believe what Intelligence had told us, that they carried long-range cannon in their floats!

Then, in December 1940, we were detached to Thorney Island, near Portsmouth, using Thorney as a starting point from which to drop landmines on the submarine pens at Bordeaux. It was a long, night-time flog, over five hours there and back, especially as, while over the target, we were coned by searchlights and suffered so much damage that back at Thorney Island we crash-landed, the aircraft being written off.

Our next trip was another landmine raid, this time on Emden; yet another long haul for a Beaufort. Then, on 1 January 1941, we were tasked for a reconnaissance-cum-bombing sortie to the North Holland Peninsula. Having carried out our patrol without sighting any ships, we dropped our bombs – four 500-pounders and two 250-pounders – on the seaplane base at Den Helder. The ground defences responded with a heavy concentration of anti-aircraft fire but after a few fraught moments we won clear and set heading for home: our good old favourite, 270 degrees – due west. Only to be jumped by two Messerschmitt Bf109s!

These fell in behind us, repeatedly attacking in sequence and peppering us for eight interminable minutes. I was left powerless, for I was unable to fire directly backwards – a cut-out guard rail prevented self-destruction caused by shooting off one's own tail – and all Jimmy could do was push the throttles through the gate and hug the waves, so preventing the fighters from getting at our belly.

The limiting speed for the Beaufort was variously given, but mainly as 260 miles an hour – 226 knots. However one chose to reckon it, though, Jimmy must have exceeded the limit by quite some margin in getting us home safe and pretty-well sound, the miracle being that despite being holed in over a hundred places nothing vital to the aeroplane – or to the four of us – had been hit. For that sortie Jimmy received a very well earned Distinguished Flying Cross.

Was I scared on that occasion? Too right I was! Indeed, throughout every single operation, and even after them, I was forced to admit to nerves. But then if any operational aircrew member says different I'd say they were either liars, or that age has mellowed their memories. On the other hand I suppose there was one chap I was to become associated with, a pilot named Campbell – Flying Officer Kenneth Campbell –, who seemed to be utterly fearless. Certainly, we tended to avoid filling any occasional spaces that offered on his crew: don't fly with him on ops, we'd tell each other, he's bound to get you bloody killed.

And, of course, we were very conscious of losses. It was hard to remain oblivious seeing that, of the half-dozen of us who had joined the squadron together, only two remained at the end of six months. Indeed, had we realized at the time that on Coastal Beauforts the chances were that only 17 per cent of aircrew would survive a first tour, and only 3 per cent a second, I wonder if I, for one, would have volunteered beyond that first tour! Not that, at that time, there was any such thing as tour length, whether reckoned by numbers of ops or hours flown on ops. Back then you simply flew as often as you were detailed to.

Raiding carried on. In March 1941 our torpedo struck a merchantman fair and square and sent her down. I especially remember that occasion because Jimmy urged me to open fire on the seamen in the water. In effect, it was an order, and one which faced me with a never-previously-considered dilemma. Yet I found that, regardless of the fact that just moments before those self-same seamen had been doing their level best to kill us, I simply couldn't fire on them in cold blood. On landing Jimmy duly laid into me, pointing out that the seamen would undoubtedly be picked up and on returning to their gunnery duties would likely enough do for any number of other Allied airmen, if not, indeed, for me. But it had been my decision, measured by my moral responsibility, and he had to accept that. As he did, and without lasting rancour.

The previously mentioned Flying Officer Campbell came to figure large in my life the very next month when eight aircraft from North Coates – two travelling as spares – were detached to St Eval, in Cornwall, to attack the German capital ships *Scharnhorst* and *Gneisenau*, at that time lying in Brest.

Scharnhorst *and* Gneisenau

One of the two previous raids on Brest

At briefing we were told that the warships were on the verge of setting sail to join the already marauding *Bismarck* and her consorts. We learnt too, that Churchill had specifically ordered that they must not be allowed into the Atlantic where the Royal Navy's resources were already stretched to capacity. With this in mind, two conventional bombing raids had been carried out. Then, with neither of these producing a significant result, our air-torpedo operation had been laid on.

The plan was that at first light on 6 April 1941 three of our six Beauforts would carry mines, arrive first, and bomb the anti-torpedo nets, so clearing the way for the torpedoes of the other three. Campbell was to lead the torpedo trio with a sergeant pilot named Lamb trailing him and Jimmy Hyde – and me! – following on. As a plan it was all very well. But Brest was known to be the most heavily defended of all the German-occupied ports. Little wonder then that the general feeling at both North Coates and St Eval was that we were being sent on a suicide sortie.

As it happened, things went awry from the outset. With St Eval being a grass field two of the mine-carrying aircraft – essential to the task, of course! – bogged down. Only the third, flown by Sergeant Pilot Harry Menary, managed to get airborne.

The scheme had been that we would all fly out in company. Then, on arrival, the torpedo-carrying machines would loiter outside the port until the three mine-layers had blown gaps in the anti-torpedo nets, for only when these were pierced would our weapons have any chance of a clear run. As it was, the weather from take-off onwards was atrocious, with high winds, low cloud, and very poor visibility in heavy rain. Even flying in loose station proved out of the question and so it was that on arrival at Brest in the half-light there was no chance of any of the aircraft rendezvousing or even, the visibility being what it was, of holding off in order to study the situation.

For our crew the plan became somewhat academic anyway, for we strayed over Ushant – the islet off the extreme tip of northwest France – where we came under heavy anti-aircraft fire. Escaping that, we set course again, but on making a landfall in the vicinity of Brest, Bill, our navigator, elected to turn in the wrong direction, so that initially we were heading away from the port. By the time we had corrected the error and arrived at the target not only was it daylight but the place was simply hopping with defensive fire.

Clearly something had disturbed the wasps' nest, from which we deduced that the others had arrived before us. Pursuing an attack seemed hopeless from the start, nevertheless we persisted with our torpedo run until we were halfway to the releasing point. By then though, with no notion of what had gone on before we arrived, or of the state of the net barrier, and with what was already a fearsome barrage intensifying, it became evident that to press on was truly suicidal. Jimmy, therefore, broke off the attack and returned to St Eval. The entire sortie to Brest and back should have taken three and a half hours. On landing we had been airborne for five and a half.

Having effectively been out of contact with the others of the attacking force since climbing aboard our aircraft, it was only then that were we able to begin piecing things together.

We found out, for instance, that Sergeant Menary's crew – the only mine-carrier to get airborne – had been shot up as they approached the French coast and suffered so much damage that, despite jettisoning their mine, they had crashed on landing back at St Eval. We discovered too that Sergeant Lamb, in the torpedo-carrying aircraft, which should have immediately preceded us in the attack, had also bogged down and had been ten minutes late in getting off. Just as we had done, his crew had then gone off course, and arriving at the target area – as their nav log showed – five minutes after us. Equally unaware of the situation but eyeing a sky full of tracer, they had weighed up the chances, then let it be, and had turned away for St Eval, taking their torpedo with them.

We waited long past the time by which fuel reserves would have been exhausted. But Flying Officer Campbell and his crew never did return.

News came in remarkably quickly, however, in the main from French Resistance sources but also from anxiously monitored German news broadcasts. We learnt that while *Scharnhorst* was still in an inner dry dock and untouched, *Gneisenau* had been seriously damaged.

The damage to* Gneisenau *caused by Campbell's torpedo

The details came later. *Gneisenau's* commander, it seemed, wary of his ship's vulnerability following the second RAF bombing raid the night before, and also concerned about the proximity of an unexploded bomb, had moved the vessel to the outer dock. Here it had been positioned so that it was protected on three sides; by a mole, but also by anti-aircraft batteries and flak ships. Moreover, as we had learnt at briefing, the whole port was protected by hills that not only made things difficult for low-level attackers but were themselves bristling with guns. Ironically, after-the-event reports also revealed that to facilitate the *Gneisenau's* re-positioning the anti-torpedo nets had, in fact, been drawn away!

The same sources, though, told us of the actual attack Campbell and his crew had made, describing how their Beaufort had skimmed the waves below the very muzzles of the guns.

It could be that, seeing by the light of flares and searchlights the absence of supporting buoys, Campbell had realized that the nets were not in position. It could also be that, arriving unannounced, he had caught the defences relatively off guard, although with the earlier raids so fresh in the mind it would only have taken seconds for the gunners to respond. Perhaps delay enough, though, for Campbell not only managed to get into position but actually launched his torpedo. Immediately afterwards, however, the aircraft, engulfed by then in defensive fire, had plunged into the harbour. There were no survivors.

The torpedo, meanwhile, had run true, doing so much damage that the *Gneisenau* had to be returned to the inner dock where repairs took over six months.

'Dickie', as the squadron knew Campbell – from the time when he had been a second pilot, or 'second dickie' –, had not been alone, of course. His crew had comprised Sergeant James Phillip Scott, Royal Canadian Air Force, the observer; Flight Sergeant Ralph Walter 'Titch' Hillman in the turret; and Sergeant William Cecil 'Prof' Mullis, the wireless operator. All four had died heroically, with Flying Officer Campbell, as captain of the crew, being awarded the Victoria Cross, the citation detailing the exploit owing much to the evidence supplied by the Resistance.

Such then, was Kenneth Campbell, perhaps, as I say, the only man I ever met who might, indeed, have been without fear.

As a coda to our involvement, when *Scharnhorst* and *Gneisenau* did break out, ten months later, on

The Victoria Cross

the night of 11 February 1942 (German Operation Cerberus), the unsuccessful bid to destroy them occasioned the loss of a further forty-two RAF aircraft and led to the award of a second posthumous VC. The German flotilla did not, however, head for the Atlantic, but for the Channel.

In July 1941, although there were still no recognized tour lengths for Coastal Command, our crew was rested. Jimmy Hyde was posted as a pilot-instructor to the Torpedo Training Unit at Abbotsinch. As for the rear crew, my original fellow WOp/AG had already gone off to be a signals officer but his replacement and I were sent as wireless and gunnery instructors respectively to No. 5 Coastal Operational Training Unit at Chivenor, in Devon. Here we operated Blenheims and Beauforts, giving training to three gunners at a time until they were proficient, after which they completed their training as integral members of a Beaufort crew.

Flying training was rarely dull, but one night when I was on my way to take over as safety wireless operator in the tower I was totally taken aback to be overflown by a landing aircraft displaying, as I put it at the time, 'bloody big crosses and a swastika'. It was, it transpired, a Junkers Ju88 whose crew, having raided Liverpool, had mistaken the Bristol Channel for the English Channel and had thought they were safely back at their base in Northern France. Chivenor's duty officer followed the aircraft down the runway in his jeep and as it came to a stop had a chock placed under one wheel so that, as its hapless occupants realized their mistake and tried to power up, their lamed machine merely turned about the chock. Eventually, realizing that they were going nowhere, the subdued crew stopped the engines, and clambered out with raised hands.

A little later, in March 1942, I was sent on a gunnery-leader's course to the Central Gunnery School at Sutton Bridge, near Spalding, in Lincolnshire. Here we learnt to co-ordinate fighting control from the astrodome of a Wellington, normally directing a vic of three machines or a box of four. I got on well here, and on passing out took with me a recommendation for a commission.

Back at Chivenor I found a letter from Jimmy Hyde telling me that he was starting his second tour, this time with No. 42 Squadron at Leuchars, in Scotland, and asking me to join him. I immediately applied for a posting but by the time it came through and I arrived at Leuchars he had been promoted to take command of No. 86 Squadron and had moved on. Nor did No. 42 Squadron have any requirement for 'such an animal as a gunnery leader', rarely detailing a formation of more than three aircraft. So I flew on with them as a rank-and-file air gunner. I also put up my flight-sergeant's crown, although I was assured that my commission would be duly processed.

I was fortunate too, in joining up with a former staff pilot from Chivenor, newly-commissioned Pilot Officer Maurice Adams, whom I knew to be very experienced. With him came our observer, Flight Sergeant Titch Reynolds, and the other WOp/AG, Flight Sergeant Tex Ritter, an RAF regular.

Shortly afterwards we were attached to No. 86 Torpedo Squadron at Portreath, near Redruth, Cornwall – *Squadron Leader* Jimmy Hyde's squadron! The squadron was then working up for anti-shipping and ground-installation raids with Beauforts. These Beauforts not only had Pratt & Whitney Twin-Wasp engines but were also fitted with Air-to-Surface-Vessel (ASV) map-display radar, a four-day course turning us into workaday experts on this sophisticated gear.

In the way of training we raided practice targets that included Sumburgh Head in the Shetlands. Additionally, we flew to Norway to seek out enemy submarines, although none were in evidence during the sweeps our crew carried out.

The attachment came to end, however, and I was back with No. 42 Squadron when, on 17 August 1942, with its aircrew operationally ready, it was posted to the Middle East, the groundcrew having set sail in the February, six months before. There was just time for me to say farewell to my fiancée, Marjorie, in Nottingham. Then the move was on.

For the aircrews, flying our own aircraft out, it proved to be some trip. We night-stopped in Gibraltar, then flew up the Mediterranean to Malta, soon to be the George Cross Island but at that time still in the throes of its aerial purgatory. We had been briefed to stand off if a bombing raid was in progress but as we were running short of fuel we landed regardless, touching down during a lull and being hurriedly manhandled into a bunkered parking bay.

A few days later we were off again. Initially we flew to Landing Ground 224, near Cairo, passing close to a formation of Junkers Ju52s on the way: we supposed they were watching us as warily as we were watching them! Next stop was Wadi Shari, in Palestine, where we had to give up our new aircraft. We were then entrained to the Middle-East aircraft pool at Alamaza where we reluctantly took possession of some outmoded Taurus-powered Beauforts which, as we well knew, would not hold level flight with one engine out. Flying these we spent our time carrying out dummy shipping strikes on the Great Bitter Lake and on the Suez Canal, not forgetting the beating-up of any gunposts we were exercising with.

It was now late August 1942 and as our CO was appointed to convert the locally-based No. 47 Squadron to Beauforts – until recently they had been operating the outmoded Wellesley – we operated alongside them. Hard upon this semi-merger, however, and still before our ground personnel had arrived from the UK, news came that the Japanese were preparing to send a fleet into the Indian Ocean. To cover such an eventuality the squadron – No. 42 Squadron – was re-assigned to South East Asia Command, located at Colombo, in Ceylon. So we decamped again, routeing via Habbaniyah, Bahrain, Sharjah, Karachi, Bombay and Bangalore – towards the tip of India – thence to Ceylon, and Colombo's Ratmalana Airfield.

On arrival in Ceylon my own crew was initially detached to, and then actually posted to, No. 22 Squadron – back to my roots, as it were. We found the

American personnel laying perforated steel plate (PSP)

squadron operating from a jungle strip in the centre of Ceylon, the runway being noisily surfaced with perforated steel plate (PSP). Our duties included naval and fighter liaison but in December 1942 we were re-posted to No. 42 Squadron, by then up on the sub-continent proper, at Bangalore, where the groundcrews had finally arrived.

Two months later, in February 1943, we converted to the old Blenheim Mk 5, the Bisley, and began carrying out low-level, close-bombing support for the Chindits – Orde Wingate's Long-Range Jungle Penetration Force – who were pushing through Burma. As a squadron we operated from Rajyeswarpar (the spelling varies), another jungle strip, this one so new that when we arrived elephants were still clearing the trees! The terrain over which we operated was thick rain forest – jungle to the non-purist – and did not easily lend itself to mapreading. On occasion, therefore, we carried army observers to locate the targets for us.

We were so far upcountry – Rajyeswarpar was, in fact, in Northern Assam, with Burma just across the River Chindwin – that it took our long-suffering, train-borne groundcrew thirteen days to catch up with us, and even then half of them went down with malaria. Yet still they kept us airborne, just as they always did; though heaven alone knows how! And despite getting so little recognition for it! For my part when I fell for malaria a few days later, taking on jaundice for good measure, the combination floored me completely and left me with an enlarged spleen for life.

In May 1943, however, I became fit to fly again, and soon found myself raiding Kelemyo, the large Jap base, bombing from 1,500 feet. As always the horizon-to-horizon, peak-to-peak, tree cover seemed impenetrable and not for the first time I remember reflecting that if ever I came down hereabouts, and found myself alive, I would not have the slightest idea of which way to walk to find succour.

June 1943 arrived, and the squadron lost its Blenheims, all our pilots converting to the bomber version of the single-seater Hurricane. For me this redundancy meant my second rest posting. *Rest*! Or so it was deemed. In fact, it was to No. 1 Air-Fighting Training Unit at Armada Road, some 150 miles south of Calcutta, my orders being to help set up a course for gunnery leaders along the lines of that at Sutton Bridge.

Liberators at No. 1 Air-Fighting Training Unit, Armada Road, India

At Armada Road two of us shared the training task, my colleague being a flying officer, Laurie Willetts. Laurie and I decided from the outset that he was best suited to handle the theoretical, I the practical side. Then we got down to work, admitting our first course within the month, in July 1943. Indeed, by November 1943 the unit was in full swing, operating Blenheims and Wellingtons together with a Vengeance dive-bomber for target-towing. In fact, I would occasionally fly in the Vengeance and so get a different perspective of the trainee gunnery-leaders' task.

Then the Americans joined us in the theatre and I found myself flying with a whole succession of 'lootenant' pilots. Pragmatically, we utilized the Liberator B-24 and Mitchell B-25 bombers they brought with them until, in due course, these were recalled by their parent units.

In September 1943, by which time I had been a warrant officer for quite a while, my commission as a pilot officer finally came through. It had been sixteen months in the pipeline but during that time a sizeable lump of back pay had accrued. Indeed, from then on my rise was very nearly dizzying. A month later I became a flying officer, and then, because I was filling an established post, an acting flight lieutenant. Similarly Laurie, who was filling a squadron leader's post, became an acting squadron leader.

Unlike my promotion, the flying-training commitment was unvarying. There were no great changes in the syllabus but although nobody was trying to shoot us down, complacency had to be fought against. This was pointedly brought home to me when I was controlling a fighter-liaison exercise, flying as gunnery co-ordinator in the centre of a twin-vic formation of six B-24s. I was in the astrodome, facing forwards, when, for no apparent reason the aircraft ahead and to my right touched the leader. Instantly each broke up and plummeted into the ground, leaving no survivors.

The aircraft ahead and to my right touched the leader …

VE Day came, and went. Indeed, it was hardly noticed in the Far-Eastern Theatre. But then came 15 August 1945, and VJ Day, with the surrender being ratified soon afterwards. Indeed, our American Allies commemorate VJ Day on 2 September, as the day when the surrender was actually signed. Whatever the date though, the war was over. And in the fullness of time I found myself back in Britain with decisions to be made about the future. One option was to extend my service in the RAF. I looked into this but did not find the terms offered satisfactory. Of course, I had a right to resume my old job with Thomas Forman and Sons Ltd, and duly found myself before the managing director.

Having chatted for some while – for I had been away for six years and eight months, and actually overseas for three and a half years – he asked me what I wanted to do on rejoining. I replied that I would like to learn more about printing and then go into the sales department. There was a silence.

I stood there as he eyed me, a two-tour veteran, erect in my flight lieutenant's uniform; bronzed, as I knew, by the Far-Eastern sun; my eyes, I was sure, reflecting the years of aerial trauma and derring-do that had been my lot since leaving the firm; proudly chesting out my AG brevet and ribbons – with Battle of Britain clasp – and my Air Efficiency Award, the latter signifying meritorious service with the RAF Volunteer Reserve. He mused a moment longer, and then said pointedly, 'You realize, young Bramley, that you're nothing but a glorified office lad?'

Then, without unbending, he said flatly, 'I'm paying returnees from the Services four pounds ten shillings a week. But I'll pay you five pounds.'

The Air Efficiency Award

I was highly gratified, and accepted at once. Besides, alongside the new wage I was being paid nearly twenty pounds a week by the RAF!

That extra payment, however, came to a stop six months later. And not long afterwards the job began to pall. I duly made another approach to the RAF, this time receiving rather more satisfactory terms. They would grant me a commission, no problem there. But only for a three-year engagement, and with no guarantee of a permanent commission to follow. There was always the chance, of course ... But if the permanent commission fell through I would not only have put myself out of a career job, but have lost three years. So it was that I reluctantly turned them down, and soldiered on with Forman's.

As it transpired, Forman's grew, became international in stature, and took me with them, so that when I finally retired after a total of forty-three years with the firm my title had long been Sales and Marketing Director.

But before that, in 1948, Marjorie and I were married, the union ushering in forty years of happiness that saw the birth of our son, Gordon, and only came to an end when Marjorie died untimely with a heart problem.

Certainly, after that, work took up much of my time, but I never altogether cut my ties with the Service. I had joined the RAF Association in 1947 – becoming entitled to the sixty-year badge in 2007; I am a member of the Blenheim Association, and of Nos 42, 47, and 22 Squadron Associations – indeed as a founder-member of the latter, I became its president. At the same time I was editor of *The Turret* newsletter, the voice of the National Air Gunner's Association. Then again, I had become chairman of the Notts and Derby Branch of the Aircrew Association. Not least, I had formed links with the City of Nottingham's own No. 504 Auxiliary Squadron whose Wallaces had so attracted me all those years before.

Such involvements have brought many Service-orientated invitations, some of them to royal occasions, to most of which, these days, I am accompanied by Pam, not only a girlhood friend of Marjorie but the widow of my best friend.

A highlight among such Service occasions came in April 2000 when a plaque was unveiled to the memory of Kenneth Campbell at Saltcoats, Ayrshire, where I had the privilege of transferring his Victoria Cross into the safekeeping of No. 22 Squadron. A proud moment indeed for a glorified office lad!

Mr Ron Bramley, AE, transfers Campbell's VC to No. 22 Squadron

Ron (Bram) Bramley, AE, 2012

10

Unloved by the gods

Acting Warrant Officer Arthur Minnitt, flight engineer

In 1934, on leaving school at fourteen, I joined the illustrations department of the *Nottingham Evening Post*. With the war looming, however, I signed on in the RAF as a prospective pilot. At Cardington, though, it was found that my eyesight fell just below the required standard for any aircrew category but, though disappointed, rather than go back to my old job I accepted the role of rigger.

Sergeant Arthur Minnitt, 1942

Duly attested, I became an aircrafthand (under training) and was sent to Blackpool for six months of courses. I seemed to progress well, getting marks in the upper eighties, in particular receiving high praise for my splicing! Indeed, I was able to report home that I had been offered a commission as an engineering officer but had turned it down, still hoping to get into the air!

Then, when I was posted in mid November 1940, my transport was routed through Coventry, and as we nosed through the blitzed streets, hope became determination: I simply had to help carry the fight back to the perpetrators.

I could see no immediate way of doing so, of course, but I stifled my impatience, working on at my trade and servicing both Battles and Spitfires at various Operational Training Units (OTUs).

The day came, however, when a notice appeared asking for volunteers for the new aircrew category of flight engineer. I applied immediately and, my eyesight notwithstanding, was accepted!

Even then, my flight commander urged me to reconsider becoming an engineering officer. I thanked him, but said that I would try to qualify as a flight engineer first, then apply for commissioning when I was rested; that is, in four months or so, once I had completed the required tour of bomber operations. It was a declaration that he accepted doubtfully enough, but which must have

Coventry city centre

struck Fate as irresistibly challenging. Only I was young, of course, and a great optimist!

My initial training posting was to No. 7 Air Gunners School at RAF Stormy Down, Bridgend, in South Wales, where we concentrated in particular on operating the Browning machine gun.

Firing at a model aircraft running around a track

Following this, we were moved to Speke, Liverpool, for the six-week flight-engineer's course itself. This, being a new syllabus, I suppose, was rather sketchy, but they crammed the requisite amount of knowledge into us so that we left Speke wearing sergeant's stripes and FE (flight engineer) brevets and only a little disgruntled to be bound for Halifaxes rather than Lancasters.

A brief spell of leave followed, after which I was posted to No. 1652 Heavy Conversion Unit at Marston Moor, North Yorkshire. The proceedings began with all the new arrivals being ushered into an enormous room seething with various aircrew and a noise level suggestive of bedlam. Hearing my name yelled out, I pushed through the throng to find myself face to face with another sergeant.

'I'm Gerry Dane,' he greeted me, hand outstretched. 'I'm your pilot. Got an oxygen mask? Good, then we'll get airborne. Don't forget to put it on when we get above 10,000 feet.'

Showing the deterioration in performance due to oxygen lack

And that was that. Climbing aboard I took my place just behind Gerry where a swivelling seat enabled me to reach my instrument panel and manage the fuel.

So it was that I got airborne for the first time and, together with an equally new mid-upper gunner, became one of 'Dane's Pups'.

Gerry, my pilot, Sergeant (later Pilot Officer) Gerald Herbert Dane, was just coming up to twenty. He and the rest of his crew had been carrying out anti-shipping strikes in Whitleys and Wellingtons. Now, converting to heavy bombers, they needed a flight engineer and a mid-upper gunner. And the mid-upper – Alf Beatson – and I were it.

There were seven of us in the crew, all sergeants: Gerry; Mick Goddard, the navigator; Len Adams, bomb aimer; John Pople, wireless operator; yours truly; then Frank Webb, rear gunner; and as I've said, Alf Beatson, mid-upper gunner.

The Heavy Operational Training Unit course lasted about a month, during which we flew cross-countries, gradually gelling as a heavy-bomber crew. At the end, having been passed as fit for operations, we were posted to No. 4 Group and No. 78 Squadron, stationed at Linton-on-Ouse, in Yorkshire.

Dane's Pups; left to right: Section Officer Pam, debriefing officer; Gerald Herbert Dane, pilot; Sergeant Alf Beatson, mid-upper gunner; Sergeant Arthur Minnitt, flight engineer; Sergeant Mick Goddard, navigator; Sergeant Len Adams, bomb aimer; Sergeant Frank Webb, rear gunner. Sergeant John Pople was away at a separate wireless-operators' debriefing. I got to know Pam very well at the time, subsequently encountering her many years later at a No. 4 Group reunion at York

That I slipped easily into operational life is reflected in a letter home dated 3 April 1943: 'Last night we did our first operation. This afternoon I've got to collect last week's washing but it doesn't take long on a bike.'

In fact, losses were particularly heavy at that juncture, indeed, by the time I had done seven ops my crew were beginning to be regarded as fixtures, with so many others falling by the way after just three or so.

Ops tend to form a pattern in the memory, with just the occasional, usually stark, incident standing out: bombs from a higher aircraft showering down around us and missing us heaven only knows how: another Halifax cutting across in front of our nose and somehow ghosting off into the night without actually colliding with us. And the awareness the whole time we were airborne that disaster might be heralded by an exhaust flare, or a solid shape, momentarily illuminated by a flash, by flak, or by a bomb burst. As for daylight, then there was simply far too much of everything. The truth was, I had all too good a view, for when Gerry didn't actually need me on station I tended to take post in the astrodome, keeping an eye on the whole upper surface of the aircraft and seeing what was going on about us.

Far too much of everything ...

Flash, flak, or bomb burst ...

Either smoke or low cloud ...

Looking back, that first op, on 2 April 1943, proved an exemplar for those that followed. It was to St Nazaire, which we bombed from 15,000 feet, aiming through what was either smoke or low cloud at the marker flares, with Len, the bomb aimer, reporting that the red target indicator was smack in the centre of the bombsight when he released. We certainly felt that our bombs had fallen close, although it was twenty minutes after leaving the target before the rear gunner and I, looking backwards, began to see fires.

Then again on 10 April 1943, raiding Frankfurt, we dropped from 18,000 feet but had to bomb exclusively on cloud markers, the ten-tenths cover extending up to at least 12,000 feet. On 20 April 1943, on the other hand, visiting Stettin, conditions were better and we bombed using a combination of markers and the river, noting five massive fires that could still be seen from 100 miles on the return.

Although it had not been my first choice, the Halifax was generally very dependable, but performance was always a problem. Indeed, when returning from Dortmund I had to warn Gerry that we were getting seriously low in fuel. As we approached Linton, however, it was covered in fog, obliging us to divert to Leeming. Only to find fog closing in there too.

Gerry put out a priority landing request, but had to press our case before it was granted. And even then, eyeing the fuel gauges, I was on tenterhooks. Luckily Gerry caught sight of the flare path and, although it was well off to one side, turned in – and arrived! I use that word advisedly. Indeed, I can still hear the wheels screeching as he slammed the aircraft onto the ground. Then we were off the tarmac and bounding across the grass. But we were down, and safe, and very glad to walk away yet again.

On meeting them the next day, however, the Leeming groundcrew seemed awed.

'Do you realize', the Chiefy asked us, 'you had less than four gallons for each engine?' Not even enough, that is, for another circuit! Yet on touching down we had long been committed, for we'd been far too low to have baled out!

In fact, baling out of the Halifax called for a lot of height. The rear gunner was not too badly placed for he could rotate his turret, grab his parachute pack and clip it to his chest before toppling out backwards. In the very front too, the bomb aimer could use his hatch, as could the navigator and the wireless op. But any supernumerary pilot would have to follow on their heels. And I mention a supernumerary for it was the practice for each new skipper to fly one or two ops merely standing behind the flying pilot and observing.

The flying pilot though, was also expected to use that hatch. He did have an alternative exit in the top of the canopy but that risked fouling the tailplane and was not normally considered viable.

For mid-fuselage crew, there was another hatch on the starboard side but that meant climbing over a spar, squeezing beneath the mid-upper turret and all its paraphernalia and then negotiating another spar before reaching the exit. Indeed, as a flight engineer I was probably in the best of all positions, for I could use either the forward or the mid-fuselage hatch.

Naturally, it is my eighth trip that stays with me most. This took place on 12 May 1943 when we were to raid Bochum, in the Ruhr. Never a picnic, the Ruhr, yet as we left briefing we were all feeling cockahoop, for an overnight claim by our rear gunner that he had shot down a German fighter had just been accepted. This feeling of elation was somewhat dampened, however, even as we came to board. As a crew we had fallen into the habit of painting a representation of the Saint – the Leslie Charteris creation – on any machine we flew and the mid-upper and I, certainly, would touch it as a talisman. It was disconcerting to find that the aeroplane we were to use for this raid was Saintless!

We duly got airborne, however, but long before reaching the target area the engines began giving trouble, causing us to fall behind the bomber stream. This left us keenly aware of how vulnerable we now were to night-fighters, for all our recent offensive prowess.

Then the starboard-inner engine began hunting, so much so that eventually it had to be stopped. Between us we feathered it, and as Gerry had decided against pressing on with just three motors, Mick Goddard passed him a heading for home. But our vulnerability became instantly apparent! The night-fighter that got us made just one pass, but an only too accurate one, leaving numbers five and six fuel tanks on the starboard side holed and spewing blazing petrol. From my hurriedly-assumed perch in the astrodome I was able to give Gerry an immediate situation report.

'The whole right wing's on fire, Skipper, with flames torching back to the tailplane.'

For I could see the lot. It was already clear that Gerry was struggling to maintain control. He gave the order to abandon but when I clambered down to him I found that he was leaning aside, wheel hard over in a gallantly-desperate, but evidently futile, effort to hold the machine in the air. It was already nosing downwards, the dive steepening with every moment. Scanning the forward hatch I could see that the others were having trouble getting it open. Also, it seemed crowded, especially as it would eventually have to accommodate the supernumerary pilot we were carrying too. Presently, the machine not having supplementary controls, he was powerless to do anything but hover, anxious to assist Gerry.

Unlike many pilots Gerry favoured a chest-type parachute – rather than the seat type, which was integral to the harness – but although I passed it to him it was clear that the moment he let go of the controls to snap it to his chest the aircraft would go completely out of control. We both – indeed all three of us huddled there – knew that.

'I'll get to the mid exit,' I told them, 'that'll lessen the jam up front for you two.'

Gerry acknowledged. And that was the last exchange I was to have with him. Doing my utmost to close my mind, I touched the supernumerary's shoulder, and turned away to begin the obstacle course to the mid-fuselage hatch.

Thinking back to actually leaving the aircraft, I always wonder that I was not terrified. For this forced abandoning of an aeroplane, where only moments before everything had been comfortingly familiar, was a terrible undertaking. The air-rush was intensifying, rising to a crescendo as the death dive steepened. Canted over, the interior of the machine bristled with suddenly alien projections, while beyond every hatch the flames were casting a lurid, quite unearthly glow.

Pushing rearwards it was to discover that Alf Beatson, the mid-upper, had the hatch opened all right, but was sitting at it, petrified. After the merest hesitation I supplied the impetus needed with my toe and he disappeared into the night. Later he would tell me, 'If you hadn't booted me out I'd have simply sat there and gone down with the kite.'

For my part, I dived through the hole he'd left and the moment I judged it safe to do so, pulled the ripcord, the canopy coming open with such a violent jerk that my right flying boot disappeared into the night: Fate's final jape, perhaps!

Gathering my senses and looking about me, I found that I was above cloud. But a short while later a great glow appeared through the paleness and I knew that the Halifax, and Gerry with it, had hit the ground. Very shortly after that I too made contact, but in a far kindlier fashion, plummeting into what proved to be a wheat field.

With my nerves rattled as they were it took a while for me to pull myself together. Taking stock, I seemed to be in one piece, although my right ankle wasn't too happy. My left boot had stayed with me for I'd kept my torch stowed there and that had held it secure. As for my right foot, I pressed my flying helmet into service in lieu of the missing boot. But what to do next?

Because we had already turned for home when we were hit I was unable to decide whether I was in Belgium or in Germany. Whichever, I formed the resolve that I must walk south, towards neutral Switzerland. And so I set off.

But it transpired that I had landed not that far from the aircraft and well within the search zone. It was with no great sense of shock, therefore, that just minutes later I found myself staring up the barrel of a gun.

My captors were neither friendly nor unduly hostile, just matter-of-fact, I suppose.

'Wounded?' asked one brusquely, in German.

'Nein,' I replied, airing most of my knowledge of the language. And little more was said.

Pay-back time for Coventry was done, my evasion bid was over, and my time as a prisoner of war had begun.

My time as a POW had begun

I was helped into a van and after a short ride arrived in a village where I was taken down a flight of steps and into the cellar of a bar. After waiting there for some while I was formally handed over to the Luftwaffe. My details were checked and everything I was carrying was brought out and recorded. Such items as a compass were confiscated, but most of the rest was returned to me. Seeing that I had lost a boot they tried to fit me up with clogs, but after it was found that I couldn't get my foot into the biggest available, they gave up.

Another van ride followed, to the village of Haasrode, near Leuven, in Belgium, where I was taken aback to see the rear end of our Halifax, sitting on the haystack it had flattened! What instantly raised my spirits, however, was to see that the rear turret was turned aside, meaning that Frank Webb had probably got clear.

On seeing me emerge from the van some of the village women actually shed tears, and one very attractive young girl – she wore a hat, I remember! – pressed me with food and drink for all that the guards shouted to dissuade her. I was more than a little shaken, however, by some of the Belgian youths who catcalled and made throat-cutting gestures at me. Indeed, I have never been able to ascertain why they showed such hostility. Certainly nobody I have met during post-war visits to Belgium has been able to throw light on it.

After that it was back into the stiflingly hot van for a much longer drive in the direction, as it turned out, of Brussels. The actual destination was what I gathered to be a German training area, gated, wired about, and with some detention quarters. I was put into a solitary cell lit by a single bulb. As a bed it contained a narrow board with its top section angled up to serve as a pillow, the result being that I kept slipping down. Here I was given water – but no food – and kept overnight.

It was a depressing, largely sleepless night – hardly surprising, of course. After all, my situation took some getting used to. I had survived. Just the same, at a stroke my life had been utterly disrupted. I knew how our loss would be taken on the squadron. I knew too that in the Operations Record Book the post-op entry would read, as it had for so many others before us, 'This aircraft took off at 1329 hours' – in our case – 'and nothing further has been heard of it or the crew since. It is, therefore, presumed missing'. By now our belongings would have been collected and our bedspaces cleared in the spirit, at least, of the old Royal Flying Corps maxim, 'No empty places at the breakfast table'.

As for the reaction at home, that was altogether too painful to think of. Only after the war would I see the telegram that had been delivered to my mother on 14 May 1943: 'REGRET TO INFORM YOU THAT YOUR SON SGT MINNITT IS REPORTED MISSING FROM OPERATIONS ON THE NIGHT OF 13/14 MAY LETTER FOLLOWS. OC 78 SQUADRON.'

After another van journey the next morning I was offloaded outside a vast building near the centre of Brussels, obviously a long-established jail. But even

Regret to inform you ... reported missing from operations ...

POST OFFICE TELEGRAM

Prefix. Time handed in. Office of Origin and Service Instructions. Words.

25

OOT 225 2/32 YO/T OHMS 35

IMMEDIATE MRS E MINNITT 40 PATRICK RD WEST BRIDGFORD NOTTINGHAM =

REGRET TO INFORM YOU THAT YOUR SON SGT MINNITT IS REPORTED MISSING FROM OPERATIONS ON THE NIGHT OF 13/14 MAY LETTER FOLLOWS = OC 78 SQUADRON as we had driven up, so had a small coach, which now disgorged five members of the crew!

What a lift to the spirits! However, of course, it was a muted lift. For Gerry Dane, I now discovered, had indeed died, as had the supernumerary pilot, twenty-one year old Sergeant James Howard Body. I was forced to notice too that Mick Goddard, our navigator, was also missing. But the tidings there were better, although it would be a very long time before we learnt that, having come down some distance from Haasrode, Mick had managed to evade the searchers and had eventually made his way to Britain, being awarded a DFM for his efforts.

Once shepherded into the Brussels jail we were lodged in cells that had tiny windows high up in the walls, far too high to reach. What sticks in the mind, though, is the system of heating pipes that ran through the cells. Clearly some communications code had long been established, for throughout the days we were held there the tapping hardly ceased as messages were passed from one regular inmate to the other.

Our next move, and a quite lengthy one, was by train, alongside ordinary, if often scowling, passengers, and our destination Dulag Luft, the Luftwaffe Interrogation Centre, at Oberursel, some miles north of Frankfurt.

Dulag Luft, Luftwaffe Interrogation Centre, Oberursel, Frankfurt

The centre was a vast place, the roofs emblazoned with the legend 'POW Camp' as a precaution against air attack, with twin barbed-wire fences, watch towers, ditches, patrolling guards, and dogs. We were kept in solitary, which wasn't very pleasant, although I suppose as run-of-the-mill Bomber Command aircrew our interrogation was relatively low key.

In my case three men came into my cell, the smallest of whom – but clearly the big I-am – proceeded to question me. I tried to waffle, at which he lost patience. Slamming a voluminous file onto the table he snapped, 'Look at that.' I opened it, and found myself viewing nothing less than a dossier of my squadron: location, personnel, aircraft types, the lot! The information was culled from every conceivable source and in such detail as to far outstrip my familiarity with it as a senior-NCO flight engineer. All I could offer was, 'You clearly know far more than I do.' At which the leader stood up and stalked out of the cell, taking his cohorts and his scrapbook with him. The other members of my crew were to report a similar experience.

There were others, though, the Germans clearly had more interest in. In particular there was an American whom we never saw but who shared the same corridor. They would ask him questions, and he would shout abuse at them at the top of his voice. We learnt, somehow, that he was one of the first Thunderbolt long-range escort pilots to be shot down. Evidently they wanted to learn all they could about the new machine and the strategy and tactics of escorting the bomber force.

I have been asked since how nervous I was during that phase of incarceration. I suppose I had expected to be rather more at ease once we were in the hands of the Luftwaffe, although the German army personnel had treated us reasonably enough. What helped me most, however, was that before getting shot down we had all become familiar with wireless and newspapers accounts of aircrew previously posted missing being declared alive and well as POWs. So I suppose I trusted to this being my case too.

It is a fact, though, that as the war went on and things got harder for the Germans, so the guards became more bitter and tended to react more violently to anything that upset them. They also reacted badly, we noticed, to specific events, nastiness that often mystified us, for it might be months before we would able to link effect to cause, the celebrated Dams raid being one such case.

We were not held long at Dulag Luft, a week or so, perhaps, but during that time I gained a new identity number. I remained 1166617 Sergeant Minnitt. Additionally, I became POW No. 1260!

Now fully assimilated as POWs, a whole group of us were moved on to a permanent prisoner of war camp, in our case to Stalag Luft One, at Barth, on the Baltic Coast. The journey started by tram to Frankfurt railway station, then by train; only not in the comfortable passenger coaches we had been allocated before but in cattle wagons into which we were packed forty to a truck.

Marching through Barth, for Stalag Luft One

Stalag Luft One itself turned out to be built on the pattern that has since become familiar from POW books and the cinema. One thing we did note, rather wryly, was that the custom-built wooden huts we were accommodated in were streets better than the canvas tents we had lived under at such RAF stations as Cardington.

Life in the camp, too, followed the pattern since made familiar to all, with goon watching and, within limits, goon baiting. As soon as the resident 'kriegies' – from *kriegsgefangener*, or prisoner of war – felt confident of us, we were made party to the escape facilities available, the forged documents, the tools, the clothing, and the various schemes already afoot.

None of my crew evinced any interest in escaping but I got together with three other lads and cooked up a scheme that aimed to get us to either Switzerland or Sweden.

Our first step was to wait for the next RAF bombing raid, for when the warnings sounded all the compound lights were switched off. We would then

Stalag Luft One, Barth

make our way through the various huts and into the toilet block nearest the fence. Our preparatory prowlings had shown us that that behind each toilet there was a flap by which the containers could be emptied from outside. Our plan, therefore, was to crawl through one of these flaps into the compound, duck under the chest-high warning wire, and having reached and cut the perimeter wires beyond, to scamper off to freedom.

On the appointed night, with bombers roaring overhead all four of us in turn pushed through a waste flap and emerged into the pitch darkness of the compound. We ducked the warning wire – pass that and the guards will shoot! – and reached the first of the main fences. Having been supplied with bolt cutters fashioned from metal bedframes we reached up for the first wire. It was taut, and parted easily enough, but with a twang that, in our tensed-up state, we felt must have been heard for miles. More so because the throbbing of aero-engines overhead was rapidly dying away. With nerves strung even more tightly than the barbed wire we clipped another strand. And were just about to clip a third when all the lights came on!

You can't credit how vulnerable we felt! Bathed in white light! Actually in what was, effectively, the death zone! And at the outer wire, clearly attempting to escape! I was fit enough in those days. But so, apparently, were the rest! By the time I'd turned about they were going like stink back the way we had come.

I arrived at the flap in a slide, one of the others reaching back to lift it for me. I thrust in head, shoulders, and thighs, expecting to feel a bullet at any instant. Only, being the last one through, there was nobody to keep the flap up off my heels. And so I was stuck there for a seeming infinity, the others pulling at my shoulders and only succeeding in trapping my feet more firmly. Finally, my lower bits came free, and we raced through the various huts, bursting into our own and throwing ourselves onto our beds, trying to control our breathing and to make a start on settling our nerves, anticipating that the doors would burst open at any moment.

But nothing happened. Where the guards had been – the dog patrols and the watch-tower sentries – heaven alone knew. But we counted ourselves well out of it. And to the best of my knowledge none of us retained the least zest for escaping after that.

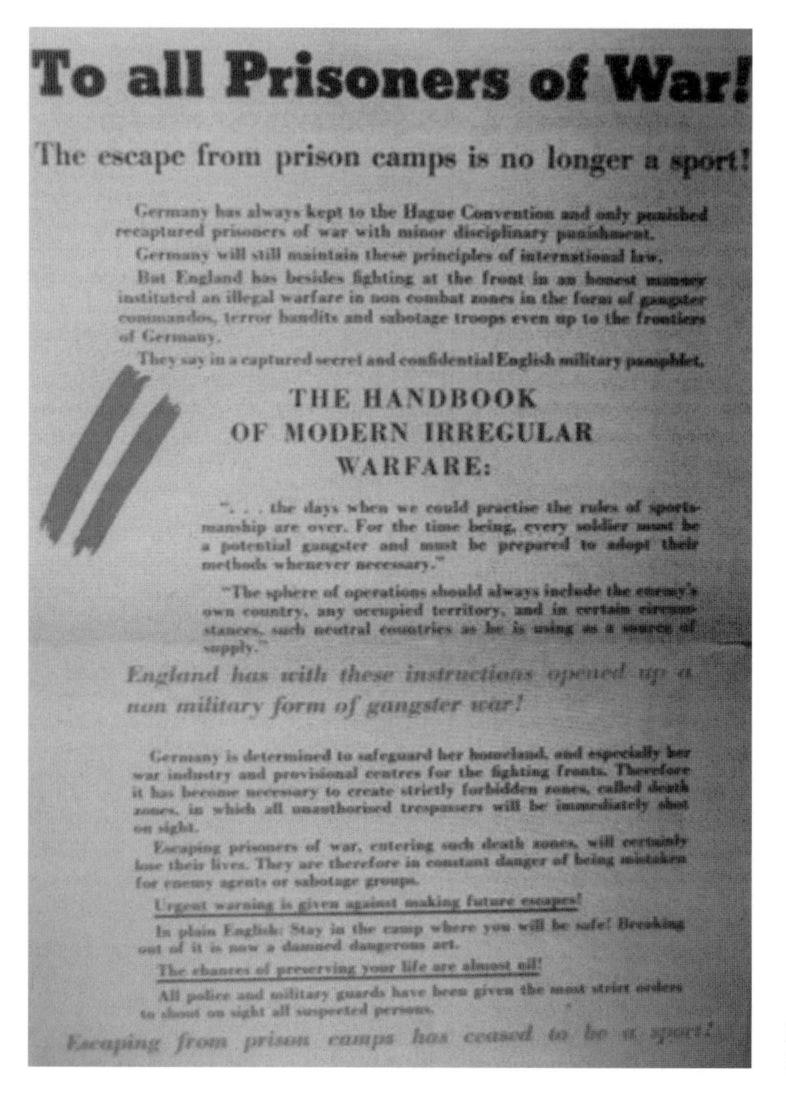

To all Prisoners of War!

The escape from prison camps is no longer a sport!

Germany has always kept to the Hague Convention and only punished recaptured prisoners of war with minor disciplinary punishment.

Germany will still maintain these principles of international law.

But England has besides fighting at the front in an honest manner instituted an illegal warfare in non combat zones in the form of gangster commandos, terror bandits and sabotage troops even up to the frontiers of Germany.

They say in a captured secret and confidential English military pamphlet,

THE HANDBOOK OF MODERN IRREGULAR WARFARE:

"... the days when we could practise the rules of sportsmanship are over. For the time being, every soldier must be a potential gangster and must be prepared to adopt their methods whenever necessary."

"The sphere of operations should always include the enemy's own country, any occupied territory, and in certain circumstances, such neutral countries as he is using as a source of supply."

England has with these instructions opened up a non military form of gangster war!

Germany is determined to safeguard her homeland, and especially her war industry and provisional centres for the fighting fronts. Therefore it has become necessary to create strictly forbidden zones, called death zones, in which all unauthorised trespassers will be immediately shot on sight.

Escaping prisoners of war, entering such death zones, will certainly lose their lives. They are therefore in constant danger of being mistaken for enemy agents or sabotage groups.

Urgent warning is given against making future escapes!

In plain English: Stay in the camp where you will be safe! Breaking out of it is now a damned dangerous act.

The chances of preserving your life are almost nil!

All police and military guards have been given the most strict orders to shoot on sight all suspected persons.

Escaping from prison camps has ceased to be a sport!

Escaping is no longer a sport …

Possibly because of that, we were rather mystified some time later when notices went up specifically warning us that escaping was no longer a joke. The mystery was solved when we learnt of the fifty escapers who had been murdered after escaping from Stalag Luft Three!

Camp life quickly took on a pattern. As we were aircrew, for whom outside working parties were not an option, life had to be lived within the wire. Every sort of sport was organized and high-standard variety shows and pantos were worked up. For me, music was important. We organized a choir, and that not only passed the time for us but provided entertainment for others.

Many people turned to study, with the books supplied by the Red Cross and St John War Organizations covering every imaginable area of relaxation and education; indeed in some camps as many as ninety subjects were on offer! Some POWs occupied themselves in producing camp newspapers, in gardening, or in knitting such things as scarves and cap comforters. Just the same, it was a pretty humdrum existence.

Along with all the other POWs I had been given a handsome notebook entitled *A Wartime Log, For British Prisoners.* It was distributed by the World's Alliance of YMCAs who – presciently – recognized that our experience would be of great significance to us in later years. A directing leaflet suggested that we might like to use the book 'as a diary; alternatively to record thoughts, jokes even, to reflect everyday life in the camp; to describe meals, or entertainments; even to write stories in ...' There were special pages set aside for any photographs we might have, or might later receive, together with adhesive corners for mounting them. Altogether, it was an extremely thoughtful initiative.

Regretfully there are few enough entries in mine, but quite a few addresses, predominantly of the Americans we were later to meet up with in Stalag Lufts Six and Four. I also began to record a reading list, and noting now that Kermode's *Mechanics of Flight* and Molloy's *Engineering Materials* are in it, it is clear that I was gleaning knowledge that would stand me in good stead after the war!

What entries do exist, however, are truly evocative. There is a sketch of our stricken Halifax, naming the crew and showing two crosses and six parachutes. Then again there is a song, *The Kriegies' Lament*, composed for a band show in February 1944, that touches poignantly upon several aspects of camp life.

Bloody wire for bloody guard, Bloody dog in bloody yard ...
Bloody tea is bloody vile, Bloody coffee makes you smile ...
Bloody sawdust in bloody bread, must have come from bloody bed, better all be bloody dead.
Bloody bridge all bloody day, learning how to bloody play ...

And an only too oft-repeated lament, 'Bloody girl friend drops me flat ... gets a Yank like bloody that ...

This theme is returned to in another entry: 'Never a mail day but comes the news, That puts a fellow in the blues, A loved one married a Yank – or worse, Back pay going in the wife's own purse.'

The arrival of the weekly Red Cross parcel was always a big event. But mail, of course, was of paramount importance to us all. And on 30 May 1943 I was at last able to write home, although by strictly-censored *Kriegsgelangenpost*. I was even able to pass on birthday wishes to family members, apologizing as I did so, 'Sorry, but presents will have to wait a while ...'

Presents from me to them, that is. But my own list of wants, as sent home, was extensive: 'Needles, cotton and wool, plimsolls, summer-type shirts, socks, toothbrushes [in the plural!], wire hairbrush, comb, nail scissors ...' At least I had the grace to interpose, 'Pause for breath' before directing Mum to contact the Red Cross who would supply her with 'coupons and gen'.

As I say, I was able to lodge my letter in late May, but official channels were slow and it was only in mid June, after a month of agonizing, that Mum received a telegram reading:

> THE NAME OF YOUR SON SGT ARTHUR POOLE MINNITT 1166617 WAS MENTIONED IN A GERMAN BROADCAST ON 14/6/43 AS A PRISONER OF WAR STOP.

And even then Air Ministry finished with the caveat:

> YOU ARE ADVISED TO TREAT THIS INFORMATION WITH RESERVE PENDING OFFICIAL CONFIRMATION STOP.

But they did assure Mum that any further news would immediately be passed on, as indeed it was.

Your son's name has been mentioned as a POW

POST OFFICE TELEGRAM

No. 1503

Prefix. 48

348 B 8.15 LONDON TELEX OHMS PRIORITY 64

IMMEDIATE MRS E MINITT 40 PATRICK RD

WEST-BRIDGFORD NOTTS

IMMEDIATE FROM AIR MINISTRY KINGSWAY PC 111

15/6/43 THE NAME OF YOUR SON SGT ARTHUR CECIL POOLE MINNITT 1166617 WAS MENTIONED IN A GERMAN BROADCAST ON 14/6/43 AS A PRISONER OF WAR STOP YOU ARE ADVISED TO TREAT THIS INFORMATION WITH RESERVE PENDING OFFICIAL CONFIRMATION STOP ANY FURTHER NEWS

Life as a POW dragged by. But in September 1943 all eight hundred of us were moved to Stalag Luft Six, situated at Heidekrug in East Prussia, near the Lithuanian border. The journey around the southern shore of the Baltic in over-crammed cattletrucks took us four days. And what a distressing trip that was, with little sanitation, no food, and virtually no water!

Heidekrug was a huge camp containing up to five thousand prisoners. These were split into four compounds, two for Commonwealth POWs with one each for Americans and Russians. We stayed there until well into 1944 during which time the guards became increasingly twitchy. Indeed, camp knowledge had it that they had shot dead one prisoner who had gone beyond the warning wire to recover a ball, even though he had raised his hands when challenged. Certainly, there came a time when they took to shooting low over our barracks. In fact, it all got very fraught. And even more so as the Red Army, long on the move westwards, came closer yet.

The outer fence and the inner 'Do not cross' fence

Then, in July 1944, we suddenly got the order to prepare to move westwards ourselves. It was back to the cattle trucks, which then offloaded us at the Baltic port of Memel (Klaipeda), in Lithuania. Here we were herded aboard a collier, the *Insterburg*, for a three-day voyage to the Swinemünde Naval Base.

Having been offloaded – and being forced to shelter from an Allied air attack on the naval base! – we were then manacled in pairs and loaded for another journey by cattle truck. Offloaded again next day, we were set to walk the four kilometres to Gross Tychow, or Tychowo, where our new camp, Stalag Four, was situated.

Unfortunately for us the local troops, both Luftwaffe and *Kriegsmarine*, had been incessantly bombed by Allied aircraft in the last few weeks and were in a foul frame of mind, forcing us to run – quite literally – the gauntlet of their rifle butts, bayonets, whips, boots, and dogs. As it happened, I was among the last unloaded from the wagons, so that, with the guards having expended much of their bile, we had a far easier passage than the leaders in 'The Run up the Road', as POWs were to dub the atrocity. Nor did things overly improve in the camp, the next six months proving to be the low point of our inside-the-wires incarceration.

This did not mean that prisoner enterprise failed to rise above conditions, not least in producing a motoring magazine named *Flywheel* with a text in model handwriting and a whole host of drawings. There was even a preview of the next year's Motor Show! Just the same, as more and more prisoners were packed into the camp so conditions deteriorated even further.

But worse was to follow. For in February 1945, with the Russians pressing ever closer, another westwards move was called for. In this instance the POWs were divided into three groups. One went by sea, another by rail, but I was part of the third group, some hundreds strong, which was forced-marched over a peripatetic route – constantly altered in order to avoid encirclement by the Russians – which was to total around six hundred miles.

It was February when we were put onto the road, in what was to be recognized as the most severe winter for many years; no accommodation was provided and food very rarely so. For my part I quickly found that raw sugar beet was relatively palatable, but after the long spells most men had spent in prison camps, the suffering was terrible, with not a few in our column dying on the way.

The fact that some of the older guards were also in a poor state was no comfort, for rifle butts, boots, bayonets, pistols, machine guns and Alsatian dogs were always in evidence. Some days we covered thirty miles, on others, rather less, and there were days when we simply stayed put. The saddest irony was that on one occasion our column was strafed by RAF aircraft, so that some POW aircrew, having survived so much, were actually killed by their comrades.

The march – a death march for far too many – eventually came to an end in May 1945, and for a short while we found ourselves interned in Stalag Two B near the Southern Baltic port of Stettin (Polish Szczecin). Shortly after this, however, we began yet another march as the guards, even more keen now to avoid being encircled by the Russians, led us directly towards the advancing British.

Having generally followed a south-westerly course through Pomerania we eventually arrived at a place called Zarrentin. That evening, having got us into the camp, the Germans called an assembly and told us that British troops would reach us within twenty-four hours. They advised us to stay where we were and not to stray. And next morning we awoke to find ourselves unguarded, the Germans having decamped overnight.

We dutifully stayed where we were for most of the morning. Then, at around midday, we heard motor bikes approaching. Motor bikes ridden by British soldiers! Then lorry-borne Tommies arrived. And our incarceration was over!

Once again we were warned about straying: stay-behind snipers were still active, it seemed. But soon enough we grew impatient and procuring horses and carts from the local area, set out ourselves. Only here was horsepower not even a trained flight engineer could control and we ignominiously finished up as the animals dictated, each beast inexorably circling back to its own village.

Eventually, however, we found ourselves homeward bound. First we were taken in Dakotas across Germany and into Holland, where we discovered that the starving Dutch were receiving food drops from Halifax and Lancaster bombers. We then found that the RAF had further arranged that some machines would land after dropping their supplies and pick up a dozen or so ex-POWs: no straps or seats, of course, but who worried! What we found wondrous, cynical kriegies that we were, was that the RAF could organize anything so successfully. I was even able to send off a gladsome telegram: 'HALLO MA HOME VERY SHORTLY EXPECT ME WHEN YOU SEE ME ARTHUR'.

In fact, I was landed at Woodley, near Reading, on 12 May 1945, two years and a month since I had taken off from Linton on that fateful eighth op.

POST OFFICE
TELEGRAM

Prefix. Time handed in. Office of Origin and Service Instructions. Words.

42

42 6.30 PM SCE PTY 20

MRS MINNITT 40 PATRICK ROAD WEST BRIDGFORD
NOTTINGHAM =

HELLO MA HOME VERY SHORTLY EXPECT ME WHEN YOU
SEE ME ARTUR +

Expect me when you see me

I was eventually demobbed from the RAF on 13 June 1946 and to earn my crust in civvy street, returned to my job at the *Nottingham Evening Post*. I couldn't settle though. Then, I worked for two years organizing flights for British European Airways, at Northolt. By 1947, however, I had met and married Mary, and as she had a good job as a shorthand typist in Nottingham, I became a fitter with Field Aviation Services Ltd, at Tollerton Aerodrome, much closer to my West Bridgford home and, at five pounds a week, paying far better than BEA. It proved to be an altogether good move, for the work furnished me with so much experience that in 1954 I was able to become an aircraft inspector at Rolls-Royce's Hucknall testing centre, starting at six pounds a week.

My entry into jet-engine testing was well timed, with many problems to be resolved – not least blade shedding – which meant a lot of trouble-shooting call-outs.

On the other hand this new employment was to bring my closest ever near-death experience – the night descent by parachute into Haasrode not excepted!

In 1958 Hucknall was heavily engaged with the development of the Conway engine using the prototype Vulcan bomber, VX770, as a test bed. When a chance came for me to be aboard for a test programme to be followed by an appearance at nearby Syerston's At-Home Day air show, I jumped at it; it was, after all a Saturday, a day when my boss never came to the works. The captain, New Zealander Keith Sturt, a Rolls-Royce test pilot, welcomed my interest. However, just as I was about to secure the hatch I found myself looking down into the face, and the summoning finger, of my boss.

Two hours later, therefore, I watched glumly as, its test programme completed, the stately Vulcan flashed by on a low-level pass down the runway at Hucknall before clearing to do the planned programme at Syerston, first a fast and then a slow run. Only during its fast run its right wing began to disintegrate and seconds later it rolled into the ground, taking the airfield-control van and its occupants with it. One of the four airmen in the caravan, though badly injured, survived. But he was the only one.

Its starboard wing began to disintegrate ...

Certainly, the disaster proved that my good fortune had not deserted me, that Fate had relented after Haasrode! Even so, according to Menander, Whom the gods love dies young. I can only conclude, therefore, on reflecting upon all the years of happiness I have enjoyed, that the gods cannot be best pleased with me.

Arthur Minnitt, 2011

Aircraft types and enemy defences

The performance figures given can only be a rough guide. Indeed, flying any one of a line-up of a given aircraft type will show all such data to be merely representative. Regarding machine-gun armament, British aircraft invariably employed Browning, Lewis, or Vickers 0.303 inch (7.7 mm) calibre guns.

Allied machines

Airspeed Oxford

The 1937 twin-engined, wooden-framed, plywood-skinned Airspeed Oxford was a general-purpose trainer that had a basic crew of three but could accommodate other trainee-aircrew depending upon the role. Typically powered by two 375 horsepower Armstrong Siddeley Cheetah Ten radial engines it had a maximum speed of 188 mph (163 knots), a cruising speed of 163 mph (142 knots), a ceiling of 19,000 feet and a range of 700 miles.

Armstrong Whitworth Atlas

This 1931 dedicated army co-operation machine was both rugged and reliable. The twin-seat, dual-control version entered RAF service in 1931 and was the standard advanced trainer until 1935 when it was replaced by the Hawker Hart. Powered by a 450 horsepower Armstrong Siddeley Jaguar 4C engine, it had a maximum speed of 143 mph (124 knots), a range of 480 miles and a ceiling of 16,800 feet.

Armstrong Whitworth Whitley

This 1936 five-crewed, twin-engined bomber was withdrawn from Bomber Command operations in April 1942 but served on in the training, maritime, paratrooping, clandestine-operations, and glider-tug roles. Typically, two 1,145 horsepower Rolls-Royce Merlin in-line engines were fitted but performance figures – many subject to wartime propaganda – vary widely. Mid road would be a cruising speed of 180 mph (156 knots) with a ceiling of 26,000 feet.

Typical armament was a single machine gun in the nose, and four in a tail turret. The bomb load was 7,000 pounds over a range of 1,500 miles.

Avro Anson

The 1935 Avro Anson began life in the maritime reconnaissance role and remained in RAF service until 1968, serving as general-purpose trainer and communications aircraft.

Two 350 horsepower Armstrong Siddeley Cheetah Nine radial engines gave it a cruising speed of 158 mph (138 knots), a ceiling of 19,000 feet and a range of 800 miles. Its design-role armament was two machine guns; a fixed, forward-firing Vickers, and a single Lewis in a dorsal turret. The nose had a bomb-aimer's station and 360 pounds of bombs could be carried.

Avro Lancaster

The seven-crewed Lancaster, developed from the twin-engined Manchester, first flew in January 1941 and was designed for ease of production and subsequent servicing, 7,737 being built by 1946. Powered by four 1,640 horsepower Rolls-Royce Merlin Mk 24 in-line engines, its maximum speed was 280 mph (243 knots). It cruised at 210 mph (182 knots) or, on three engines, at 140 mph (122 knots), operating up to 22,000 feet over a range of 2,500 miles. Armament was eight machine guns; four in the tail, and two each in nose and dorsal turrets. The standard bomb load was 14,000 pounds or, if modified, one 22,000 pounder – in a comparison often made the Flying Fortress's standard load was 6,000 pounds.

Avro Manchester

The 1936 spec Manchester was withdrawn from operations in June 1942 after its twin Rolls-Royce 1,760 horsepower Vulture engines proved unsatisfactory. While in service it had a maximum speed of 265 mph (230 knots), a range of 1,630 miles and a ceiling of 19,200 feet. It had three power-operated turrets with two machine guns in the nose and dorsal turrets and four in the tail. Its maximum bomb load was 10,350 pounds.

Avro Shackleton

The typically ten-crewed 1949 Avro Shackleton used many of the Lancaster's strengths but was constantly updated, notably with the tricycle undercarriaged 1955 Mark 3. In 1971 the Comet-derived Nimrod assumed the maritime task, the Shackleton continuing in the search-and-rescue role until 1972 and serving as an early-warning platform until 1991 when the Boeing E3D Sentry took over.

Shackletons were typically powered by four 2,455 horsepower Rolls-Royce Griffon Mk 57A in-line piston engines which gave a maximum speed of 300 mph (261 knots) and a cruise of 180–240 mph (156–209 knots) depending upon the task in hand. They had a ceiling of 19,000 feet, a range of 3,500 miles and an endurance of nearly fifteen hours. Typical armament was two 20 mm (0.79 inch) calibre cannon in the nose, and two machine guns at the tail, with an ordnance load of 10,000 pounds of bombs or depth charges.

Avro Vulcan

This 1952 five-crewed, long-range (strategic), delta-winged medium bomber was typically powered by four Bristol Siddeley Olympus engines. Average performance figures give a maximum speed of 0.92 M (625 mph), a ceiling of 56,000 feet and a range of 4,600 miles. The 1958 accident at Syerston was attributed to the cleared speed having been exceeded and a rolling pull-up overstressing the wing.

Avro York
A 1942-designed four-engined, long-range transport manned by five crew and carrying up to twenty-four passengers.

Boeing B-17 Flying Fortress
The perceived role of the 1935 B-17 was that of a long-range outpost capable of defending America beyond the range of its shore defences, hence 'Flying Fortress'. The enormous tail fin ensured that it remained a stable bombing platform up to its 40,000 foot ceiling, while its formidable defensive armament and its capacity for absorbing battle damage, was held to make up for its relatively small bomb load.

The upgraded B-17G version relied for its defence on up to thirteen 0.5 inch (12.7 mm), heavy-calibre Browning machine guns, this firepower being enhanced by the formation strategies employed. With so many guns to man, the standard crew complement was ten. This comprised pilot, co-pilot, navigator, bombardier, flight engineer, and radio operator. In combat the flight engineer would man the top turret, and the wireless operator the dorsal turret. The remaining four crew were dedicated gunners to man the ball-turret, the left and right waist positions, and the tail turret.

The B-17 was typically powered by four 1,200 horsepower Wright Cyclone R-1820-65 nine-cylinder air-cooled engines which, with Hamilton three-bladed, constant-speed, fully-feathering propellers, gave it a cruising speed of 225 mph (196 knots). It had a normal range of 3,000 miles and a standard bomb load of 6,000 pounds, although this could be increased to 12,800 pounds, and over a very short range, to 20,800 pounds. For a comparison often made, the Lancaster's standard bomb load was 14,000 pounds; if modified, however, the Lancaster could carry a 22,000-pound bomb.

B-24 Consolidated Liberator
This long-range heavy bomber and maritime reconnaissance machine was manned by eight to ten crew depending upon the role. Typically powered by four 1,200 horsepower Pratt & Whitney Twin Wasp engines the Liberator had a cruising speed of 220 mph (191 knots), a ceiling of 36,000 feet and a range of 2,500 miles. It was armed with up to fourteen 0.5 inch (12.7 mm) calibre machine guns in four turrets and two waist positions and it could carry 8,000 pounds of bombs.

Bristol Beaufighter
The two-seater Beaufighter was initially employed as an AI-equipped night-fighter. It also served Coastal Command as a long-range strike fighter and torpedo carrier.

Typically, two 1,770 horsepower Bristol Hercules radial engines gave a maximum speed of 303 mph (263 knots), a cruising speed of 249 mph (216 knots), a time to 5,000 feet of 3.5 minutes, and a ceiling of 15,000 feet. Range was 1,470 miles.

A common armament fit was four forward-firing, nose-mounted 20 mm (0.79 inch) calibre Hispano cannon and six forward-firing, wing-mounted Browning machine guns supplemented by a single Vickers in the rear. Each cannon gave a rate of fire of 550 shells a minute, and each machine gun 1,100 rounds a minute.

Either a 2,127-pound torpedo could be carried or a 1,605-pounder, or alternatively, eight 90-pound rockets together with two 250-pound bombs.

Bristol Beaufort

The four-crewed, twin-engined Beaufort was Coastal Command's standard torpedo bomber from 1940 to 1943. Typically powered by two 1,130 horsepower Bristol Taurus engines, it had a maximum speed of 265 mph (230 knots), cruised at 200 mph (174 knots), had six hours' endurance and a range of up to 1,600 miles. Typically armed with a machine gun in the nose and another in the dorsal turret, it carried 1,500 pounds of bombs or a 1,605-pound, 18-inch torpedo.

Bristol Blenheim

In 1935 the prototype Blenheim proved faster than any fighter. By 1939, however, it was outclassed by most German types but, although swiftly withdrawn from bombing operations, it served on as a radar-equipped night-fighter, and later, as an advanced crew trainer.

Driven by two 905 horsepower Bristol Mercury Fifteen radial engines, a representative Blenheim had a ceiling of 27,000 feet, a cruising speed of 198 mph (172 knots) and a range of 1,460 miles.

Armed with two machine guns in a power-operated dorsal turret, with two remotely-controlled guns below the nose, and a fifth in the port wing, it could also carry 1,300 pounds of bombs.

Consolidated Commodore

This 1931 commercial transport flying boat was the progenitor of the celebrated Catalina. Powered by two Pratt & Whitney Hornet 575 horsepower engines, it had a range of 1,180 miles, a ceiling of 16,100 feet, and a maximum speed of 139 mph (121 knots). It could carry up to 32 passengers with three crew and Pan American Airways primarily used it on the 9,000-mile route from Miami to Buenos Aires

De Havilland Comet

The 1949 Comet was the world's first commercial jet airliner. Metal-fatigue failures led to the type being redesigned, after which it flew for many years, notably as the maritime Nimrod.

De Havilland Dominie (civilian Rapide)
The long-lifed, twin-engined, biplane light transport was developed during the 1930s and used by the RAF as an eight- to ten-seater communications machine, and as a five- to six-seater navigation and radio trainer. Rapides were still flying in 2012.

De Havilland Mosquito
The private-venture, two-crewed de Havilland Mosquito, conceived in 1938 as a fast, high-flying bomber, first flew in November 1940. The wooden construction saved on scarce alloys, the 1,620 horsepower Rolls-Royce Merlin 25 in-line engines giving a cruising speed of 325 mph (283 knots), a ceiling of 33,000 feet and a range of 1,650 miles.

It filled many roles: photo-reconnaissance (often unarmed), bomber, intruder, fighter-bomber, night-fighter, and communications-cum-freighter. Armed versions typically carried four 20 mm (0.79 inch) calibre cannon and four machine guns in the nose; a typical bomb load was 2,000 pounds.

De Havilland DH82A Tiger Moth
The 1934 tandem two-seater biplane de Havilland trainer was used at over eighty wartime elementary flying training schools. A 130 horsepower de Havilland Gipsy Major in-line engine gave it a cruising speed of 93 mph (80 knots), a ceiling of 13,000 feet and a range of 300 miles. To maintain the centre of gravity a solo pilot sat in the rear seat. Although demanding to fly accurately, and invariably giving a freezing-cold ride, the much revered Tiger Moth had no vices.

Douglas Boston, or Havoc
The American A-20 – the RAF's Boston, or Havoc, and its first tricycle-undercarriaged operational aircraft – was variously employed as medium bomber, fighter-bomber, night-fighter and night intruder. The crew comprised pilot, navigator, and gunner. Twin 1,600 horsepower Wright Cyclone engines gave a top speed of 304 mph (264 knots), a cruise of 250 mph (217 knots), a ceiling of 24,250 feet and a range of 1,020 miles.

Representative armament was four fixed machine guns in the nose with another two pairs in the dorsal and ventral positions; two 1,000-pound bombs could be carried.

Douglas Dakota (DC-3)
The 1935 Douglas DC-3 Dakota, basically an airliner manned by a crew of three and carrying twenty-one passengers, was still flying commercially in 2012; its roles, however, have been infinite.

Two 1,000 horsepower Wright Cyclone radial engines gave a cruising speed of 194 mph (169 knots) and a ceiling of 21,900 feet; the stalling speed was 67 mph (58 knots) and the range 2,125 miles.

Fairey Battle

The 1936 single-engined light bomber was swiftly withdrawn from first-line service but served on as a trainer and target tug. Accommodating a pilot, bomb aimer/observer, and a wireless operator/air gunner, and powered by a 1,030 horsepower Rolls-Royce Merlin Mk 1 in-line engine, it cruised at 210 mph (182 knots), had a ceiling of 25,000 feet and a range of 1,000 miles. It carried a Vickers machine gun in a rear-cockpit mounting, and another in the starboard wing, its bomb load being 1,000 pounds.

Fairey Seal

A 1930 biplane, basically a naval type, but used by the RAF as a target tug. An Armstrong Siddeley Panther 605 horsepower radial engine gave it a maximum speed of 145 mph, 600 miles range, and a ceiling of 22,145 feet. It carried one fixed, forward-firing Vickers, a rear-facing Lewis, and 500 pounds of bombs. It was superseded by the Swordfish

Handley Page Halifax

The 1940 seven-crewed, twin-finned Halifax heavy bomber found favour with its versatility, for besides its design role it was employed in both transport and maritime duties, also as an ambulance, a glider tug, and as a clandestine and paratroop-delivery vehicle.

Typically, four 1,615 horsepower Bristol Hercules Sixteen radial engines gave it a cruising speed of 215 mph (187 knots) and a ceiling of 24,000 feet. It had a range of 1,030 miles and could carry 13,000 pounds of bombs. It mounted nine machine guns, one in the nose, and four each in dorsal and tail turrets.

An unfortunate characteristic of early Halifaxes was that fully-laden aircraft could enter an inverted, and effectively irrecoverable spin. A retrospective modification of the tailfin leading-edge shape from triangular to quadrilateral helped overcome this stability defect.

Handley Page Hampden

After the outbreak of war the 1936 four-crewed Hampden was swiftly removed from bomber operations and employed in torpedo-dropping, minelaying, night operations, and leaflet dropping. Pilots found it pleasant to handle, although the crew, isolated from one another in flight, found their positions cramped.

Handley Page Hastings

This 1946 four-engined transport was powered by four Bristol Hercules radial engines, which gave it a maximum speed of 343 mph (298 knots), a range of 2,850 miles, and a ceiling of 26,700 feet. No. 202 Squadron, Coastal Command, featured within, operated the weather-reconnaissance version.

Handley Page Heyford

The 1933 twin-engined, basically four-crewed Heyford was a biplane-bomber of all-metal framed construction whose speedy 143 mph (124 knots) earned it the appellation, 'Express'. Withdrawn from first-line service in 1939 the type still gave good value as a crew trainer until 1941, being stable, and pleasant to fly.

Powered by two 575 horsepower, Rolls-Royce Kestrel Mk 3 engines, the Heyford had a ceiling of 21,000 feet. For defensive armament it carried three Lewis machine guns mounted respectively in dorsal, ventral (belly dustbin), and nose positions. Its full bomb load was 3,500 pounds and with half that load it had an operational striking range of 920 miles, or as Handley Page 'spin' preferred, it 'carried a very large load of bombs for 2,000 miles'.

Hawker Hart

From 1930 to 1935 this was the RAF's standard light bomber. With two crew and powered by a Rolls-Royce 525 horsepower Kestrel it had a maximum speed of 184 mph (160 knots), a range of 470 miles and a ceiling of 21,320 feet. Armed with two machine guns, a Vickers forward and a Lewis aft, and carrying 500 pounds of bombs, it was superseded by the Hind.

Hawker Hind

The Hawker Hind biplane day bomber was a refined version of the Hart, its fully-supercharged, 640-horsepower Rolls-Royce Kestrel engine giving it a maximum speed of 186 mph (162 knots). It had a range of 430 miles, a ceiling of 26,400 feet, could carry 500 pounds of bombs, and was armed with two machine guns; a Lewis to the rear and a forward-facing Vickers.

Lockheed Hudson

The 1938 twin-engined, twin-finned, five-crewed Lockheed Hudson was the military version of the Lockheed 14 Super-Electra airliner. The RAF intended it as a navigational trainer, but it was pressed into the maritime-reconnaissance and anti-submarine roles, carrying an air-droppable lifeboat while on air-sea rescue duties. It was also used as a bomber, and as a clandestine delivery vehicle for supplies and agents. Finally, once superseded as a first-line aircraft, it served as both trainer and transport.

Typically, two 1,100-horsepower Wright Cyclone engines gave it a cruise of 170 mph (148 knots), an endurance of six hours, a range of 2,160 miles, and a ceiling of 22,000 feet. Its normal armament was five machine guns, two below the nose, a pair in the rear turret, and a moveable dorsal gun, but two beam (waist) guns could also be mounted. It carried 900 pounds of bombs.

Percival Proctor

A 1939 single-engined, three- to four-seater monoplane used for communications and radio training.

Short Stirling

With its cockpit rearing a lofty 22 feet 9 inches above the tarmac the Stirling was the first of the RAF's heavy bombers. Shorts re-used their successful

Sunderland-wing profile but Ministry requirements limited the span to 100 feet (not, as widely stated, to fit into RAF hangars, which were 125 feet wide). Such modifications detracted from the design performance to give the Stirling a ceiling of only 17,000 feet.

It was very manoeuvrable, however, and powered by four 1,650 horsepower Bristol Hercules Sixteen radial engines, had a maximum speed of 270 mph (235 knots), a cruise of 200 mph (174 knots), and a range of up to 2,000 miles dependent upon bomb load, itself a maximum of 14,000 pounds. It had eight machine guns; four in a tail turret, and two each in nose and dorsal turrets.

Though popular with its seven- to eight-man crews its bomb bay could not be adapted as bigger bombs were developed and it ceased bomber operations in September 1941. It was then very successfully employed in the glider-tug, transport, and clandestine-operations roles. There was also a transport variant.

Short Sunderland
A 13-crew, long-range general reconnaissance and anti-submarine patrol flying boat. Four 1,200 Pratt & Whitney Twin Wasp engines gave a maximum speed of 213 mph (185 knots) and a ceiling of 17,900 feet; endurance was 13.5 hours and range, 2,980 miles. Crews loved its luxury.

Supermarine Spitfire
The 1936 Spitfire metamorphosed through over a score of variant Marks. Representative performance figures for early versions with the 1,030 horsepower Rolls-Royce Merlin Mark Two in-line engine, driving a two-bladed, wooden, fixed-pitch propeller, give a maximum speed of 350 mph (304 knots), a cruising speed of 265 mph (230 knots) and a ceiling of 30,500 feet. Range was 630 miles and armament eight wing-mounted machine guns.

The later 2,050 horsepower, supercharged Griffon engine, gave a maximum speed of 448 mph (389 knots), time to 20,000 feet of seven minutes, ceiling of 44,500 feet, and range, with an external tank, of 850 miles. A regular armament fit of two 20 mm (0.79 inch) cannon and four machine guns was upgraded when the latter were replaced by two guns of 0.5 inch (12.7 mm) calibre.

Vickers Valentia
The 1934 Valentia was basically a two-crew biplane troop carrier. Two 650 horsepower Bristol Pegasus radial engines gave it a maximum speed of 130 mph (113 knots), a cruise of 117 mph (102 knots) and a ceiling of 16,250 feet. Range was 800 miles. It could carry 2,200 pounds of bombs on underwing racks.

Vickers Virginia
From 1924 to 1937 the four-crewed, biplane Virginia was the RAF's main heavy night-bomber. Its two 570 horsepower Napier Lion Five engines gave it a maximum speed of 108 mph (94 knots) and a ceiling of 15,530 feet; range was

985 miles. It was armed with three machine guns, one Lewis in the nose and twin Lewis guns in the tail. Its bomb load was 3,000 pounds.

Vickers Wellington

In designing the 1937 Wellington, the celebrated Barnes Wallis used repeated junctions of Meccano-like alloy channels to form a cocoon of great strength. This geodetic structure (see Glossary) was then covered with doped fabric. The operational crew of four comprised a pilot, a navigator/bomb aimer, a wireless operator/air gunner, and a rear gunner.

The German defences soon took the Wellington's measure, after which it was switched to night bombing. Wellingtons, however, were also employed in the maritime role.

A typical power fit was two 1,500 horsepower Bristol Hercules Eleven radial engines, which gave a ceiling of 19,000 feet and a maximum speed of 235 mph (204 knots).

Representative cruising speeds vary with source, ranging from 232 mph (202 knots) to 166 mph (144 knots). A former-Wellington pilot suggested 173 mph (150 knots), with a normal bombing altitude of 12,000 feet.

The armament comprised eight machine guns; four in the tail turret, two in the beam, and two in the nose. The bomb load was 4,500 pounds.

Westland Wallace

The Wallace was a 1931 development of the 1927 Westland Wapiti biplane bomber used by the Auxiliary Air Force as a general-purpose machine. It was metal structured and fabric covered, with an enclosed canopy for pilot and gunner. A 680 horsepower Bristol Pegasus 4 engine gave it a cruising speed of 135 mph (117 knots), a maximum speed of 158 mph (137 knots), a range of 470 miles, and a ceiling of 24,100 feet. Armament comprised two machine guns, a fixed Vickers forward, and a swivel-mounted Lewis aft. The bomb load was 580 pounds. An especially modified Wallace was one of the two Westland aircraft that overflew Mount Everest on 3 April 1933.

Enemy machines

Focke-Wulf Fw190

This 1941 fighter evolved through forty variants but is typified by a maximum speed of 408 mph (355 knots), a time to 29,000 feet of twenty minutes, a ceiling of 37,000 feet, a range of 500 miles, and a combat endurance of one hour. Many carried four 7.92 mm (0.31 inch) calibre machine guns and two 20 mm (0.79 inch) calibre cannon; later versions employed 30 mm (1.18 inch) cannon and a wide range of underslung rockets. A comparison flight with a relatively early mark of Spitfire showed the FW190 to be superior in all respects except for turning capability.

Junkers Ju88
This 1936 four-crewed bomber was eminently successful in many roles, a typical fit of two 1,400 horsepower Junkers 211J liquid-cooled inverted V12 engines giving it a maximum speed of 295 mph (256 knots) and a ceiling of 26,900 feet.

Representative armament was three forward-firing 7.9 mm (0.31 inch) calibre machine guns and a 20 mm (0.79 inch) cannon, together with two 7.9 mm machine guns in the dorsal and ventral turrets. The bomb load was four 550-kg bombs.

Junkers Ju188
This five-crewed, high performance, medium-range bomber was a development of the Ju88. Powered by two BMW or Junkers Jumo engines giving some 1,776 horsepower, early versions had a maximum speed of 325 mph (282 knots), a range of 1,360 miles, and a ceiling of 33,000 feet. As armament it had a single 20 mm (0.79 inch) calibre cannon and three, variously mounted 13 mm (0.51 inch) calibre machine guns. Its bomb load was 6,612 pounds.

Messerschmitt Bf109
The 1935-designed, much modified Messerschmitt Bf109 was typically powered by a 1,475 Daimler-Benz twelve-cylinder, liquid-cooled engine, which gave it a maximum speed of 386 mph (335 knots), an initial rate of climb of 3,346 feet a minute, a ceiling of 41,000 feet and an endurance of about an hour. It had a range of 620 miles and commonly carried two 7.9 mm (0.31 inch) machine guns and a 20 mm (0.79 inch) cannon; later, a 30 mm (1.18 inch) cannon.

Trials found the Spitfire and the Bf109 to be evenly matched between 12,000 and 17,000 feet with the Bf109 performing better above 20,000 feet.

Messerschmitt Me262
This single-seater twin-jet fighter was powered by two Junkers Jumo 0004B engines, each giving 1,984 pounds thrust to produce a maximum speed of 540 mph (470 knots), a rate of climb of 4,000 feet a minute, a ceiling of 37,730 feet and a range of 650 miles. Its standard armament fit was four 30 mm (1.18 inch) calibre cannons but later versions carried rockets.

V-1 (*Vergeltungswaffe*) Flying Bomb [popularly Doodlebug, or Buzz-bomb]
The German *Fern Ziel Geraet*, (effectively: Long-range Aiming Apparatus), their *Vergeltungswaffe 1*, (Reprisal Weapon Number One), was a pilotless flying bomb that carried a ton of amatol high-explosive. It might be politic to emphasize that the V-1 – nowadays so-often termed 'V-1 *rocket*' – was a pulse-jet aircraft.

First tested in December 1941, the main assault on Britain and Belgium began in June 1944 and lasted eighty days. Of 10,000 V-1s launched against England, 7,000 impacted on the mainland.

The V-1 was propelled up a railed launching ramp by volatile hydrogen peroxide, and then accelerated to 410 mph (356 knots) by an Argus AS14 pulse-jet engine developing 660 pounds of static thrust. This engine was provided with 750 gallons of petrol, adequate for the 150-mile range. Some 825 V-1s, however, were carried beneath Heinkel One-Eleven bombers and air-launched.

In flight, an auto-pilot held the heading and height, while a propeller-driven timer decided the range. At the pre-determined time, a linkage would set the elevator to dive. The abrupt nose-down impetus had the effect of cutting the engine, so leading to the cessation of sound, which warned the initiated that an explosion was imminent.

V-2 *Vergeltungswaffe* 2 (Reprisal Weapon) A-4 ground-to-ground rocket
Essentially, fuelled with water and alcohol activated by liquid oxygen, the rocket carried a 1,000 kg (2,000 pound) warhead up to 200 miles but had a circle of error of 11 miles.

V-3 *Vergeltungswaffe* 3 (Reprisal Weapon)
The barrel of this 150 mm (5.9 inch) calibre super-cannon was 150 metres long and rocket-boosted along its length to give the 150 kg shell greater impetus and a range of 550 miles. The guns, intended for bombarding London, were constructed in caves in the Pas de Calais but were bombed before completion.

Enemy defences

Anti-aircraft guns

Germany's main anti-aircraft weapon was the 88 mm (3.5 inch) calibre flak cannon which, even in the early years, could effectively fire 15 high-explosive shells a minute to a height of 26,000 feet: 2,000 feet above the average bomber's ceiling. This was soon raised to 37,000 feet at a firing rate of twenty rounds a minute. Early shells produced shrapnel, but later, incendiary pellets were sprayed beyond the shrapnel burst.

15,000 flak guns formed successive ten-mile-wide defensive belts across Holland and Germany, the guns being integrated with a control system whose master searchlight would lead up to 30 others to cone any bomber illuminated.

The heavier calibre 128 mm (5 inch) guns, capable of firing ten rounds a minute to 35,000 feet, were characteristically sited in permanent flak towers in Germany's main centres.

Searchlights

In 1941 acoustically-directed German searchlights were found to be grouped in bands ten to twenty miles deep and capable of illuminating aircraft flying at some 5,000 feet. By 1943 many searchlights could reach well over 18,000 feet. It was held that an aircraft coned for 20 seconds was at maximum risk.

Glossary

Ab initio: from the beginning. This referred to aspiring flyers who had passed aptitude selection but were yet to be tested for suitability in the air.

Ack-ack: see **Flak**.

Aircrew: on 19 January 1939, airmen aircrew (observers and gunners) were effectively afforded the status of sergeants, although the situation was not regularized until early 1940 when heavy bombers appeared. World War Two aircrew categories comprised: pilot; navigator (observer, pre 1942); wireless operator/air gunner; air gunner; flight engineer (post 1941); bomb aimer (post 1942); air signaller (post 1943). There was also the observer radio (radar) of 1941, the navigator/wireless operator category, and similar combinations involving navigators.

Aircrew Europe Star: a well-regarded award for air operations carried out over Europe from Britain between 3 September 1939 and 5 June 1944 inclusively. The qualifying time was two months during that period, meaning that many aircrew operating after D-Day did not receive the award. Although they received the France and Germany Star, this did not reflect their aircrew status.

Air Efficiency Award (AE): a medal recognizing 'Ten years exemplary service in the auxiliary and volunteer air forces of the United Kingdom and Commonwealth'. Holders are entitled to the postnominal AE.

Arriving, arrival chit: when reporting on posting, 'arriving' personnel would check in, on signature, at every section on the station relevant to them (clothing stores, accounts) so that they were known to be on strength for issues and services. Similarly, personnel would 'clear' with their 'clearance chits' on being posted away.

Astrodome: a perspex hemisphere set on the top of the fuselage, designed for taking sextant readings, but also used as a viewing station and, often, as an emergency hatch.

ASV (Air to Surface Vessel): a map-presentation radar, similar to H2S, designed for maritime use.

ATS (Auxiliary Territorial Service): the women's army; from 1949 the WRAC (Women's Royal Army Corps).

Biggles: fictitious World War One single-seater scout/fighter pilot. Although his creator, W. E. Johns, did not fly single-seaters during that conflict the early books provide fine atmospheric source material for the period.

Blighty: home, the United Kingdom, derived from Hindustani.

Black (putting up a): gaining a discrediting – black – mark, normally for a minor infringement.

Brown jobs (alternatively Pongoes): army personnel, to the RAF and the Fish-heads (aka Royal Navy). Just as the RAF are Blue jobs or Crabs.

BOAC: the British Overseas Airways Corporation, the state's long-haul airline until 1974, when it became British Airways.

Bombs: in general, these become armed only when a time-delay mechanism has operated.

Bullseye: a sortie designed to simulate an operation. It might involve photographing a UK target or approaching an enemy coast as a diversion.

Carnaby: an emergency airstrip, see Woodbridge.

Chiefy: familiar form of address for flight sergeant.

Circuits: a 'circuit' – circuits and landings – involves taking off into wind, turning downwind parallel to the runway, flying past the airfield, then turning back, touching down, and rolling to a stop before clearing the runway. A 'roller' (circuits and bumps), on the other hand, requires the pilot to touch down but, without coming to a halt, to put on full power, reconfigure the aircraft for flight, and take off again.

Civil Air Guard: a government scheme, initiated on 23 July 1938, to provide a reserve of civil pilots, men and women, by subsidizing flying training.

Cook's tour: flights laid on after VE Day, often to show non-aircrew personnel the former target areas. Derived from the 1841 travel firm, Thomas Cook, of Melbourne, Derbyshire.

Corkscrew: an evasion manoeuvre that involved steep diving and climbing turns in alternate directions.

Crossbow: an anti-V-weapon sortie (V-1 and V-2).

Crown: flight sergeants displayed a brass crown above their sergeant's stripes.

Cucumber: sea-mining sortie.

D-Day: 6 June 1944. The invasion of Europe in the Cherbourg-Peninsula area.

Dicey: dangerous.

Doodlebug: (see ***V-1***) **Popular name for the V-1 pulse-jet flying bomb. (***Not* a rocket.)

Dorsal: as with a turret, on the back, or the upper surface of the fuselage. (Ventral, the belly.)

Dreadnoughts: the 1906 HMS *Dreadnought* revolutionized battleship design by mounting nothing but heavy 12 inch calibre guns and being powered by steam turbines that gave a speed of 21 knots (24 mph). She provoked an international naval arms race, the name passing to all such battleships.

EFTS (Elementary Flying Training School): basic flying was taught, but the unit could also be used as a Grading School, where aspirant pilots were allowed fifteen hours' flying during which their suitability for further training would be assessed.

Empire, or Commonwealth, Air Training Scheme: set up in 1939 to take advantage of the favourable flying conditions in various Commonwealth countries: discontinued in late 1944.

Expedite: without delay. Used as a procedural word by air traffic control to order an aircraft to commence take-off immediately, alternatively, to immediately clear the runway.

Expeditionary Venture (Norway): British forces entered Norway on 9 April 1940 but despite some success in the Narvik area were evacuated on 9 June in the face of German air superiority and a greater concern for operations in Belgium and France.

Feather: to electrically or hydraulically turn the blades of a propeller edge-on to the airflow to cut down the drag: as with an oar in rowing. The propeller of a failed engine left blade-on to the airflow, and therefore said to be 'windmilling', creates an inordinate amount of drag.

FIDO (Fog, Investigation and Dispersal Operation): a poor-visibility landing aid in which burning petrol was used to locally heat the air along the runway to temporarily disperse the fog. It took twenty minutes to become effective.

Flak: enemy anti-aircraft gunfire, from *flugabwehrkanone* (aircraft defence cannon). The Allied equivalent was ack-ack, after the then-current phonetic for AA (anti-aircraft). The 'modern' term anti-aircraft-artillery (AAA) was, in fact, contemporary to the period, though rarely used.

Forty Millimetre Mercury Test: a medical endurance test, introduced by researcher Martin William Flack in 1920 and highly rated by aviation medics. It required the candidate to sustain a 40 mm column of mercury in a U-shaped manometer for as long as possible with a single expiration. Pulse-reading variations showed the patient's response to the stress of the effort and to discomfort (breathlessness) generally.

Gardening: codeword for mine-laying operations.

Gazetted: *The London Gazette (Published by Authority)* promulgates awards.

Gee (Ground Electronic Equipment): a radar aid by which master and slave ground-station signals were plotted on a lattice chart to give a very accurate fix. Gee's range was 350 to 400 miles.

Gen: information, genuine, or pukka; as opposed to duff, or inaccurate

Geodetic: the structure developed by aircraft designer Sir Barnes Wallis and employed in the Wellington bomber. Essentially, it comprised triangular grids made up of aluminium strips to form a mutually-supporting shell of great strength. More properly, the component parts formed 'parts of a circle' – that is, geodetic, alternatively geodesic – curves on the structure, each element taking the shortest line across the curved surface.

Gharri (Gharry): Indian horse-drawn cart, hence lorry, or transport.

Gilbert and Sullivan: in their operetta *The Pirates of Penzance* a singular coincidence is supposedly caused by 'the agency of an ill-natured fairy'.

Good conduct stripe: an inverted chevron worn low on the left sleeve.

Gosport Tube: a pre-electrical-intercom voice pipe.

Gremlins: manikins whose *raison d'être* was to harass aircrew by creating technical problems. They appeared in 1940, got into print in the *RAF Journal* in 1942, indoctrinated fighter pilot Roald Dahl a little later and subsequently Walt Disney. They were known to be 'green, gamboge and gold; male, female and neuter; and both young and old', yet there were fliers who thought them fictitious.

Harris: Marshal of the Royal Air Force Sir Arthur Harris, Baronet, GCB, OBE, AFC, LLD (1892–1984), Air Officer Commanding-in-Chief, Bomber Command, 1942–1945.

Hedy Lamarr: (1913–2000) Austrian-born American film actress, famed from the 1930s to the late 1940s, on occasion known as 'The world's most beautiful woman'.

H2S: map-presentation radar. Originally, BN: Blind Navigation until a scientist observed, 'the whole thing is stinking through not having been done years ago.' Hence, H2S, the hydrogen-sulphide smell of bad eggs.

Hitler Youth: see **SA**.

ITW (Initial Training Wing): the training unit teaching drill and elementary air-related subjects.

Jerry-built or Gerry: poorly or hastily constructed. Long predates Jerry or Gerry for German.

Joe'd (to Joe): someone proved both willing and able who is then made a convenience of. From Joe Soap, rhyming slang for dope.

Kriegie: *Kriegsgefangener*, prisoner of war (POW).

Krupps: after Friedrich Krupp, whose family steel business at Essen became Germany's largest manufacturer of arms and ammunition.

Lady in White: throughout the Second World War, South African singer Perla Siedle Gibson (1888–1971), clad in a white dress and wearing a red hat, would position herself on Durban harbour and, using a megaphone, sing in and sing out troopships, not even missing the day when she learnt of her soldier son's death in action. The commemorative statue was unveiled by the Queen in 1995.

Line-shooting: mock-heroically bragging of experiences: typified by, 'There I was, upside down and nothing on the clock'.

Link Trainer: a flight simulator originally designed in 1929 by Ed Link, an American organ maker.

LMF (lack of moral fibre): the term the RAF used during the Second World War for combat fatigue or post-traumatic stress disorder. Since the 1700s also known as Nostalgia, Melancholia, Hysteria, Wavering, Shellshock, and Flying Sickness D (debility).

'Lootenant': American usage of lieutenant, which for the British services remains 'leftenant'.

Mae West: an inflatable lifejacket with two frontal lobes eponymously named after the celebrated, and busty, American actress Mary Jane West (1893–1980), stage name Mae West.

Mag drop: ignition in piston aero engines is supplied by a pair of electrical generators known as magnetos. Before getting airborne each of these is earthed in turn to ensure that the other is serviceable. The falling-off to be expected in engine revolutions during this test – one magneto producing slightly less electrical power than two together – has to conform with certain limits.

Maginot Line: France's in-depth system of defences along its border with Germany. Named after André Maginot, the Minister of Defence who lobbied for its construction in 1929.

***Memphis Belle*:** in May 1943 Flying Fortress B-17F 41-24485, became (effectively) the first American bomber to complete 25 missions. The 1944 documentary is well worth seeing.

Menander: Greek dramatist (342–291 BC). 'Whom the gods love dies young' is from *The Double Deceiver*.

Mention (in Despatches): recognition of a job well done, but not meriting higher award. Denoted throughout the period by a bronze oak leaf (since 1993, by a silver one).

Missions: see **Operations – ops**.

Monica: a rearward-looking radar for detecting attacking fighters whose use was discontinued because German fighters could home onto it.

Monty: Field Marshal Bernard Law Montgomery KG, GCB, DSO, PG, First Viscount of Alamein (1887–1976). In early 1945, overall command having passed, by prior arrangement, to the Americans, he commanded the 21st Army Group.

NAAFI (Navy, Army, and Air Force Institute): the organization, created in 1921, to run recreational establishments for the Services.

Nickel: a propaganda leaflet drop.

Oboe: a blind-bombing aid employing two ground stations. Essentially, one provided a beam to lead the aircraft over the target, while the other told it the bomb-release point. Using stations at Dover and Cromer, it was first employed against a Ruhr target on 21 December 1942 with an accuracy of some 80 yards. After the invasion twenty-four mobile stations were placed on the continent.

Operations – Ops: throughout the Second World War, offensive sorties by the RAF against the enemy were termed operational flights, or ops. The equivalent term employed by the United States Army Air Force was missions. While there were variations in the rules by which RAF operations were reckoned, even within Bomber Command, the standard operational tour required may be taken as thirty. It is noteworthy that in 2012 modern usage has the RAF flying missions (that similarly, wounded personnel are injured, and stations are bases).

OTU (Operational Training Unit): the unit at which aircrew were made familiar with the machines and the techniques of the commands they were to join.

PSP (perforated steel plate): interlocking metal sheets used for hardstandings and runways.

Plain sailing: (from plane sailing triangle) refers to the normal assumptions made when using a flat map to represent the spherical earth, as in walking: hence, straightforward.

PLUTO (Pipeline Under The Ocean): a fuel pipe laid under the Channel to support the invasion.

Port/starboard: left and right, viewed looking forwards.

Prang: a crash. But very strictly Second World War slang.

Predicted flak: anti-aircraft fire directed at a specific aircraft singled out by searchlights or radar: as opposed to a box barrage, aimed at a specific area of sky.

POW: prisoner of war.

Psycho device: this encoded plain language into five-symbol groups for transmission by morse.

Pundit beacon: a light flashing the airfield's code letters in morse, for example, HL for Hemswell.

Q-Code: a three-letter brevity code for often-used messages in morse. As shown following, some linger in R/T usage. (There was also an X code, and a military Z code.)

QDM: the brevity code for the magnetic heading to be steered.

QFE: the brevity code to denote the atmospheric pressure that will make an altimeter read zero at the location in question.

RCAF: Royal Canadian Air Force.

Retrospective recognition (awards): in 2005 the Malaysian Government awarded the *Pinjat Jasa Malaysia* to all Commonwealth participants in the Malayan Emergency (1948–1960). Though Her Majesty, the Queen, accepted it at that time, Authority only approved its wearing by UK recipients in late 2011. In 2008, Authority recognized the services of the Women's Land Army (1939–1950) with a commemorative badge. Hard upon this, in 2009, similar awards were made to the codebreakers of Bletchley Park, to the Bevin Boys, and to the Air Transport Auxiliary. It is just possible, then, that aircrew status will someday be recognized for all operational fliers of the Second World War, including those of Bomber Command.

RNZAF: Royal New Zealand Air Force.

R/T (radio telephony): voice.

SA *Sturmabteilung*: the brown-uniformed Nazi paramilitary organization formed in 1921 from which the black-uniformed SS (*Schutzstaffel*) developed. Though formed in 1925 as Hitler's personal guard, the SS became increasingly powerful after 1933 under Himmler, eventually embracing police, security, paramilitary, and military branches. The Hitler Youth (HJ, *Hitlerjugend*) was founded in 1922 and accommodated young people aged from ten to eighteen.

Service ceiling: effectively the highest altitude obtainable by a given aircraft. Essentially, the density altitude at which the rate of climb falls to 100 feet a minute

Spiv: a flashily-dressed dealer in suspect or black-market goods.

Sprog: inexperienced.

SS: see **SA**.

Standard Beam Approach (SBA): in essence, this was a radar landing aid that transmitted a 30-mile long, very narrow radio beam down the extended centre-line of the runway. This told a pilot receiving the aural 'on-the-beam' signal that he was somewhere along the projected centre line of the runway. To furnish an exact location *along* the beam, an 'Outer Marker' radio beacon was sited at a known distance from touchdown. This sent a coded signal vertically upwards to tell an inbound pilot that he should commence descending on his final approach. SBA developed to become the Blind Approach Beacon System (BABS) and was, therefore, the forerunner of the Instrument Landing System (ILS).

Sten gun: a British 9 mm calibre sub-machine gun hurriedly produced when invasion threatened and the supply of Thompson machine guns dried up. Utilitarian and cheap it had a 32 round magazine. The name is an acronym contrived from the surnames of the designers, **S**heperd and **T**urpin, and **E**nfield.

Stratus: horizontally-layered cloud, low-sitting; basically lifted fog.

Synoptic observations: meteorological readings to be plotted on a geographical chart; the basis for the prediction of future developments.

Tallboy L(arge): a 22,000-pound bomb, designed for deep penetration: Grand Slam.

Tallboy M(edium): a 12,000-pound medium-capacity bomb.

Trailing aerial: when operating with stations using high frequencies, a wire fixed from fuselage to tailfin gave the standard RAF wireless equipment a satisfactory range. Getting a reasonable range on medium frequencies required a wire to be streamed beneath the aircraft.

U-boat: *Unterseeboot*, submarine.

Upward-firing cannon (*Schläge Musik*): widely used by Luftwaffe aircraft, which positioned below a bomber. The guns characteristically employed a mix of 30 mm calibre rounds whose tracers left only a vestigial trail.

V-1: *Vergeltungswaffe* 1 (Reprisal Weapon) unmanned Fiesler 103 pulse-jet flying bomb. (*Not* a rocket.) Popularly known as the Doodlebug.

V-2: *Vergeltungswaffe* 2 (Reprisal Weapon) A-4 ground to ground rocket.

V-3: *Vergeltungswaffe* 3 (Reprisal Weapon) rocket-boosted, long-range gun.

VE Day: 8 May 1945. Victory in Europe, end of hostilities in Europe.

Ventral: as with a turret, below the fuselage, or belly. (Dorsal, the back.)

VHF: very high frequency.

VJ Day: in the UK, 15 August 1945. Victory over Japan, end of the Second World War. (The date is 14 August in the Pacific/Americas area due to the time-zone difference; also 2 September 1945, when the surrender was actually signed. Written too as V-J, and V-P [Pacific]).

Windmilling: see **Feather**.

Window: Aar-dropped strips of paper-backed aluminium foil cut to some correlation with the wavelength of the enemy's air-defence radars and designed to confuse their controllers.

Wings for Victory Week (1943): one of several national fund-raising initiatives to aid the war effort. Others were Salute the Soldier Week (1944) and Warship Weeks (from 1941).

Woodbridge (Suffolk): along with Manston (Kent), and Carnaby (Yorkshire): emergency airfields, 3,000 yards long, 250 yards wide, in three strips, with extensive grassed under- and over-shoot areas.

Wooden horse: in October 1943 three POWs escaped from Stalag Luft Three using a vaulting horse to conceal their tunnel. In March 1944 the three-tunnel Great Escape enterprise led to wide repercussions, including the execution of fifty escapees. Two fine POW books resulted but a travesty of the latter escape was to be become a widely-shown feature film.

Z-Code: similar to the Q brevity code (see above) but for military communications, and therefore restricted.

Selective references

Air Ministry (1937) *Royal Air Force Pocket Book, AP1081*. London: HMSO
Air Ministry (1943) *Elementary Flying Training, AP1979A*. London: HMSO
Air Ministry (1948) *The Rise and Fall of the German Air Force (1931 to 1945)* . London: HMSO
Air Ministry (1954) *Flying, Volumes 1 and 2, AP129.* (Sixth edition). London: HMSO
Bennett, D.C.T. (1936) *The Complete Air Navigator.* London: Pitman
Fellowes, P.F.M. (1942) *Britain's Wonderful Air Force.* London: Odhams
Handley Page Ltd (1949) *Forty Years On*. London: Handley Page
HMSO (1944) *Target: Germany*. London: Air Ministry
Monday, David (1982) *British Aircraft of World War II*. Chancellor Press: London
Stewart, Oliver (1941) *The Royal Air Force in Pictures.* London: Country Life
Tait, Andy (2008) Vol. 3, nos. 1 & 2, Article 18, p. 20 *'Boy and Apprentice Training at Cranwell'*. RAF Publications: *Spirit of the Air*
Terraine, John (1985) *The Right of the Line.* London: Hodder and Stoughton
Thetford, Owen (1958) *Aircraft of the Royal Air Force 1918–1958*. London: Putnam